Before and After Zachariah

Before and After Zachariah

A Family Story About a Different Kind of Courage

Fern Kupfer

DELACORTE PRESS / NEW YORK

Published by
Delacorte Press
1 Dag Hammarskjold Plaza
New York, N.Y. 10017

Manufactured in the United States of America

First printing

Designed by Judith Neuman

Library of Congress Cataloging in Publication Data
Kupfer, Fern.
  Before and after Zachariah.
  I. Title.
PS3561.U618B4   813'.54   81–12510
ISBN 0–440–00507–8   AACR2

For My Family: Joe, Gabi, and Zachariah

Contents

Acknowledgments

For the sake of privacy and clarity, some characters in this book have been fictionalized and some names and places have been changed.

I am grateful to all the many mothers of severely handicapped children who shared with me their most painful, private feelings. Most especially to J.K. and Ellen Donnelly.

I am thankful to agents Gayle Benderoff and Deborah Geltman for making that first call; to my editor, Sandra Choron, for her passionate intelligence; to Marj Whitney, who met all those awful typing deadlines and whose kindness and enthusiasm for the project never flagged; to my friend Maggie McCarey for her gift of poetry; and to Andrea Fooner, who saw a special "young mother's story." My family and friends have supported me unwaveringly. To my husband, Joe, who read and reread, who gave gentle criticism, who lived with me through the worst of times and claims to love me still, I offer a lifetime of gratitude.

And, of course, Joe and I are forever thankful to the people of Hills and Dales Child Development Center, who continue to care for and love our son.

He is carried in a floating basket
Unflinching at the lapping of his days
No dreams of marbles, cats, or greater stuff
And yet, his being has been a tantara:
A fanfare, a loud and lusty trumpet blast.

Before, we played so green and golden
Sometimes I don't remember who we were
But after Zachariah, oh, after
How tenderly we touch our scars
How mindful of that chancy evil eye.

Introduction

Promise me, Fern, just promise me; you are not going to write a happy book.

—Wanda

Zachariah at five—now palely, sadly beautiful. A baby who cannot sit, or use his hands or say "Mommy." Still an infant who needs to be rocked and held. Damaged goods. This is a story about a child and the tragedy that is his small life, about surviving in a family seared by the pain, about a change in my life so powerful, so enduring, that I define myself every day by its consequence.

Change comes upon us, not slowly, gently evolving, within our control, but suddenly, abruptly, within hours, sometimes moments, the course of our lives so turned around, turned about, inside out—a slick road on the way home from work; in the night, the discovery of a lump. Lives are smashed and rearranged without any preparation on our part. The rug is pulled out from under us, the roof comes caving in—domestic metaphors for catastrophe. Oh, the capricious nature of tragedy. Sometimes it's hard to plan beyond what's for dinner.

I am part of a community of women who share a common pain. When I first knew that "something was wrong" with Zach, I would seek out these women; I wanted to hear their stories because I thought they could help me understand and make decisions about my own life. Mothers of "children" who were now thirty years old themselves could talk about their pregnancy, their child's infancy, with such freshness and clarity that it would seem only a few months rather than a few decades had passed. For most of us, having a profoundly handicapped child is the single most defining feature of who we are.

As I began to write my story the voices of other women spoke to me. And the other voices spoke as I changed Zach in his crib, as Joe and I went to another doctor, saw another social worker, attended another evaluation.

They spoke as we left Zach in the arms of strangers so many miles away.

Part 1

BEFORE ZACHARIAH

1

I filled out a survey the other day and as I checked the right boxes I thought about who I was: Female, white, 30–35 years old, Democrat, college educated, married, Catholic, children (three), homemaker, twenty-five-to-thirty-five-thousand dollars a year. But there was no box which asked if any of my children were not normal . . . and how did that affect my life?

—Erica

In a speech class I teach, I ask the students, for their introductory presentations, to "bring themselves to class in a paper bag," to select three things that best show or symbolize who they are as people and share these with the class. My students at the community college bring record albums ("music plays a big part in my life") and family pictures and schoolbooks. One boy takes out a six-pack of Bud ("this is what I do every weekend"); a girl displays her checkbook and its balance of ninety-three cents ("being poor is my identity," she explains).

I, too, am going to participate, to introduce myself to the class. The night before I think of what to put in my paper bag and think of "who I am."

I am thirty-four but part of a generation who heard that this age could not be trusted. I see small lines around my eyes and the boy at Safeway who puts the sacks in the back of my station wagon calls me "ma'am."

My friend Barbara calls from New York. We have been friends since junior high; her first period began in my house, her exuberant shouting from the upstairs bathroom, "I got it! I got it!" Then, more restraint, compassion, because I, her best friend, had not yet "got it."

At college we shared sweaters and graphic sexual secrets. And years later, hundreds of miles apart, we talk of the security and constraints of monogamy, the joyful births of our first children, our daughters; we swap teaching stories

3

and give each other book lists. We talk, even on Ma Bell's discount rates, long into the night, at least fifteen dollars' worth. We say at different times in the conversation, "Oh, my God, this will be some bill," but we continue on the telephone, that intimate connection for women, ear-to-ear, mouth-to-mouth, heart-to-heart. Tonight Barbara calls and says how the young mothers around the pool at her apartment complex that summer are *really* young. She's thinking about covering the gray that has begun to thread itself through her thick, dark hair.

"I mean, really, Fernie, I think we have only a few good years left!"

I am a New Yorker, now living almost a decade in the Midwest, a Jew surrounded by Gentiles who see this identity and my New York accent as somewhat exotic. (My students ask, "Are you from Boston?")

I have adapted to a certain midwestern civility and earnestness. Here in Iowa people smile at strangers they pass in the street; they say "hi" or "how ya doing?" or "sure is hot." And I have gotten so used to this cordiality that on our frequent visits "home" to New York, I feel uncomfortable assuming that blank subway stare, looking past invisible faces in crowded elevators. It does indeed feel more natural to smile, to connect in a human way, although it is only madwomen and hookers who address strangers on New York streets.

Easterners talk, sometimes scornfully, of the "culture shock" when they move to the Midwest. It took me a while to make the adjustment. The first time I went shopping here in Iowa, the cashier said, "Hi, how are you today?" with such a warm interest that I spent the rest of the afternoon trying to figure out where we had met before.

Sometimes clerks smilingly help you to the car with heavy packages; garage mechanics have really said, "Oh, it's nothing, I'll fix it right now, no charge"; delivery boys look dumbfounded at gratuities ("What's this for?"); the garbage collectors say "Have a nice day" if they see you on the way out the door as they empty your pails.

But midwesterners also lack—and because I grew up with it, I miss it—a certain passion, an intensity, an abrasive honesty, a capacity for easy intimacy. "How are you?" Always "fine." Even if things are really shitty, the ulcer's acting up, the kids are on dope, the husband falls asleep every night in front of the TV, I'm growing old, I'm growing lonely, I hate my life. "How are you?" "Fine."

Midwestern parents neither bite the behinds of their children in adoration ("so good, I could eat you up") nor do they ever shrilly scream "get over here or I'll kill you" across a crowded playground.

Midwesterners can admire a dress, or a dinette set, or a new Persian rug, but they rarely ask, "Where did you get it?" (And never, ever, "How much did it cost?")

And most midwesterners do not respond to sarcasm— that staple for East Coast repartee, leading an English professor here at Iowa State to observe, "There is no irony in Iowa."

So part of my identity has to do with a view of myself as a visitor of sorts.

I am a feminist; I have survived in a marriage and grown and changed because of it, no small accomplishment nowadays. I remember one time, nearly twelve years ago, when Joe and I had dinner at his mother's apartment. Joe wore jeans and an unironed cotton shirt. His mother looked at me. "Aren't you ashamed of the way he looks?"

"Why? I'm not wearing a wrinkled shirt," I said. It would not have occurred to me, even as a newlywed in preliberation America, that my standards were reflected by my husband's dress. At that time I was seen as a rebel, and a lazy rebel at that—one who wouldn't do the ironing. Later I did that modern-woman juggling act, trying to find a balance between graduate school or work and family, wanting to have it all, knowing that it's never possible; that to be grown up is to understand the nature of compromise; that now I was not going to be "discovered" as I had secretly dreamed even throughout college.

(A woman I know, in midlife after three children, one divorce, and a new marriage, went back to school to become a reference librarian. I met her for lunch one day and asked her how she liked the job. She confessed that she'd really "rather be a ballerina."

"Why, I never even knew that you danced," I exclaimed.

"I don't," she said. "I never have.")

Oh, our fantasies die hard and late. Part of the problem with the women's movement is that it tells us that we can be anything we want to be. I mull this over, driving to work in subzero temperature, on icy Iowa highways, to teach English composition and speech to a group of girls at a community college who are going to become dental hygienists; it is a job for which, because I am part time, I receive no benefits and am grossly underpaid.

I still wasn't sure what to put in my paper bag for my introductory speech.

I think of hobbies. The truth is, I really don't have any hobbies, a fact that I find disconcerting only when I have to fill out applications or surveys. Then I usually put down "reading," an activity that never does seem appropriate. My students all seem to have hobbies. Along with the beer and family portraits, they bring in needlepoint and motorcycle helmets and old comic books.

The next day I introduce myself to the class and give a brief personal narrative. I don't mention my age, or my feelings about being New York Jewish in the Midwest, or the complications of the women's movement. I take a red pen out of the bag and talk about being a teacher as part of my identity. Then I take out a book (a Margaret Atwood novel), which I unwrap from a pillowcase and tell them about my keenness for reading in bed—my ersatz hobby. They laugh. Finally, I take out a copy of *Redbook*, which has published a story I wrote for their "Young Mothers" series called "A Place for Zachariah." I tell this class, whom I have never met before, that I am the mother of a multiply handicapped child. I wrote the story about him and about my decision not to have him live at home. I talk about how being the mother of such a child has changed me and my vision of the world. The class is very quiet now and there are a few girls, scattered in different rows, whose gentle faces turn toward me, glowing softly like flowers in the sun.

Saying this is difficult, even now, and my voice still catches. The admission gives me a vulnerability I'm not sure I like. When I first made the assignment, some student in the back yelled up, "You do it, too. We want to get to know you." Right away I thought about Zach. Oh, Zach. I could never, with any honesty, omit Zachariah from a description of who I am. I am the mother of a retarded child, of a severely physically handicapped retarded child. Zach's gross limitations help define me in a way that is perhaps ineffable, but permanent. My relationship to this child defines me, not only as I present myself to the world, but in a way that reaches deep within. Because of Zach, certain moments of everyday life—a small boy running through a shopping mall, a woman lifting a baby from a car—stand out with such brilliance that even these most ordinary events reveal the intense fragility, the beauty and pain of life.

Zach has changed me and sometimes I can no longer think of who I was before I had this identity. Then again, there is a part of me that does not truly believe that this really happened at all.

Radicalized, I have fought for Zach's rights and for our rights as a family to survive. I know I am stronger for the struggle, and perhaps I am a better person. A woman who has a Down's syndrome child told me that "having a handicapped child is the best assertiveness-training course there is."

But oh, I did not sign up for this course. This was an elective not of my own choosing. No matter how we long for the silver lining in even the most ominous thunder-cloud, I cannot say that this has been a positive experience.

There is a lot of talk with parents of retarded children about "learning to accept it." We get praise and admiration from the "handicapped professionals," from the teachers and social workers about how well we've "learned to accept it." Parents themselves spend a lot of time denying like crazy ("He's only a baby, he'll catch up"), choking back the anger, and crying in the night as we bend over to cover our children in their beds. It is true that just as all children are good when they are sleeping, so all children look normal when they are sleeping. I do not know a parent of a re-tarded child who has not had this thought and made silent pleas in the dark.

There are days I suppose that I don't want to "learn to accept it." On one of our early social-worker evaluations, it is written "the parents have difficulty in learning to accept the situation." I thought, That's true. That's right. And oh, God, who wouldn't?

A few years ago I hurt whenever I saw a baby crawling and cooing and doing cute baby things. A few weeks ago I saw a blond, curly-headed little boy in overalls and tiny red sneakers running across campus toward his mom. The image, recalled over and over again that day, tore at me. I wonder if I'll feel the same pain later when I see ten-year-olds playing ball in the street or teen-age boys showing off to their girl friends at the beach. I think so. There is a deep-down sadness that will be with me for the rest of my life. I don't know if you ever totally learn to accept it. I'm getting better all the time. I can talk about Zach to an inquiring stranger who asks if I have any children, without tears coming to my eyes. I no longer awaken at five in the morning, cold and frightened, with my heart pounding un-controllably. I don't always feel as if I'm on the verge of throwing up. I know that no doctor is going to find an operable brain tumor, to fix Zach and make him better. I know that Zach is irreparably damaged. I accept that. And yet, at the very core, I still find the whole situation some-what unbelievable and, yes, unacceptable.

I look at the picture on our kitchen bulletin board of a smiling, dimpled Zach, blue eyes with dark fringy lashes, his hair a mass of golden curls, and think of the kid he could have been. So there is still that voice in me, protesting and rejecting, angry, hurt.

Once, at a parent support meeting for "new parents" of handicapped children, we had as speakers a husband and wife who had a retarded teen-ager. They were talking about learning to accept the fact that your child is retarded. "Well," said the mother, smart in a black tailored pantsuit, her long red hair caught up in a barrette, "it took me a long time, but I *have* learned to accept it—about twenty-eight days out of the month."

There are studies that show that many families of retarded children experience a grief akin to that felt when a child dies. I talked about this with a friend of mine who has a severely brain-damaged daughter. She said, "Of course it is horrible when a child dies. It is one of the worst things that can happen—for the parent to outlive the child. You will always feel the pain. It is not something you can ever really 'get over,' but at least the act, the death, is an *ending*, a finality. And the parents' wounds can begin to heal. I feel as if I am always enacting Cathleen's death. As she becomes older and less appealing, her problems become more pronounced. When we go back to the neurologist, when I go to her special class for the evaluation, I feel as if the coffin is being wheeled in again. And I am split open all over again."

Yet the books we read about life with a handicapped child and the programs we see on TV are not truth-telling for how a number of parents live their lives. The thing is, we like miracle stories. We like inspirational tales of courage and conviction, the spirit of never-say-die. We like to hear of children who learned to walk when the doctors said "never," children who laughed and sang and became whole when the doctors said, "There is no hope." And the moth-

ers of these children, who patiently nourished and sac-
rificed and never lost faith that their special children would
bloom slowly in their own time, these women were held up
for all of us to see.

But what about those women who have such children and
who cannot stand one more Sunday afternoon alone in the
house with a child who doesn't know how to play; or wake
to another day to find the bedroom walls smeared with
feces; or feed another blended supper to a child who must
be fed spoonful by chokey spoonful? What about these
women? Mothers of normal children can say aloud, "These
kids are driving me crazy," after a long August of car pool-
ing and spilled sugar on kitchen counters and kids whining
about nothing to do. But the woman whose handicapped
child is really driving her crazy can admit this to no one.
The lamenting, the anger, the tears—this is experienced
behind closed doors as we put on our "good mother" faces
while we sit through therapy sessions and social-service
evaluations, while we wait hour after hour in clinic waiting
rooms. Seemingly we have "learned to accept it."

There are certain myths that go with the territory: That
we were somehow "picked," chosen by God to play this
noble role. We are patient; we are strong. Our children,
however deficient, are always lovable and joyful in the good
care they receive; they are always rewarding and enriching
our lives; indeed, they are "special" children.

Every so often people write to Ann Landers requesting
that poem "Heaven's Very Special Child," telling us that
our retarded child is a gift from God. I want to write her
a letter and tell her how it *really* is. (She'll probably print
it and say, "You're very angry, dear. I suggest you get
counseling!") Even Erma Bombeck did the same thing on
Mother's Day (Mother's Day—what a stab in the breast)
with her column "A Holy Tribute for Mother's Day." She
actually said that mothers of handicapped children were
saints. Oh, no, I thought. *Et tu,* Erma.

The more modern myths talk about "normalization" and
"mainstreaming" and tell us how easily our retarded chil-

dren can fit into our families and our lives if only we could reject those nasty prejudices, those stereotypes that "project such negative images."

My friend Bob, who is a regional coordinator for mental-retardation services on the East Coast, tells me that "being retarded should not be viewed negatively. The retarded are just like you and me." But Bob has no retarded child of his own. And of course he would not ever want one.

There are no myths about the maddening eternity of babydom, the suffocating effect of constant need. And of course, I can talk about what this life is like for me, for our family. Sometimes I tell it to professionals, always well meaning, who offer advice but have no idea what my family life is really like.

"Swimming is very good for Zach because it builds up his tone. You can take him to the community pool near your house; Gabi will be home and that will be extra stimulation as she plays with him; this will be a really neat summer. . . ." Zach's physical therapist went on with her idealized description of our family.

I stopped her.

"Gabi doesn't play with Zach because he doesn't really play. She talks to him and pushes the wheelchair sometimes. But mostly she has her own friends, her own life. And," I went on (oh, be tough, be honest, tell it like it really is), "getting in and out of a swimming pool carrying a thirty-pound child who cannot sit or hold a toy, who cries when you lay him down on a blanket, is *not* my idea of a 'really neat summer.' "

I am not so patient, and I am not so good, and Zachariah did not at all fit easily into the scheme of things. So I must always explain who I am. And now when we go, hours away, to pick Zach up and take him "home—for a visit," I still flutter when I see him there among all those so severely handicapped children, children lying on prone boards, rocked by loving arms. No talkies. No walkies. Wheelchairs of different sizes line up against the wall like bicycles.

I suppose I have yet to make peace with who *he* is.

2

I never thought about having a child who was not normal. In fact, I can remember one time when I was about eight months pregnant with Katie; I was coming out of the bathroom of a downtown department store and a woman was standing there with a little boy in a wheelchair. The mother asked if I would just watch him for a minute while she went to the bathroom. I stood next to the boy, not saying a word, watching him suck on his fingers. I kept thinking, "Oh, God, that poor woman." I never, ever, thought I could have a child like that.

My pregnancy and delivery were normal, and of course I thought Katie was a normal baby. Even now, after all the tests at Mayo Clinic, we still don't know what caused the brain damage. My theory is that at some time between birth and three months "something happened." I don't know what it was. I can't remember her having a high fever or her hitting her head, but I think she changed. I suppose that I wanted to think of her as being born normal—or me not giving birth to a child who was retarded. She looked just like a normal baby. I suppose I really want to think that something happened to her.

—Marjorie

Questions on the record:
Q. Do you have any other children?
A. Yes, a girl. She was four when Zach was born.
Q. Was the second a planned pregnancy?
A. Well—sort of—unplanned. But not unwanted.

I have told Zach's prenatal history so many times to so many people that I feel I should list it on my résumé right after "colleges attended" and before "other professional

experience." But there is a psychological as well as a medical history that includes expectations and decisions, which
explains relationships, which defines guilt.

Recorded as an unplanned pregnancy. At best, an iffy
start in life.

I need to give an explanation, a family history. Well, for
example, no doctor has ever asked me, "And how did you
meet your husband? . . ."

I met Joe in 1962 at a high school sorority party. In he
came, out of a cold December night, peeling off a navy pea
jacket, then a white fisherman's sweater; underneath he had
on a sweat shirt: STUYVESANT HIGH SCHOOL SWIMMING
CHAMPS. We looked across the floor at each other, à la *West
Side Story,* and danced in steamy silence to Johnny Mathis
singing "The Twelfth of Never." Later we discovered that
we both loved J. D. Salinger.

After the party Barbara said, "Oh God, Fern, I bet you
marry him."

"Don't be ridiculous," I said as I started writing "Mrs.
Joseph Harris Kupfer" all over my world history book.

Joe was an only child who felt, because of this status, both
special and alone. He wondered as a boy what it would be
like to have a sibling.

At sixteen, when I met him, one of my attractions had
been Ray, my thirteen-year-old brother, who could ex-
change sports statistics with him and who accepted Joe's
"summer reading list" with enthusiasm. Two bright jocks.
Saturday night, Joe would come a little early so he could go
out and "toss a couple around" with Ray. Then they'd
come in an hour later, Joe sweaty in his good clothes, a rip
here, a scrape there. I'd wait for him to wash up. We were
late for every movie we ever went to.

One time one of our dates was a double-header at Shea
Stadium. Those were the days when *Seventeen* magazine
suggested that you "share his interests," and so Ray spent
hours engaging me in preparatory clever baseball repartee.

Later, when Joe found out about the duplicity, he said, "What a waste. Those games were so good. I should have taken your brother."

That summer Joe, in his Stuyvesant-High-School-Swim-Champ capacity, worked as the lifeguard at a local pool. He sat up on his stand, blond, caramel-colored, flashing a white smile, the whistle dangling provocatively between two muscled shoulders: a golden boy. Hanging languidly about the stand were gawky fourteen-year-old girls, proffering 7 Up and compliments. Unlike the other lifeguards, Joe took his pool watch seriously, staring across the blue water with an even gaze. On his ten-minute breaks he would come and lie with me in the sun, reading Shakespearean sonnets. I thought he was the smartest person I ever met—and I loved the boy-sweet smell of him, the feel of his strong back against my open palm.

I went away to college to "test our love" by going out as often as I could to college mixers and gropey blind dates.

Spring break of my freshman year I wanted to go to Fort Lauderdale with a couple of friends; visions of *Where the Boys Are* danced in our heads all winter, of angular, preppy boys in Harvard sweat shirts jogging across white sands. Oh, none of us would meet poor Yvette Mimieux's fate: seduced and abandoned in some cheap motel. We were too smart for that.

My father said I could not go.

"But I'm eighteen," I screeched. "And I have the money to pay for it myself! You can't tell me I cannot go."

"Well, let's put it this way," my father said. "You cannot go and come back to this house." (Had he seen *Where the Boys Are,* too?)

Somewhere during my sophomore year I started asking "What does it all mean?" and wore only dark turtlenecks, jeans, and Fred Braun sandals. I hung around with people who drank wine instead of beer, scorned the fraternities, listened to Bob Dylan, read Kahlil Gibran, and acted in the school plays—a real bohemian. I told my mother I had tried pot. "Oh, no," she lamented, "next it will be marijuana."

At the end of four years, our love nurtured by holiday good-byes and summer romance, I knew Joe was really "the one," and we were married the weekend before finals of my senior year. We drove to Niagara Falls, and I spent my wedding night reading *The Way of the Hopi* (I had an anthro final on Monday) while Joe watched a hockey game on TV, massaged all the while by the bed's twenty-five-cent "Magic Fingers."

We lived for a few years in Rochester, New York, where Joe went to graduate school in philosophy (My father asked, "What do philosophers *do* for a *job?*"), and I taught English in an all-boy vocational high school.

We thought a lot about the army, about "'Nam," as the boys in my rough school would say (they all had brothers who wore flashy satin jackets with "I've Been to Hell and Back" emblazoned across the shoulders). There were a few graduate-school deferments; then right before his induction physical, Joe badly broke his ankle playing basketball. The physical was rescheduled, then shifted as we moved across the country; but Joe was already becoming "too old" at twenty-six.

We moved to Ames, Iowa, in 1971, where Joe had gotten a job as an assistant professor of philosophy at Iowa State University, and I got pregnant the first week we were there —the fumes from the most fertile soil in the U.S.A. I was home for a few months, taking care of Gabi, a beautiful baby whom I adored; but I was driving across town one afternoon because Pampers were fifty cents off at Target, and I said aloud in the car, "This is not the way I want to spend my time." So I applied to graduate school and got an assistantship teaching English composition.

The marriage was enduring and solid—it had been a while before I thought "divorce" following a wrenching fight; trauma did not follow every disappointment. Our marriage grew in a milieu where separation, termination, was seen as an acceptable (if painful) alternative when relationships were no longer "meaningful" or "fulfilling." In fact, out of the eight couples who were friends with us in graduate schools at the end of the sixties, Joe and I were the only ones who were still together—all the other couples had dispersed: some, realigned as individuals, grew up, grew apart, outgrew; women found themselves; men found others. Some sadness, some rage, but mostly an acceptance that keeping a marriage together is wearing work and there are always alternatives.

Joe and I came that far. And I still warmed to his voice over the phone (grown from our long-distance romance while I was away at college; me sitting in a phone booth at the end of a dormitory hall, longing across the wires); and even in the fiercest fights we could still make each other laugh.

Though both of us tend to be showy, our personalities are often complementary. Joe is moody, quick to anger, quick to apologize, forgive and forget. While I am more dependably cheerful, I can also nurse a grudge and am never the first to say "sorry."

Joe wakes cranky and irritable. He says he is just not a "morning person." ("What! There's only goddamn white bread for toast! I *hate* goddamn white bread.") I say there is no excuse for being nasty to people you live with no matter what the time of day. Soon I am loathing him. But before noon he calls from the office, affecting a suave French accent.

" 'Allo, Messis Kupfer?"

"What do you want, Joe?" I say, my anger already ebbing.

"Ah, Messis Kupfer. I 'ave seen you in—how you say—la supermarket, squeezing melons and I would like to say that I think you 'ave very nice melons yourself."

So he knows I'm already smiling and he's got me.

"I'm sorry, honey. I was so grouchy this morning."

We had survived the effects of the women's movement, changing and growing (I no longer made Joe sandwiches

and snacks while he watched the ball game; more important, I stopped feeling guilty about it). It was during these
years that I felt truly, for the first time in the relationship,
that Joe and I would grow old together.

Teaching and graduate school gave us a flexible enough
schedule to share child care.

Gabi had been in a small cooperative play group that I
had helped organize when she was about eighteen months
old; then there was a part-time baby-sitter while I was in
school with a teaching assistantship. When she was two and
a half, we started her out in a regular nursery school three
days a week, but soon she was up every morning, chirping,
"School today, school today?" So we moved her to five
mornings and Joe and I shared caring for her in the afternoon. Sometimes I'd drop Gabi off at Joe's office if I had
a class in the same building. He had a bottom desk drawer
filled with crayons, paper, and Golden Books, and Gabi
would solemnly do her "work" alongside her dad. Sometimes he brought her to class, and she'd sit, quietly coloring, as Joe lectured, even though she didn't understand it
when they "talked philosophy instead of just plain."

Gabi was adaptable: we could take her with us wherever
we went and she'd take naps comfortably on friends'
couches, in sleeping bags, on the backseats of cars. Always,
she woke cheerfully. The summer after Gabi was two, we
took a thirty-hour car trip to stay with my brother and his
wife, Lynn, at a beach house they rented on the Carolina
coast. Thirty hours in a car with a two-year-old! But Gabi
was a terrific traveler, playing happily in the backseat, singing nonsense rhymes to herself until she fell asleep. At
night, in Peoria, Illinois, we stopped for gas and Joe woke
Gabi, carrying her to the bathroom, she in her pink bunny
suit. "We're going to pee in Peoria," he sang as he whirled
her around the parking lot. She thought this was gloriously
funny and for every toileting stop thereafter asked, "Are we
in Peoria?"

Joe is really a great daddy. Well, he's a "kid-person." He

likes to talk baseball with our friends' twelve-year-old son; Joe was the good-night-story-man for other friends' daughters when we stayed for a week at Thanksgiving. On Gabi's third birthday he came home from work to give horse rides around the living room and dining room, until finally his knees gave in.

But Joe is also old-world tough when it comes to discipline: rules for bedtime and table manners and not interrupting adult conversations, for keeping feet off the couch. I'm easier—I don't get upset if a kid tracks mud on the kitchen floor, or dallies before going to sleep. Sometimes I'd say that Joe was too rigid; he'd say that I was too lax (once he wrote me a poem, "Slip-shod and sloppy, my Pekingese poppy . . ."). I would always say, "She'll outgrow it," whatever "it" was. Had he ever seen a teen-age girl with a security blanket? But we didn't clash; we came on like a team, supporting whoever had the parental ball at the time. I think we also appreciated the other's parenting skills. Joe loosened up some, realizing that Gabi wouldn't fall apart if she missed a nap once in a while; and I liked the results of Joe's discipline—a child who behaved well because it was expected.

But we were never arrogant enough to assume all the credit. We looked at friends who had colicky, screaming babies or determined toddlers given to tantrums and breath-holding. No matter how much psychologists say about the influences of environment, most parents recognize that babies are born with their own distinct personalities. Gabi had been a happy, "easy" baby and was growing into a nice-to-be-with little girl. I felt we were lucky. (Maybe part of me was also scared that our luck would run out.) Should we have another baby?

Why not have another child? Have a *real* family. The threesome—me, Joe, and Gabi—struck me somehow as an inauthentic representation, too much camaraderie there. *Real* families needed that sibling interaction, the rivalry, the loyalty. I remember seeing my little brother, Ray, weepy and scared in the principal's office one day when we were both in elementary school. I stuck up for him with fierce sisterly devotion. "He gets in trouble all the time 'cause he's bored, 'cause he's smarter than half the teachers in this dumb school, that's why."

(Later, in junior high, I taught Ray how to comb his hair with a proper flat top—it had to stand straight up, coaxed by coats of Butch Wax—and to wear pennies in his loafers. We role-played meeting girls at dances—sometimes I'd make him be the girl, and I'd be the cool stud commanding a dance—long before Ray was really ready or interested. He much preferred the basketball court to the dance floor. Still, I had him groomed, and I did a good job. Clearly, the years of teasing and torment—"Hey, Mr. Big Ears, hey, Dumbo," I'd yell, focusing on his only physical defect, but never in public—didn't matter all that much. I was a big sister worth having.)

Gabi would be a super big sister, an interested companion, a teacher. Was that a reason to have another baby? Once, I casually mentioned to my dad that we might "have just one child." I said it defensively, to test him out. The look he gave me I recalled from childhood—when I'd eaten the last of the potato chips and put back the empty bag in the cabinet. A head shaking with sorrow, disgust, disbelief. This child whom he had so nourished—a monument of careless selfishness. My traditional and loving father, by his own admission a strict "family man," viewed choosing to have only one child about as alternative a life-style as living in a bisexual Buddhist commune.

During the spring of '75 I was writing my master's thesis ("The Concept of Androgyny in the Novels of D. H. Lawrence"), and Joe was offered tenure at Iowa State. We were settled, rooted to a community, to good friends. We had a house, an old house shaped like a barn, a little leaky but with a fireplace for Iowa's winters and a screened-in front porch for Iowa's summers. Joe loved his job.

Sometimes we even felt guilty about how comfortable our lives were.

After graduate school I could teach English by quarterly appointments; but Ames was an academic community flooded with people with innumerable degrees and talents. It was a buyer's market, a master's in English was as vocationally useful as a membership in the Book-of-the-Month Club. Why not have another baby? Joe wanted to.

It was, in part, my putting off decisions about what to do with my own life (almost thirty years old and still not sure what I wanted to be when I grew up), that our methods of birth control became increasingly slipshod. After a year of crampy, free-flowing periods, I had my IUD removed. We alternated—sometimes condoms, sometimes a diaphragm; we used rhythm on the "safe" days around my period. (The old joke: Q—What do they call people who use rhythm as a birth-control method? A—Parents.)

Maybe I wasn't gutsy enough to say I really wanted a second child just yet. But by the end of the summer I was sure I was pregnant.

I put off taking a pregnancy test because sometime around when my next period was due I began staining. The spotting continued for the next couple of weeks. One night I was lying on the couch trying to read, trying to ignore that "funny feeling" that came over me, a rush, a mix of nausea and dizziness. The phone rang and I got up shakily to answer it. As I spoke (a student of Joe's, could I tell Dr. Kupfer that the paper would be late . . . a death in the family), I watched watery red blood gush from me onto our kitchen linoleum. It must have come out with force because I remember hearing a terrible *splattt.* I finished the conversation (. . . sorry to hear that . . . yes, I'll tell him), holding my new purple robe above my waist, hung up, then tied the robe diaper fashion under me (better to mess the robe than the carpeting), and made my way up the stairs to wake Joe from a nap.

"I'm bleeding," I said softly, trying not to panic either him or myself as I stood by the bed.

Joe, not an entirely coherent waker-upper, sat up with a start, took one look at me, and said, "You've ruined your new robe."

I started to cry. "I couldn't help it," I blubbered, holding the soppy cloth bunched between my legs.

Joe got up—calmly. "It's probably just your period. Look, you're not hemorrhaging or anything." Efficiently unzipping the robe, he went to the bathroom to run a cold-water bath to remove the stains. I stood naked, looking dumbly down between my legs. I was no longer bleeding, not even a trickle. Joe came back and looked me over authoritatively. "You're probably not pregnant, you're late, that's all. It's nothing major." Easy enough for him to say, having missed the scary splat on the kitchen floor.

"Call the doctor tomorrow if you're worried," he said, getting back into bed.

The next day I was back to staining, no real period at all, and at the doctor's office I previewed the whole story to a sympathetic nurse. "I thought I was pregnant," I told her.

"I don't think you are now, dear," she said. "Maybe it was your period or maybe you miscarried."

Reiterating the tale to the doctor, my legs up in the stirrups, I began thinking that maybe my "funny period" was caused by an ovarian cyst, perhaps anemia.

He looked over at me through my knees. "You're pregnant," he said with finality, overriding both Joe's and the nurse's diagnosis. "Let's take a test just to be sure."

I waited in the front room, reading *Mother-To-Be,* surrounded by peaceful women in various stages of pregnancy. I could not stop smiling.

Meeting again with the doctor, the test confirming his positive diagnosis (miracles of technology; all this within less than one hour and no dead rabbits), we talked about the bleeding and what it meant. "Bleeding in early pregnancy is very common," he said, "especially at what would be the time for normal menstruation, but if the staining continues, I would recommend that we do a D and C."

A D & C. I *was* still pregnant, so that really meant an

abortion. How did I feel about that? Politically I supported the right of choice. Abortion was the final step when other birth-control methods fail. It seemed obvious to me that women should *not* be pregnant if they choose *not* to be. I remembered Sally, a pretty blond girl in college (before abortion was legal) for whose abortion we all chipped in and whom we sent away on a bus to some motel in Pennsylvania where she was to meet a man named "Ted" who was to take her to a "doctor" who would abort her for eight hundred dollars. (We raised part of the money making a collection throughout the dorm; the rest she paid with her National Defense Loan.) Sally came back to college on the bus, bleeding and dazed with stories about how "Ted" offered her a discount on the operation if she would have sex with him in the motel room ("You're pregnant anyway, ain'tcha?") and how later "Ted," with his hand on her breast, watched the entire procedure. Even then I thought, this is crazy—no woman should have to endure that. If men were the ones to get pregnant, abortions would never have been illegal in the first place.

On a personal level, however, I did not particularly want an abortion myself. This was a baby I wanted, and I took more seriously the miracle of conception and pregnancy—having gone through the process before. Even if I didn't think that a fetus was a life, removing a potential baby was not the same as removing a wart. Joe was no help. He said, "It's your body . . . you have to do what you feel comfortable with."

If my doctor felt there would be any danger whatsoever to the fetus because of the staining and bleeding, I would choose an abortion without hesitation. I did not want anything wrong with my baby.

My doctor termed it an "unstable pregnancy" and I was to go home, see how I felt, see if I was still staining, see if I wanted to go along with having a D & C.

"We'll make an appointment for next Monday," the doctor said. "Don't eat anything after twelve midnight on Sunday, just in case."

I spent the week ruminating—"yes baby or no baby"—and going to the bathroom every hour to check for discharge. Gabi listened to my phone conversation to friends and parents and asked, "Are we having a baby or not?" not quite comprehending my fluctuating state. "Well I'm pregnant now," I told her, "but I might not stay that way."

I was so depressed. I must really want to have a baby after all, I thought.

That Sunday, a peculiar thing happened. All bleeding completely stopped. Not a trace of the reddish-brown stain I had been so used to for weeks. I felt great, as if something had clicked in place. I thought to myself, Well, this little guy has decided to stop this nonsense after all.

The next day at the doctor's I told him how I was no longer staining, how good I felt.

"Well," he said after examining me again, "the pregnancy appears to have stabilized."

I was still concerned. (The notes on my obstetrical history ominously read, "Mother worried, 9/27/75.")

I gave him the old "what-would-you-advise-your-wife/-daughter" line. He looked thoughtful. "I'd tell her to go ahead with the pregnancy."

"Okay," I said, "I'll go ahead."

The rest of my pregnancy may be recorded as "normal" or "uneventful." I took my vitamins, I did not smoke or drink or shoot heroin into my veins. I didn't run a fever or cough or wheeze or develop a funny rash. I didn't swell up with water or come down with tired blood.

That fall, I bloomed, plump and proud, loving being pregnant, feeling my usually little body growing into a substantial self.

And I began that second nesting. I painted the upstairs yellow, and I brought in firewood from the garage to settle in for the long winter.

A year later I relived those minutes in the doctor's office when I decided to go ahead with having this baby, those seconds with my feet up in stirrups when I held my breath, crossed my fingers, and said okay. I blamed the doctor; I blamed me; later on I blamed our genes. Who could be sure what the cause was anyway?

But I always knew that Zach's damage did not occur at birth, but before. He just didn't move around much, and he rarely kicked. "This will be a gentle baby," said my doctor when I told him. But I remember eight months along, standing at my sink doing dishes: I banged some pots and waited for the jump in my belly. It never came. No matter how loudly I banged.

Part 2

THE FIRST YEAR

1

I often wonder what I would be like if I never had Tommy. I would like to think I wouldn't be the shrew I am now. I believe that my nerves are shot forever (I come from nervous stock anyway and didn't need this). It has cost me my religious faith. I was so deluged with religious advice and reminders ("You must be very special to God," "The Lord never asks more of you than you can bear . . ."). That view has caused such tension in my family.

I have become a compulsive house cleaner. Things were so out of control here that I have a terrible need to control every little thing now. I hate that in me.

There is a song that goes, "Oh, how I long to be the girl I used to be." I think of that a lot. We have made some very dear friendships; I have learned a lot about myself and other people. If pain makes one "grow," I've certainly "grown," but on the whole it's an experience I would pass up every time!

I'm beginning to think that this whole experience has twisted or warped me in some way—oversensitized me to the pain of others. I was sitting watching a show in Las Vegas on our vacation last year; and when the topless dancers came out, I found myself wondering if there were any mastectomies in the audience feeling wounded all over again.

I think of myself before I had Tommy. I know I will never be the same again.

—Patricia

Both my babies were born in the spring, Gabi in March, Zachariah four years later in April. Good times for births, especially in Iowa, where everything, it seems, begins to grow.

Gabi weighed more than nine pounds; her bottom-first breech position necessitated a last-minute cesarean. After a couple of hours of labor I swore, "The hell with Lamaze. Just get this kid out."

Having Zach was like making an appointment to go to the

beauty parlor. I went in, nighties and a trashy novel all packed the night before, and hung around, bloated, listening to the cries from the nursery, waiting for the knockout gas, the swift slice of the knife, my second child.

I awoke earlier than the doctors said; Joe had gone out to make the calls (It's a boy!!), and I writhed and cried in great pain. Already there were flowers in the room and an index card, with Joe's jabby little scribbles, propped against the phone.

Coming Out Poem

Our humid summer fruit-filled and new bound
Under a limitless sky:
    Whirlwind moons and warm wind days
    Has left a happy seed
    Grown big in autumn's labor
    Wintered by nests of fire
    (Your gentle lap laughing)
Sweet Sprung
    Full and bursting in the Spring
    Our young.

Minutes later Joe appeared in the doorway. "What are you doing up?" he said dumbly, and sat on the edge of the bed.

"What a poem!" I said, bringing his hand to my lips.

"What a baby," Joe said, bringing his lips to mine. "Wait till you see him, Fernie. He's so beautiful."

The nurse brought Zachariah to me wrapped in soft white blankets, smelling of Johnson's Baby Shampoo. A new life. The miracle of being "in there" for so long, and then no longer a part of me, looking so perfect, so complete.

Most C-section babies *are* beautiful because their heads don't get squooshed or bruised from the difficult time of getting themselves born. I checked all the parts: the round, soft fingers and toes (I counted and recounted just to make sure), the tiny ears, the penis (bigger than I thought—I had never seen a newborn boy). I traced gently the fine eyebrows, felt the fragile breath. It was all there. Buzzy from the drugs that were just beginning to take hold (someone's body was in great pain, but it didn't seem to be mine), I sighed with relief. A good job.

But I remembered when Gabi was born. Despite the cliché of common occurrence, it was the happiest day of my life. Or at least I remember saying so aloud after I first saw her when I came out of the anesthesia. I had had no romantic notions about having babies. I thought, Oh, well, the end of late-night movies and afternoon sex. I had friends who had babies, and I knew that they meant loss of freedom and lots of work.

I had not been prepared for the gushy rush of maternal love that I felt when Gabi was placed in my arms. Immediately that unseverable bond, that fierce protective surge. During the following days in the hospital, still drug-high and with postoperative pain, I'd look into her eyes as I fed her, so close, then falling asleep together, never sure where I left off and she began . . . flesh of my flesh, bone of my bone.

Why was it different with Zach? Perhaps because it was a second child, perhaps because he was a boy. I don't know. I just didn't feel the same kind of connection. I remember saying to a friend that when I first saw him, he could have been just any baby off the street. I saw that he was beautiful and perfectly formed. I was glad we had a boy. But I did not have that primitive response of maternal passion. Surely many mothers felt this about even their firstborn: Who is this guy anyway? Am I supposed to love him?

In retrospect I don't know that I would have felt any differently if Zach had been normal. He certainly looked normal enough for those first few months to fool us all, to fool the obstetrician who told us what "terrific babies" we made. Though sometimes I think that unconsciously, intuitively, I *knew* something was wrong with Zach and so couldn't take him in completely.

Zach was a cranky, unresponsive baby. He took such a long time to finish a bottle. (Now, from hearing so many other stories, I know that difficulty in sucking is one of the signs of brain damage.) Joe and I would always have to walk Zach *as* he nursed or it would seem that he would get all chokey and gaspy. After every feeding he would be so uncomfortable. He would still be hungry, but he couldn't drink fast enough. And he was always constipated. He didn't seem to have enough control over these muscles to make everything work right.

Once when Zach was about three months old (and before we knew), Joe and I went out alone for pizza. I was tired, feeling housebound, anxious for this time of night feedings and colicky crying to be over. I asked Joe if he loved Zach. Joe looked surprised, stopping before he took a swallow of beer. "Of course," he said. "Don't you?"

"I don't know," I replied objectively. "I'm physically attracted to him. I think he's beautiful. I like holding him and smelling him and kissing him. But I don't know if I love him."

When I went to my pediatrician for Zach's three-month checkup, I tried to put it into words, but I couldn't really explain what was lacking with Zach. I told him of the constant, irritable crying, the constipation, how hard I thought it was to take care of him. "Frankly," I said, "I just don't know what *to do* with Zach all day."

"Feed him, take him shopping, play with him," the doctor replied inanely.

I had never had these questions with Gabi. But Zach really couldn't *be* "played with." He was either crying until he was picked up and carried about or asleep. Awake, we could not seem to attract his attention.

One morning in July I was driving Gabi and some other children to their half-day nursery play session, and as I honked in front of Joshua's, his dad opened the back door to get a peek at Zach.

"Hi, you rascal," he said, sticking his head in right next to Zach in his car seat. Zach was awake, but he did not even look at John.

"I guess he won't smile for me today." John shrugged apologetically.

The car motor was running. I felt the uneasiness spread. Where was I in those early months? Going unconsciously with Zach from feeding to feeding, from nap to nap, feeling slightly disconnected, something monstrous and dark hidden from me, waiting.

In New York that summer to see my parents, the visit was fraught with tension. Joe's mom was recovering from an operation that took out 80 percent of her stomach. It was cancer, Joe's stepfather told him, the day we flew into New York. Joe exhausted himself by running back and forth from my parents' home on Long Island to visit his mom in a hospital in Manhattan.

My brother and his wife, Lynn, and their new baby, Abram, were also staying with my folks that July ("Come on, one big happy happy family," said my mother).

Zach slept a lot and cried a lot. Abram slept a little and cried a lot. Between taking care of crying babies and inviting friends over for Gabi and soothing Joe's hurt, I managed to push away the growing suspicions about Zach's lack of response, though Abram at six weeks seemed quicker, more alert. I noticed that he turned his head to face Lynn as she stood by the side of the changing table.

One time I remember hearing my parents' friends talk about a neighbor's child who was retarded ("going from doctor to doctor; they never would admit it . . ."). I felt a pressure against my chest as I went over to cover Zach, who was sleeping in a portable crib against the dining-room wall.

Before we left New York, my father asked me when I was going to see the pediatrician. "Zach really doesn't hold his head up very well, Fernie. Ask the doctor about that the next time you go."

Zach at five months . . .

I was tired from all the crying, waiting for some of the
rewards: the smiles and giggles when I entered the room
. . . reaching, playing.

It wasn't coming. When my parents called and asked
what Zach was "doing," I could only reply that he looked
at his mobile (he did) but still cried an awful lot. That was
an understatement. He cried all the time he wasn't being
carried by Joe or me. I was beside myself—holding on only
because I still knew this would pass. I told people that he
seemed "slow" to me. Everyone said I was just spoiled after
having Gabi, who had been a joyful, contented baby who
laughed heartily when we made faces, who could sit in an
infant seat for hours just listening to adult conversation.
Once I asked a friend if Zach looked retarded. She was
amused. "Not any more than you do."

I knew something was wrong, knew in an intuitive, un-
definable way. And yet, on another level, I never really
believed that he could be retarded. Retarded people
"looked funny," glazed, slack-mouthed, drooling. I
thought they must "look funny" as babies, too, and act
bizarrely—hitting themselves in the heads, making strange
sounds. There was Zach, soft blond curls just beginning to
form, long lashes on his blue eyes. He looked good; he just
didn't do much. I began to look more carefully at other
babies I saw, but since none of my friends had young babies, I couldn't really compare.

One autumn day I was doing the food shopping while Joe
was home with the kids, and I noticed a woman with torn
white sneakers wheeling a baby who was sitting, propped
with some blankets behind him, in the shopping-cart seat.
She talked to him occasionally; he gooed back and smiled.
I followed them up and down every aisle, blindly plucking
items from the shelves, leaving my list in my jeans pocket.
When she went to the cashier, I went up behind her, watching her baby as she unloaded a high cartful of groceries, six

loaves of Wonder bread balanced on top. I smiled frozenly and chucked the baby under the chin. He smiled back. I offered him a crinkly wrapper from one of my packages. He took it and began examining it industriously, passing it from hand to hand. Then the baby turned as the cashier noisily rang up the mother's total, leaning forward in his seat to inspect the contents of the money tray.

"He's darling. How old is he?" I said to his mother, trying to appear casual. She scooped him up, setting him astride an enormous hip. He held his head straight and reached for her glasses. "Just six months today," she replied jauntily, and she waddled out through the electric eye of Safeway's door. I felt as if I was going to throw up.

At home, I was scared; alone with Joe at night I told him something was wrong with Zach. I told him about the baby in the supermarket. "Come on, honey, you can't compare him to other babies."

Patronizing but kind, he got down Dr. Spock from the shelf. It had been well read all through Gabi's infancy but we hadn't looked at it since Zach was born. He read: "Every baby's face is different from every other's. In the same way, every baby's pattern of development is different. . . ." He went on but I didn't hear him. Afterward we went in and looked at Zach sleeping peacefully, his cherubic mouth in a pout—he looked like the baby on the Pampers box. "How could you worry about him?" Joe asked. (How could you not? I thought.)

I had bought some teething biscuits at Safeway a few trips earlier and had stored them away. How old was Gabi when she held one? When I put the biscuit in front of Zach, he just stared blankly at it. When I put the biscuit in his hand, wrapping his fingers around it, he dropped it, seemingly unaware of the connection his hand could make to his mouth. I put the biscuits back on the shelf . . . different babies—different patterns of development. Why was I getting so scared?

One night I had a dream of a moon-faced mongoloid sitting in front of our fireplace watching the flames. I explain to our company (I've never seen any of them before) that, although I know it is odd to have a fire in the summer in Iowa, "it always soothes the boy and keeps him from crying." So we all eat dinner by the fire, and a lady in a formal gown fans herself as she takes delicate mouthfuls of her crab casserole. "Delicious," they all say, sweating profusely. Joe comes down from upstairs with two blond children. "Gabi and Zach would like to say good night." Oh, I am so relieved. "So this is not Zach," I blurt out, pointing to the thick, blank child at my side. Joe flashes me a dirty look before carrying Gabi and Zach to bed.

In October the Iowa sky was a blazing blue, and the air smelled of earth and wet leaves. Gabi was in nursery school, and I was not teaching that quarter, so I spent a good deal of time chauffeuring Gabi to school, home for lunch and a nap, to pottery lessons or ballet in the late afternoon. I spent my time holding Zach and walking him so he would not cry . . . and waiting.

We had been calling Joe's mom in New York almost every day. What is there to talk about? Some days there is less pain than others; some meals she could manage to eat half a chicken sandwich, a little broth. Jack is at work, fall is such a busy season in the garment district. Muriel spends the day watching TV and doing crossword puzzles. She won't take the chemotherapy treatments any longer. They make her too sick and even the doctors now admit that they don't think they are doing her any good.

One time on the phone Muriel says, "The only thing about dying is, it's so goddamn lonely."

Muriel asks about the children and I try and think of amusing little anecdotes about them, realizing how little I have to say about Zach.

One Saturday a group of close friends was over, and Joe was talking about his mom sick in New York and him feeling

so removed from her here in Iowa, so powerless. We discovered (well, we always knew but never put it together)
that all four of the men—Joe; Arnie, a psychology professor; Norm, a social worker; Mel, a poet and teacher—are
Jewish, in their thirties, and had mothers who died (or as
with Joe's mom, were dying) in their fifties, of cancer.

"Gee," Joe said jokingly. "You thought we were just
friends, and we're really a support group."

The next day Mel called Joe and asked him when he was
going to go back to New York to see his mom. "Go now,"
he said, "while you can still have a nice weekend together.
Before she's back in the hospital with tubes up her nose and
you sit around waiting for her to stop breathing. Go now
so you'll have a last time you'll want to remember."

Good advice, we thought. Joe took off two days from
school, and the next week he and Gabi flew to New York.

As soon as they left, I called Zach's pediatrician to change
the appointment for his six-month checkup to the next
afternoon. He was five months, two weeks. "It's sort of an
emergency," I told the nurse calmly.

I took great care getting Zach ready for the doctor's
appointment—a bath, baby lotion, a shampoo to fluff those
new curls, a light-blue jump suit that matched his eyes.
Again, an unconscious deliberation, as if Zach's beauty
could blind the doctor to his deficiencies: the fact that he
still could not hold up his head, that he never used his
hands, that he did not look across a room.

Zach and I spent ten minutes alone in the small examination room before the pediatrician came in; I stood up with
Zach, rocking him, reading the signs on the bulletin boards:

"Do not give children under three years of age carrots or
nuts. These are difficult to chew and . . ."

"Parents of toddlers should keep syrup of ipecac in the
house. In case of poisoning . . ."

Until Dr. Lawrence knocked and entered. He had been
Gabi's pediatrician for four years, a brusque man who
never looked terrifically happy with his job; well, maybe he
was bored answering the same old questions of anxious

mothers about colic and teething and potty training. And having to make kids cry all day.

He laid Zach down on the examination table and drew him up by his arms. Dr. Lawrence's brows knit when he saw Zach's lack of head control. Then he took out a tape measure and put it around Zach's head. "Hmmmm," he said. "We might have a little hydrocephalus here."

Hydrocephalus. Water . . . fluid . . . on the brain. Was that what it was?

Something burst in me. Despite the sick feelings of dread that had lain within me in the past few weeks I was still shocked to hear him say the words, to say that there actually could be something wrong.

I pounded the wall with my fist, crying and shrieking at Dr. Lawrence. "How can you say that so casually? You're not talking about the carburetor in my car. You're talking about my child!"

Now Zach, lying flat on the table, had begun to wail.

"Well, one of us has to remain calm," said Dr. Lawrence, ignoring the fact that it was his offhand manner that precipitated my tantrum.

He returned to his office and called the Department of Pediatric Neurology at the university hospital in Iowa City and made an appointment for that very afternoon. I didn't stop to think that Iowa City was two and a half hours away, that it was a Friday afternoon, that Joe was in New York. Dr. Lawrence made it seem (even in his casual way) that if Zach *were* hydrocephalic, if he did have fluid building up in his brain, that I had to get him to Iowa City as fast as I could.

Two nurses fluttered sweetly about, gathering my diaper bag, jacket, pocketbook, dressing Zach first in his blue jump suit, then in his white sweater. One asked if I would be able to drive home all right, and I assured her that I would, although by the time I loaded Zach into the car and pulled out of the clinic parking lot, I was crying so hard that I couldn't see out the window.

At home I called my friend Mary Beth, sobbing incoher-

ently on the phone. She called Mel at school. I don't remember what I said but in minutes they appeared, two
separate cars pulling up to my driveway, as if in a police
movie. (Did Mary Beth leave her four-year-old playing in
the yard? Did Mel walk out in the middle of teaching a
composition class? I never asked.)

Mary Beth scooped up Zach in her arms and danced him
around the living room. He smiled and managed a chuckle.
"There's nothing the matter with this baby," said loyal
Mary Beth.

I packed more diapers, a jar of strained peaches, some
more milk, and Mel, Zach, and I drove off to Iowa City,
Mary Beth waving good-bye from my stoop.

What can I tell about those two days? It ended up that
Zach was admitted overnight for "observation"; Mel and I,
toothbrushless, had to hunt around Iowa City for a motel
room during what was a big football weekend. There was
only one room left in the entire city; and as we were regis-
tering, Mel turned to me sheepishly, "How should I sign
the register?"

"Well, use both our names," I said. "We're hardly here
for an affair." The man behind the counter blinked and
looked away.

It took me a while to catch on to the game at the teaching
hospital. Different doctors at different times would come in
and start asking me questions about my family history, the
pregnancy, was Zach ever dropped on his head, etc. I kept
thinking that each was *the* doctor, but no, then he or she
would gather up the notes, and minutes later a new person
would appear. "Look," I said impatiently after the third
one. "Why do I have to keep repeating this same story; why
don't you get together with this?"

What I didn't understand then was that all these people
were medical students, interns, residents; Zach was part of
their curriculum. So, of course, they didn't answer any of
my questions. They were interested in asking their own.

With every new person I had to keep interrupting my

story to explain about Mel, sitting politely in the corner. "No, *he's* not the father." One time an enthusiastic resident came in and started measuring Mel's head before we stopped him.

I remember I was sorry that before we left Ames, I had not changed into something more presentable than the faded overalls and black turtleneck I had worn to the pediatrician's that morning. There I was in old hippie garb with a man who was not the father of my child—what if the doctors didn't believe me when I had answered that no, I had never dropped Zach on his head?

I don't remember how many residents and interns I spoke to that day—they all seemed eminently forgettable; they blended into a sameness like the door-to-door Jehovah's Witnesses who have knocked over the years.

Finally when we saw *the* pediatric neurologists, I was disappointed when all they did was hit Zach with little rubber hammers, shine some lights into his eyes, and measure his head. The examination seemed primitive to me. I kept thinking, "This is it? This is years and years of medical school?"

It was later, on other subsequent visits, that the more sophisticated tests began: the bloodletting, the machines, later the genetic evaluations.

That visit I learned nothing. Except that there was no real emergency. Zach was not hydrocephalic. "Well, what can it be?" I asked one neurologist.

"Oh, there's so many things that it can be," she said.

"Name three," I pleaded.

"Why don't you just treat him like a normal little boy unless you find out for sure that he's not?"

I made an appointment for more tests, and Mel and I drove back to Ames. Zach, tired after being prodded and pounded, slept peacefully the whole way.

It was Saturday. Joe and Gabi were supposed to be coming home on Monday, and I was hoping he wouldn't call. I didn't want to ruin the last weekend he'd ever have with his mother. I planned to fake it if he did call: there was no emergency and so no reason to tell him until he came home. I needed him so much then that I felt a certain nobility and strength in making the decision not to tell him.

But I was not prepared to walk into the house after Mel dropped us off to hear the ringing phone and Joe's worried voice: "Where have you been, honey? I've been calling you since late last night."

"Oh, Joe," I cried, my voice breaking; he must have heard my heart as well.

"Oh, God, what happened, Fernie?"

I told him everything, brave resolve melted by my tears. He and Gabi took the next plane out of New York.

It's a romantic myth that tragedy brings families together. I think that we can endure tragedies and, yes, perhaps grow, but most of us with ordinary marriages are not soldered or strengthened by these trials. Never did I feel more alone than on those autumn drives with Joe back from Iowa City Hospitals during Zach's first year. Another specialist, another test, revealed only "delayed development: etiology unknown." I would press the doctors. If I couldn't have guarantees, I wanted percentages.

Zach at six months . . . lying on an examination table, surrounded by residents who had come to learn. I pointed as if Zach was some specimen from a lab, not a child who has my pale blue eyes. I heard my own voice, clinical, detached: "You say he could be perfectly normal?" I was talking to Dr. James, one of the Midwest's most respected neurologists, a soft-spoken man who looked down at the floor when he spoke to me. I wanted to shake him, hold his face in my hands, "Tell me the truth, damn it! Tell me what you know! Look at me!" (Later a mother of a brain-damaged child explained about Dr. James. "Perhaps what he has to say to parents is so painful that he can never look them in the eye. If he did, he would crumble every day.")

After Dr. James examined Zach, he answered me. "Yes, your son could be normal."

We were standing very close in that small examination room; I could smell the laundry soap from Dr. James's lab coat. Silence.

"But," I continued, "Zach could be severely retarded." I moved in closer, turned my head to try and get in under his gaze. I wanted to connect with this man.

"Yes," said Dr. James, still looking at his shoes. "He could be severely retarded."

Joe said later, "Oh, Fernie, how could you say that? Why must you always think the worst?"

I was always having to defend myself. I thought Joe was trying to protect himself by not facing the truth.

We made four trips to Iowa City within three weeks that fall, Joe canceling classes, me palming Gabi off on neighbors and friends. Zach had brain X rays: EEGs and CAT scans. Once we made the two-and-a-half-hour trip only to find out that the EMI scan, this special machine that examines the brain layer by layer, was broken. We'd made the trip for nothing. The machine had been broken all night, but no one had called to tell us not to bother to come. When I found this out, I screamed and pounded the desk, scaring a poor young nurse who had nothing whatsoever to do with the mishap. Then Joe and I, feeling numb and powerless, drove back to Ames.

No tests that Zach had that first year reported any abnormalities. The brain tests, the nerve tests, the blood and urine tests—nothing. Once we kept him overnight to collect a twenty-four-hour urine sample. Joe dropped us off and went back to teach his classes; I would take Zach back on the bus the next day. Then I found out that the plastic bag that they had taped around Zach's penis had accidentally leaked; they would have to collect the urine all over again the next week.

I suppose I wanted the doctors to find something that they could *fix,* or at least something that had a *name.* When we called our folks in New York after each of the tests, they always seemed relieved that the tests came back normal. I kept saying, "Well, that really doesn't mean that Zach is okay." Me, the perennial doom-sayer.

After each visit to Iowa City, Joe and I would drive home in sullen silence, starting already to close off from one another, to nurse our own pains. Joe's mother was dying at fifty-six, and he, an only child, felt guilty about not being able to give her his full emotional attention. I had no reserve for sympathy, for when I saw Joe gaze out the window distractedly, his eyes filled with tears, I knew he was thinking of his mother and not of Zach.

"My mother is dying," Joe would tell me, "just now when her life was going well, just now when she was happy. Zach is here and he's alive. Which is the more tragic?" I was too afraid to answer him.

So part of Joe's hearty optimism with regard to Zach's condition was an attempt to balance a bearable amount of pain. He had a mother dying of cancer a thousand miles away, a wife on the verge of nervous collapse, and a son with "developmental delay: etiology unknown." It was necessary for Joe's own survival to think that Zach was going to be all right.

Muriel died just a month after that first trip to Iowa City.

Joe still feels guilty about running off that weekend in New York and leaving her. It was that old fantasy come to life: The boat capsizes—who do you save, your mother or your wife?

I've told Joe something to assuage his guilt and said it so often that now I've really come to believe it myself: There is nothing more self-involved than the act of dying. To be able to get out of yourself, to think and worry about another, to be able to give something when your own life is shriveling to nothing, is a true act of love. When Joe and I spoke on the phone that day, Muriel said, "Go to Fern now, she needs you." There are so few things that a dying person can *do* for someone else. And this, I told Joe, was something his mom *could* do. I think this made her feel valuable and good, I really do.

I was thirty that fall, and all the hesitations and compunctions I had about reaching this age were brought forth with striking clarity: You've had a good life, you've had it easy . . . the fun's all over, my girl. The shit has really hit the fan.

For me that autumn was the end of something. Since that weekend in Iowa City I divide my life into *before* and *after* Zach. During that first year I'd go around the house and look at *this* photograph, *that* wineglass. I'd say, "This was taken before Zach was born. . . . Oh, I bought that after Zach was born."

What I was really doing was seeing two lives, separate and distinguishable.

I think people often do this when they have an event in their lives of such cataclysmic proportion, and they feel themselves so changed by this event, that forevermore they see lives as before and after, measuring time, remembering occasions, by whatever so turned them around.

I had a friend, Rose, whose mother had been in a concentration camp during the war, a timid, nervous woman who could never complete a full sentence without a sigh, who shook when she held a teacup. Once Rose showed me a picture of her mother as a young girl in her twenties: a ballerina in a famous European troupe, her arms held boldly aloft, her plumed head at a jaunty angle facing the camera.

"Oh, well, that was before the war," her mother explained. "I don't dance anymore."

During Zach's first year I, too, stopped dancing; so steeped in gloom was I, in self-pity, so scared of what the future would bring, so sure I would never be "myself" again, altered forever by this child who it seemed was stopped in time as a very young baby.

Zach at six months, at ten months, then a year; he was the same: a fretful newborn. Growing bigger, even prettier, I thought, but developmentally into a holding pattern, going nowhere . . . slowly.

Friends were always trying to buoy my spirits. Well-meaning people were telling tales of babies who were slow to develop and then turned out "perfectly normal." Joe's secretary regaled him with such stories about a friend's son: "Lay like a log until he was ten months old; didn't walk until he was two. Now he's a corporal in the marines."

"The *marines*," Joe reported distastefully to me. "He probably *was* retarded."

I thought that my pain and Zach's deficiencies were as glaring when we were out in public as the yellow Star of David that Jews had to wear during the war. So I was always surprised when we were not so branded. One time I ran into Jean, a good friend-of-a-friend whom I had not seen since Zach's birth.

We were wheeling down a supermarket aisle, Zach in his stroller because he could not sit up in a cart, when we ran into her.

"Well, well," said Jean, kneeling down face-to-face with Zach. When you got right into his line of vision, he did look you in the eye and connect. "He looks just great!" said Jean.

I thought she meant "he looks just great *considering* that something is wrong, you've been going for all these tests . . . blah, blah, blah." But as we talked some more, I realized, slowly, that, no, she didn't *know* anything was wrong at all. She was saying that Zach looked great on his very own steam.

Jean was shocked when I told her about going back and forth for all those hospital tests (probably thinking, "Is he as bad as all that?"). I was shocked that he could still pass for normal. (Was he as good as all that?) People forget what year-old babies can do, I think. When you don't have a year-old baby yourself, you forget how they're supposed to act.

During Zach's first year I spent many hours in the univer-

sity library reading medical journals I could barely understand, texts on development and neurological dysfunction.
I sat alone at a desk in the back of tier 4, poring over
pictures of children with grotesque, misshapen bodies,
mottled skin, dull eyes, expressionless faces . . . the prison
photos of a netherworld. The older books had pictures of
babies labeled "morons" and "imbeciles."

I would read about exotic diseases, match up Zach's
"symptoms" and try my diagnosis. Coming home from the
library, shaken and sick, I'd tell Joe about what I read. He'd
be watching a ball game; Zach would be peacefully sleeping
in the next room. I'd look at beautiful Zach, think of the
cruel pictures in those books, and cry until my chest hurt.
Joe told me to stop going to the library. "You're making
yourself crazier than you already are."

I remember the last day I went. I was reading a book
entitled *Development: Normal and Abnormal.* There was a picture of a round, healthy-looking baby with blond curls,
lying on an examining table; a doctor was lifting him to
sitting position by his arms. The baby's head flopped down
his back—just like Zach's did when we tried to pull him up.
The caption underneath the picture read, "No head control
for this severely retarded infant."

Joe remained optimistic about Zach. When he would
speak to friends and family on the phone, he would say that
"Zach was improving, using his hands a little more, holding
his head better." Then when people talked to me, they
must have thought that we lived in two different families.

I started teaching again that winter and spring. In the
mornings, three days a week, a handicapped preschool
teacher and a physical therapist would come out to the
house for half an hour, and I had time to get dressed and
eat some cold cereal. Zach would cry and fuss almost the
whole time they worked with him, and in my room, getting
dressed, I'd turn up the radio to block the sound, but the
knot in my stomach never did go away.

Later Millie would come by bus. Millie, an older woman

with three grown sons, had been Mary Beth's baby-sitter while she was finishing her dissertation. "Millie's youngest son was retarded," Mary Beth told me. "He was home for ten years. She knows what it is to have a hard time. Why don't you call her?"

Ask any woman, and she'll tell you that calling for baby-sitters is on the bottom of any chore list, under ironing even. Why do we hate it so? It always seems as if we are asking for favors—maybe because the pay is so low. Or the teen-agers are too rich today, and they never sound enthusiastic. "Oh, all right," they'll say laconically. And then, if they say no and you have to call a few of them, it's such a lousy feeling. Maybe we think they are rejecting our children.

With Zach this baby-sitter business was blown completely out of proportion. Unless I was sure he would stay asleep and we would be right in the neighborhood, I had to make sure to get very competent people. Someone with strong arms for rocking, someone who wouldn't panic when he started to choke when he was being fed. Probably it was easier for us never to go out. I dreaded making the calls.

But now that I was teaching again, I needed a baby-sitter for several days a week. I was overjoyed when Millie said yes.

It is hard to explain Millie's special relationship to our family for the next two years. I cannot imagine how we would have survived without her. Millie loved Zach, holding him, kissing him, making him smile, content to join him in his small world. Working with Zach, Millie was as smart as any special-education teacher. She'd tie balloons to a chair and help Zach bat them with his hands; she'd play endless games of peek-a-boo, trying over and over to attract his attention.

On warmer days, as spring came soggily to Iowa, Millie would be outside on the stoop, holding Zach, waiting for me to drive up from school. I'd see him from the car; Millie would be trying to straighten his head, telling him Mommy was home. He looked dazed in the sunlight, lying back, his arms and legs so floppy, as if he were floating underwater.

Funny, as I'm writing this, I don't even remember Gabi at the time. She was five that March, still in nursery school. I don't remember her teacher, or saving anything she made at school. She was always just playing in the periphery; Zach just loomed so large.

I tried to do all the right things that first year.

To save Zach I fought the schools to get him physical therapy; I got him into a handicapped preschool program; I bought him every toy that was colorful enough to catch his eye, was light enough to catch his hand; Joe and I read books about infant stimulation and held Zach's hands in trays of rice and Jell-O; we built scooter boards and positioning tables; we fed him each mouthful by moving his spoon from left to right, making him follow it with his eyes; we covered his fingers with peanut butter and honey and placed them toward his mouth; we stood him up every day, although his legs buckled; we sat him down every day, although his neck folded; at night Joe put on music after dinner and danced Zach around the house; we kissed him all over and held him tight.

To save myself I joined a parent support group; I bought new clothes; I saw a therapist; I went back to teaching.

But I still, always, had a lump in my throat; I feared it would go to my breast, sick as I was, always tired, susceptible now to tragedy, not at all the girl I was *before* Zach.

And sometimes in that first year when Zach slept too long into a nap and I'd think "crib-death" and then, yes, the disappointment that I felt when I finally heard his stirring, my death wish for him having surfaced again, I'd run to pick him up and cry, ashamed, into his soft hair.

2

It seemed so horrible to me. It took me a long time to say "retarded."
"Carol is retarded." I felt sick. For a long time I would wake up in
the morning and throw up.

My own parents, I think, had more trouble than I admitting that
Carol was retarded. They'd make up some excuses for themselves;
we'd talk about Carol's bad heart. Sometimes this was harder for me
because I felt as if I was helping them. It was so devastating for
them. This was the first grandchild that they had that was "defec-
tive." But they hurt for me, too. I know I would feel the same way
if my daughter Jill had a baby like this because I couldn't stand to
see her in such pain. I think for grandparents it is doubly hard. For
their child and for their grandchild. They hurt twice.

—Beth

Ever since college I have lived far from roots, from family,
from home-grown friends. All my adult life I have had
astronomical phone bills—it is my one extravagance. Other
women can go to beauty parlors—I dial area codes.

When Gabi was a baby, I would call often, sometimes in
the afternoon when my father was still at work. "Hi, Mom,
what's that recipe for potato *kugel*?" Chatty as if I were
around the corner instead of halfway across a continent.

Although I was in graduate school and Joe was getting his
first article published, most of the talk was about "important" things: What was Gabi doing? I called the first time she
stood up in her crib, her fat legs quivering, pudgy hands
gripping the side of the bed. I called to let my parents hear
"da da da da" as Gabi began nonsense vocalization. I called
for her first bowel movement deposited in the toilet bowl,

and as I pressed the phone to Gabi's ear, I heard my mother's voice, "Are *you* wearing big-girl panties? Grandma's going to send you some new big-girl panties!"

All the totally trivial wonders of normal childhood development were greeted with *kvelling* and cooing and thunderous applause. And it made me so happy to share this joy.

Now the phone calls were always painful. What is there new to tell? What did another test show? Zach was having physical therapy. Was he holding his head up a little better? "Yes, he is," Joe would say.

"I don't see any difference," I would say.

"What is he eating?" my mother would say when conversation got sticky and slim.

She had stopped saying "things will be all right" a few phone calls back.

"Things are *not* all right now. I'm not sure that they *will be* all right," I had told her sharply.

Sometimes my mother would hear my sad voice, dull and hollow—Fern, the chirpy storyteller, now with no more stories to tell—and she would cry. My father would be angry at her—"Get control of yourself"; she had promised him that she would not cry on the phone. Joe would be angry at me for being so negative and painting them such a gloomy picture of Zach's disabilities. "He doesn't 'do nothing.' He smiles. For chrissake, he's only a baby. Give him a chance."

And every so often my parents would suggest other hospitals, new doctors. "Why Iowa City? How about the Mayo Clinic?" But they never would have suggested Woodward State Hospital School, even if they had known about it, because Woodward was the state institution for the retarded. And *retarded* was not a word that any one of us was saying easily in those days.

Still, we were tired of seeing doctors who were little more than expert technicians, who, if they wouldn't give medication or operate, were useless in telling us what to do. And I was tired of the two-and-a-half-hour trip to Iowa City,

tired of the machines, the tests, the doctors who looked at
Zach for only minutes at a time, pulling him up by his arms
and watching his head flop back, tapping his knees and
elbows with little rubber hammers, and coming up later
with nothing new to tell me, nothing I did not know from
already living with him. One time Joe and I waited, enter-
taining a fretful, crying Zach in a bare cubicle for more than
an hour, when the same pediatric neurologist whom we had
seen twice before walked in and after a brief examination
concluded, "You're right. This child does have delayed
development."

"Well, *I* would be retarded if I didn't know that," I responded nastily.

After a visit to the hospitals Joe and I were always more
depressed than ever. The doctors knew nothing more than
here was a baby with "delayed development: etiology unknown."

At night I'd look into Zachy's eyes as I put him to bed.
He'd meet my gaze, deeply, warmly, and smile as I sang him
his bedtime song. He couldn't sit or hold his head; he
didn't look across the room when you came in. But alone,
face-to-face, in his darkened bedroom, his eyes would
search my face.

"Shhh," I'd say. "Listen. Do you hear Daddy watching
TV downstairs? He's going to come up and kiss you good
night."

Zachy's eyes would widen, and he'd smile. He knew what
I was saying. Could he be retarded? I tested him all the
time. Holding him in my arms, I'd turn on the wall switch
and point and say, "Light, light, look at the light with your
eyes." I could almost see the *click-click* in his head as he
made the connection. After a while he had a small, receptive vocabulary: light, TV, music (the stereo in the living
room), and Mommy, Daddy, and Gabi. We worked on these
every day, the three of us sitting in the living room after
dinner. "Look at Gabi with your eyes." Slowly, *click-click,* a
smile would come into focus and Zach would turn toward

Gabi, sitting next to him on the couch. Joe and I would be elated when he responded, and Zach, himself, would be proud when he got a proper identification, and all of us clapped and cheered. Joe would say, "This kid may be retarded, but he sure is smart!"

I got confused about what the word *retarded* really meant. Sometimes, especially when he was outside, Zach looked unfocused and blurry. Sometimes in photographs, his head down, his eyes crossed, he did look retarded. Other times, when he was held a certain way and his eyes met yours, he looked very normal.

The president of the Association for Retarded Citizens here in Ames has a mildly retarded sixteen-year-old boy who reads *Time* magazine, follows the weather report, and talks about the high and low fronts. So what makes him retarded? I have students in my classes at the community college who can't read *Time* magazine. I don't know, I think it has something to do with some kind of social appropriateness: knowing when not to giggle, keeping a composed face.

A family on our street has a retarded five-year-old who can pick locks, unscrew cabinet doors, untie knotted ropes —a regular Houdini. But he'll walk right into the street, oblivious to the dangers of cars. If you ask him how he feels, he cannot tell you. I look into his eyes sometimes, and he looks away.

Zach was a year old, and no doctor had ever said for sure that he was retarded, even though at a year he was like a three-month-old baby—at least physically. What did go on in his head?

The spring that Zach was a year old, I made an appointment with a social worker to get him evaluated at Woodward State Hospital for the retarded.

I went to the social service office here in Ames, laden with all Zach's medical records, and waited, reading signs about food stamps and day care that were posted on the bulletin board. Next to me sat a stringy-haired woman—maybe in her twenties. She had one baby on her knee who was cooing and giggling as she bounced him up and down. At her feet a two-year-old played with Matchbox trucks. Both children had smeary faces and runny noses. I scooted one of the runaway trucks back to the little boy and made a *varroom-rooom* sound. The woman smiled at me; she was missing all her bottom teeth, and I smiled back, feeling some kind of camaraderie with her—both of us waiting, asking, needful. So now I was on the other side; the social workers (God, how many of my college friends were social workers?) became "they."

I was called in and was led behind a maze of partitions to a middle-aged woman with sad, kindly eyes who was sitting behind the messiest, most paper-strewn desk I had ever seen. I told her about Zach, showed her the records from Iowa City. I'd told "the story" so many times, but it was still so painful to me. I began to cry, and she searched among the ruin on the desk to find me a tissue. Was I mistaken, or were her own eyes filled with tears?

Her name was Lauren, and she said that she needed to make a home visit before she could complete the request for the Woodward evaluation. We made a date for the following week at a time when I would be at a class but Joe would be home with Zach.

She came the next Thursday, walking in to witness Joe on the floor with Zach, giving him a suppository. Zach had fussed and cried all morning and Joe thought that he was constipated.

Then the three of them went into the living room to talk while Joe held and rocked Zach. Joe told me how Lauren kept saying, "How lucky Zach was!" I didn't quite know what to make of it, except that perhaps the sight of a father so dedicated and concerned that he involved himself with the intimate bodily functions of his child touched a certain sympathetic chord. When I came home from class that afternoon, Lauren was still there, drinking tea with Joe. Zach was upstairs napping, and Gabi was sitting on the living-room floor cutting out paper dolls. I'm sure by any social-work standards, we were an ideal family, more than ideal —actually a husband who could change diapers and make tea.

We signed all the necessary forms for Woodward and then signed releases for all of Zach's records; Lauren finished her tea and said she'd call us when a date was set up. I thought of our forms burrowed in that pile on her desk and said that I'd call her next week, just to check. I figured that a gentle nudge would not hurt us any. A month later (what happened to people who didn't nudge?) our appointment was all set. We were to bring Zach to Woodward, some thirty miles away, early Monday morning and stay during that time to meet with the therapists, psychologists, social workers, doctors, and then leave Zach there for a week while the staff observed and tested him. We would pick him up on Friday and have a formal staffing. We could bring toys and his own crib blanket, but we were not to bring any clothes, since they might get mixed up with the institution's laundry.

I thought of Gabi at a year old, of leaving her alone for five days in a hospital with strangers. I would never have done it; I would have had to stay with her.

Zach would cry when he woke up alone. It pained me to think of him there crying, confused. Well, how confused would he be? I didn't know. I also felt relief about not having to take care of him. And that made me sad.

It was sunny and cold the Monday we drove to Woodward. I held Zach wrapped in his patchwork crib blanket, in my arms, and the sun shone through the windshield across his sleeping face. Joe was silent and gloomy, and I felt an approaching dread as we drove down the rows and rows of trees that formed the entrance to the institution: Woodward State Hospital-School. "Woodward," I said. "The name sounds like Auschwitz to me." As soon as I said it, I was sorry. Joe glared hostilely. "If you're going to be melodramatic, just keep it to yourself. I feel fine, and you're always bringing me down."

I continued silently with my comparison. I felt like here, in this beautiful Iowa countryside, we were driving Zach to his death. The old brick buildings glared ominously from behind the rows of sturdy trees. What was inside?

We were to go to a building called the "medical center," but all the buildings looked alike to us and we didn't see any names.

There were people walking around the grounds; it looked like a college campus. "Let's ask someone," I suggested, pointing to a man who was raking leaves under a nearby tree. We stopped the car, and I rolled down my window. "Excuse me," I called, and heard my voice carry in the wind. The man, dressed in green fatigues and a nylon windbreaker, came over to the car. I saw that he was retarded. His eyes had a dull cast, and his mouth was askew as if he had pulled his lip down by one finger, and it somehow stayed that way.

How would he know the way? Did he even talk? But he was looking into the car and smiling at Zach, who lay still sleeping in my arms. "Do you know where the medical center is?" I asked. He turned himself around and pointed. "Make a sharp right there and the second left. It's the last brick building on your left," he said.

Joe and I drove off, smiling at each other. "Good directions," we both said as the building came into view.

The staff at Woodward were exuberant and warm: they said things like "neat" and "okey-dokey."

I held Zach in my lap as we sat at a long table with a social worker, a hearing and speech therapist, a physical therapist and a careworker, a psychologist and a doctor. Unlike the doctors at Iowa City, they seemed to have time for us. They ohhed and ahhed over Zach—clucking and touching his cheek. "Boy, are the girls going to love taking care of him. He's a doll."

Joe and I talked for a while about what Zach could and couldn't do, feeding habits, etc. I felt easy leaving him there with that eager group, who all seemed as if they couldn't wait to get hold of him.

I warned them about his irritable crying, wanting to prepare them that all was not cuddles and smiles with this guy;
oh, yes, they understood all about that. Zach was really
tired, so I rocked him a little before I put him down in the
crib they had set up in the D and E Unit, a short-term care
ward for diagnosis and evaluation. There were six other
children there. In the next crib was a tiny boy named Tate,
whom the workers called "Tater." At three he was about as
long as my arm and just as thin. He had braces around his
waist and legs and his tiny arms were rigid, his hands fisted.
Now Tate was in an infant seat, his head propped forward,
and a giant bib covered his whole body. He was being fed
mashed rice and gravy with little bits of meat by a young
girl who was smiling with him and chatting, "Mmm, that's
a boy, Tater; this is *soooo* good." Tate had a gag reflex and
a tongue thrust; like Zach, he really couldn't chew but sort
of sucked his food, pressing on his palate with his tongue.
Because of his tongue thrust much of it came back out, but
the girl who fed him scooped quickly around his chin and
put it back in. It took a long time for him to get down each
mouthful, and he coughed and choked a lot.

I watched as I stood rocking Zach and Tate looked back
at me with piercing, bright eyes. "You really like that
stuff?" I whispered to him. "That doesn't look so good to
me."

Tate gave me a broad smile and a mouthful of mashed
rice plopped out on his bib. The girl smiled, too. "He
understands everything you say to him."

I laid Zach down in the crib and patted him until he
drifted off to sleep. Then Joe and I said good-bye to the
horde of workers; we'd be back on Friday for the meeting
following the evaluation. I turned and saw a cherubic Zach,
sleeping peacefully under a mobile whose stringed butter-
flies fluttered gently above his head.

The week passed too quickly. For the first time in a year
I didn't need a nap during the daytime, I didn't walk around

with my stomach in knots. I understood what it meant to "unwind," that expression we use, usually following that "hard day at the office," etc. Unwinding came as a gradual stretching out and up toward a plateau of stability and peace. I missed Zach, missed holding him, cuddling him—the empty crib in the room at the end of the hall made me ache—but I had a relaxed energy; for the first time in a year the heaviness of depression that had sat on my shoulders like a great shawl was lifted.

I had so many plans for that week. In a burst of energy I cleaned out closets, rearranged furniture; I went through all my teaching materials and labeled and filed and threw out. Those times after supper when we'd drink coffee and read the paper seemed so sinfully easy. Gabi, at five, was a pleasure to be with. I read to her and played Go-Fish, and we'd take long bubble baths together and write invisible soapy letters on each other's backs and wash each other's hair. For a long time I could not see how people could ever complain about taking care of normal kids.

When Friday came, Joe was whistling around the house, eager to start the trip to Woodward. I felt the heaviness closing in on me. In the car Gabi and Joe were chatting. "Do you think he'll know us, Gabi?" Gabi said that she thought he'd missed us. She asked if we thought he'd cried a lot there. Joe said he didn't think so. Gabi said, "Well, he cries a lot at home."

We drove down the rows of trees toward the medical center and parked the car in the side lot. I got out and took a deep breath, assumed a bracing stance, and gave myself a little pep talk . . . be strong . . . no tears . . . no complaints. Okay, let's go. We pushed the steel door and headed to the second floor to meet the experts and find out the verdict. Joe wanted to see Zach first thing, so we walked to the end of the corridor where all the children were who were in for diagnosis and evaluation. In a crib toward the far wall Zach was being diapered by a pale young girl who looked no more than sixteen. When we walked over, he was still fussing, but his eyes seemed to click in with ours. Did he know us? I picked him up, and his cries ebbed, then stopped as I began to walk him around. I knew he would stop crying no matter who was walking him, as long as he was held and moving. His head smelled of institutional soap, harsh and medicinal. I held Zach as we went to meet the group that had evaluated him all week; we sat around a wooden table and waited. I don't know what I expected from them. The therapists said that he was at a two-month level in most physical skills, perhaps a five-month level in some receptive skills. Well, I knew that. I lived with him; I didn't want them to tell me what he was now; I wanted some assurances about what he could become.

The thing is that with a very young child there is no real "verdict," and I could understand why they were loath to give us one. Brain damage, unlike enlarged tonsils or infected ears, often cannot be "seen," even with the most sophisticated equipment. Also, the behavior associated with brain damage varies so greatly; a child who is "slow," a child whose learning disability makes him transpose letters, can be brain-damaged. The hyperactive child who fidgets and drums and knocks down the other kids' blocks can be brain-damaged. The child in the wheelchair who must be fed all his meals can be brain-damaged. The physical disabilities confuse appropriate labeling even more. The child who is nimble and physically quick but who makes little cognitive connections. The child who can neither walk or talk, but who "knows." And then seizures. All the doctors we've ever seen have asked us questions about seizures. Does Zach ever go rigid, his eyes blinking or turned up in his head? (No.) Does Zach ever seem unfocused, far off, unresponsive to surrounding stimuli? (Yes.) At one year of age Zach had had enough pages in his medical records to rival any file the FBI has on criminals, terrorists, or spies. Now this, the "Woodward Evaluation" —a composite opinion from the doctors, therapists, psychologists, clinicians—again told me what I knew: that here

was a year-old baby who acted like a much younger baby—
"delayed development: etiology unknown." It was a fairly
common diagnosis.

But unlike the doctors in Iowa City the therapists at
Woodward did not pronounce it "cased closed—come back
for reevaluation in six months." In fact they seemed eager
and excited to "get to work to get Zach in therapy, to get
him 'programmed.' " Nan, the head therapist, said that,
although Woodward did not legitimately take "outpa-
tients," she would like to continue to see Zach for therapy
sessions. She said she could call them "follow-ups." Also,
she herself was later starting an infant-stimulation program, and she could continue to see Zach in that capacity.

Nan was so exuberant, so confident, that for the first time
I felt that we could positively influence what Zach could
"become" physically and mentally in the same way that
parents influence their normal children with opinions and
values. I felt that perhaps we really could make a difference.

The emphasis at Woodward was "developmental" rather
than medical. To me this meant that instead of taking blood
and urine, X-raying his head, and passing him from machine to machine, they treated him as a little boy; they
watched him awake in the morning; they held him and
played pattycake with him; they knew he liked bananas.
They said, "Oh, Zachy, whassa matter?" when he fussed
and pouted. They treated him like a little boy whom they
wanted to help.

Meeting in Nan's office at the end of the evaluation, she
told us about a program that summer in Virginia, the
Neuro Developmental Therapy Program. "It's based on
the Bobath neurodevelopmental approach; it's one program I went through, and it taught me about handling
these kids; it really changed my life around. I want you to
just think about going to Virginia this summer. The program is really for the therapists, so that they can become
trained in the Bobath method. [The Bobaths, a husband-
and-wife team, were both therapists from England.] But the

parents can attend all the sessions and learn a great deal. There's a lot we can do for these kids, you know."

Even before we got to the car, our minds were made up. This was the first time that anyone had ever offered an opportunity to do something, and we had to take it. Besides, it offered us something to do for the summer besides watching Zach lie there and listening to him cry. I reasoned, At least he'll be getting therapy while he's crying. Another plus was that Joe and I would actually split the time in Virginia, thus dividing up the chore and giving each other a much needed break. Because I was teaching the first session of summer school, Joe would fly down to Virginia for the first three weeks; I'd come down later, getting a friend to give out my finals and mail them to me. Joe would then "fill me in" over the weekend we'd spend together and fly back to Iowa to start teaching the second summer session, having a friend fill in for him for the first week he missed. During the weekend that we'd both be gone, Gabi would stay with her friend Ann. We seemed to have it all worked out. Thank God we had lots of friends!

When we got him from Woodward, I called another friend, a doctor. Would he call and check into this NDT Program? He sounded suspicious and started asking all sorts of questions. What exactly did they "do" with the kids? Who ran the show? How much did it cost? Actually I didn't know too many of the answers, so trusting was I of Nan's integrity and honest concern for our welfare.

Later our doctor friend called back. Virtually all the therapists who had heard of neurodevelopmental therapy agreed to its merit. Of course, the doctors had never heard of it, but I was so antidoctor by this time that even that seemed like a plus.

"Well, you know," he said to me, "it's going to cost a lot of money for both of you to fly to Virginia, stay there for six weeks. It's also a big investment of time and energy. To split up your family like that for a summer, Fern, I just don't want you to think that something like this is going to work miracles."

I met all of his objections. Joe and I had done a lot of reading. We knew what we were doing, I said, and we wanted to help Zach as much as we could. We didn't expect miracles.

In my heart, of course, I longed for one. And at night my dreams were filled with babies who could crawl and babies who could pull themselves up. One night Joe and I had the same dream. That Zach was standing up in his crib when we went in in the morning. We took that as a special omen.

Joe was so excited about going to Virginia. He felt that if you worked hard enough for something, it could happen; if he worked hard enough with Zach, his child would become "better." I didn't really agree, leaning more toward a neurological model. If Zach's brain damage was severe, what could we really do? I didn't want to rain on Joe's parade, so I kept quiet.

Zach was fourteen months old that summer when Joe took him to Virginia.

3

For years, whenever I'd meet someone and they'd ask me how many children I have, I'd say "Five. The youngest one has Down's syndrome and she's severely retarded." Why did I think I had to do that? I would never dream of giving my other kids' IQ scores to someone just like that.

I guess I thought that to not say it—that Marie was retarded— was to hide her handicap. I fought being ashamed of it. That's why I named her Marie. I gave her my name to show that she was a part of me.

—Ann Marie

I always feel compelled to tell the truth and perhaps too much of it, so when people, strangers at a party or on a plane, ask me innocently enough if I have any children, I usually tell them about Zach. It's a conversation stopper, all right, or at least it's a small-talk stopper. But just as often it's a beginning, an opening for a peculiar shared intimacy with those who usually will pass through your life like shoppers, pausing and moving on to the next store window.

Two particular intimacies I recall—with two different men, on two different plane trips, going to two different cities.

The first—right before the Woodward evaluation—was coming back from my parents' new condominium in Florida. I was alone with Gabi and Zach, who was almost a year old. Joe had left Florida a few days before, having to get back to work, and I stayed on. It was supposed to be a vacation, but spending all that time with Zach, of course, was not a vacation. We knew then "something was wrong." But what? And how bad would it be? Zach had been having physical therapy, and although my parents tried so hard to help, my mother's hands were nervous and her eyes were sad for the whole visit. The mystery about Zach's lack of development shrouded me with gloom, impenetrable by the bright Florida sunshine.

On the plane back to frosty, gray Des Moines, a place where I could feel more comfortable with my depression, I sat next to a salesman with a gleaming bald head, cat's-eye pinky rings, and a black appointment book, open in his hand and into which he was checking off items of "business: things to do today." On the opposite page, headed "personal," I saw in fastidious print: Karen's birthday, garage door, tickets for Stevie.

After the final check, his life in order, he snapped the book closed, placing it in his inside jacket pocket, and turned to us good-humoredly.

"How old are you, sweetie?" he said to Gabi. She gave me sidelong, self-conscious glances. "Five," she said softly.

"Five? I bet you go to kindergarten. I have a little boy who's five, and his name is Jimmy. Do you like school?"

Gabi nodded, but she kept her eyes down in her lap. She needed some warming-up time, and he was coming on too strong, too fast.

He decided to try his luck with me. "Oh, kids, God love 'em. I have four of my own. The oldest one's in high school. I can hardly believe that. I travel so much that I don't get to see them as much as I'd like. My son's on a hockey team, and I hope I'm home early enough to see him play tonight. Last week we circled O'Hare for an hour and a half. Do you believe that? He's a beautiful baby. Look how good he is. Boy, my youngest son was a terror to travel with; he'd be always wanting to crawl around."

Zach sat dully on my lap, looking sleepy and sweet.

He went on, "That's a great age. Boy, they're really starting to come into their own. Boy, after those first few bad months, then they're a delight. They're just learning something new every day. They change right before your eyes. Is he walking yet?"

"No, he's not," I said. Should I go on? What's the diagnosis, what's the label? Should I just keep mum, having poor, floppy Zach pass as normal all the way to Chicago?

The words slipped out. "He may be retarded; we don't really know. He's just not developing normally." I turned toward the man and saw in those few seconds his fleshy face soften and droop.

"I used to have five," he said quietly.

"Excuse me?" I asked, confused at the non sequitur.

"Children. I used to have five children. Our middle boy, Jason, was nine when he died of leukemia. Well, he would be twelve today. The pain never goes away." He turned to me, his eyes rimmed gently with tears, and shook his head as he looked at Zach. "He's such a beautiful baby," he said again.

We talked for the next two hours, and he bought me a Scotch, grateful for the chance of something he could do. We talked about his wife's depression following the boy's death and about the advice the psychologist gave the family when they all went in for counseling. We swapped stories about doctors who didn't know and thought they did. And doctors who were kind or careless.

A few minutes before we landed at O'Hare, he took out a brown leather wallet and unfolded picture after picture in clear plastic—of sunny-faced blond children, studio shots with autumnal backgrounds; one, of his wife seated demurely on a gold velvet sofa, legs crossed at the ankles. A plump, pretty woman with carefully coiffed brown hair.

"And this was Jason," he said, carefully removing a black-and-white photograph of him from between two others in the plastic. It was a picture of a little boy in a baseball uniform, a bat over one skinny shoulder, dark eyes squinting against the sun.

"Look," the man said to me as he was getting up, collecting his briefcase and blue overcoat from the overhead compartment, "you either make it or you don't. We've had rough going, but all I can tell you is, you either make it or you don't." I nodded silently.

I don't know why this tautology seemed so profound, but years later I replayed those parting words.

Only last week, as seasons began to shift in Iowa, and I was sorting out our summer clothes from where they are stored under the big window seat in the yellow bedroom, I came across something in a paper bag pressed down into the back corner of the big chest. I knew immediately what it was: a baseball glove my father had bought for Zach when he was only a few weeks old. I took out the glove, rubbed the soft palm, smelled the leather of that tiny glove. I felt such a rush come, the pain so engulfing that I could no longer stand upright, and I dropped on the bed and lay amid the halter tops and jean cutoffs and terry beach robes, bellowing and crying in rage and despair. Then lying spent in soggy grief, I watched the second hand on the clock radio go around for the third time and said aloud, "You either make it or you don't." I put the glove back in the bag among turtleneck sweaters and put it all back in the chest. I took all Gabi's summer clothes and put them in her drawers, leaving two sweaters and long-sleeve shirts to guard against Iowa's changeable weather. I put my clothes away and left Joe's in a pile on the dresser so that he could go through them himself.

Then I went downstairs and started thinking about supper.

The next plane encounter happened the summer Zach was fourteen months old and I was going to Virginia to meet Joe, really to "relieve" Joe and spend the last two weeks of the therapy session with Zach while Joe flew back to Iowa to teach summer school and take care of Gabi. I drove myself to the airport, leaving the car in long-term parking for Joe to pick up the next day. So I was really going solo, free, traveling on an airplane for the first time in years without a big bag stuffed with diapers and wet naps and Magic Markers. I had also had a three-week vacation at home with Gabi, teaching two morning classes at the community college. I thought about how little I really missed Joe. The last year had been so tense, both of us palming off this crying baby on each other, forever waiting around in hospital corridors.

I'm sure in front of the professionals we seemed like interested parents, supportive and kind. Alone, our own relationship was crumbling. I was weepy and withdrawn, Joe blindly optimistic but raging at trifles. Now for three weeks there was no crying in the house, and no one barking orders. I savored each peaceful day.

The last few days I had felt the dread begin to build again. I went out to dinner a lot trying to fatten myself up (for the kill?), knowing that when I was alone with Zach I would not be able to eat well. Before I left, I bought a new skirt, a muted purple print, and wore it on the plane; my legs, in wine-colored high-heel sandals, were tanned.

The man I sat next to was fortyish and attractive in an old-college-basketball-player sort of way. Short, sandy hair and a strong nose and holding a drink (a martini), which must have been poured en route from wherever this plane had taken off. He was reading *The Hite Report.* Leaning toward him, even before takeoff, I felt daring and flirty. "Better than Kinsey?" I ventured.

The man looked up quizzically and gave a wide, boyish smile, putting the book in his lap. Maybe he was embarrassed reading about multiple orgasms in public. Perhaps he was taken aback by my boldness. We got to talking—or I should say *he* got to talking—as I nodded and smiled and asked leading questions in a manner perfected by years of college mixers, blind dates, and fraternity parties. I almost asked him what his major was.

And I made bright, nonthreatening jokes and laughed softly at his.

This I learned over our snacks of cold roast beef on cold buttered rolls: that he was a biochemist doing research on cloning (something to do with Salmonella—I tuned out for some of this); that he played high school but not college basketball because he had surgery (an appendectomy) during the season and never really "caught up"; that he loved Woody Allen movies; that he was not friends with many scientists because they were "so narrow"; that he knew of many fine and wonderful restaurants and night spots in D.C. and—hesitantly—he would really love to "show me around."

By now the plane was unloading at O'Hare, and Stan and I (after the Woody Allen confession, he told me his name) stayed on, cozy in our seats as we watched the backsides of departing passengers go down the aisle. It was the first time in a long while that I was feeling attractive, that I didn't think of myself first as "Zach's mother."

Although Stan and I talked about our jobs and books we liked, neither of us had mentioned who we were in connection to any other people—ah, the anonymity of the friendly skies.

I was sure that Stan, although ringless, was married. He had a comfy, lived-with look, hands that I knew turned pages for a child's good-night story.

There were no leering, no unctuous, sidelong glances. A

little nervousness at the "show-you-around" part, but otherwise a friendly, sexy man.

Stan asked how long I was going to be in Washington. What was I doing there? Now the question was, should *I* pass as normal? I could just say (sweetly) to his invitation, "No thanks, I'm meeting my husband." True enough. And I *was* wearing my wedding ring.

I could say, "I'm in Washington on business," leaving the message veiled, and ask to meet him for dinner one night next week. I could get a sitter at the dorm for Zach and wouldn't it be nice to look forward, after days of crying Zach and therapy sessions and parent seminars on feeding skills, to be alone and anonymous, and getting dressed up (I'd have to buy another outfit; I only had my "mommy" clothes—cutoff jeans and T-shirts that Zach could drool on) and going out to an elegant restaurant. I ran through this fantasy quickly before I turned back to Stan with a sigh. I told him about Zach, about what the whole trip was for. And then all the games were over, and we both stopped saying clever things, and we both stopped wondering how we looked to each other and met each other's gazes easily. The sexual tension, the energy that was in the air only moments ago as his knee brushed against my skirt, was gone, evaporated—*kaput.*

As a scientist Stan was interested in the probable causes of Zach's brain damage. It was such a mystery, the brain. His daughter (he was married and had three children) had a reading disability that (although he was quick to say this was in no way comparable to Zach's problem) made her feel like a failure even though she could pick up and play virtually any musical instrument without reading a note.

And on to Washington we continued to talk about our children and our families as two people who simply met on a plane and before we departed and I ran into Joe's arms, so truly glad to see him, Stan and I shook hands and he wished me luck.

Joe was at the airport with Pat, one of the teachers from the NDT Program. He looked so tired, but I knew he wouldn't tell me how really hard it had been, alone with Zach, having sole responsibility for three whole weeks. Joe is not a complainer, but sometimes I wish he were, because his anger and disappointments are often secreted away only to emerge later at inappropriate times.

Still, he was excited to see me. The three of us went out to an all-night pancake house and drank coffee and talked about the program, what they had learned. Joe was still really enthusiastic about the whole therapy business; he had a notebook filled with observations about Zach, about proper positioning and handling, feeding tips.

Under the table we held hands.

Later that night Joe and I made love, but it was a mechanical, empty coupling, disappointing for both of us because we had not seen each other for three weeks and Joe was flying back to Iowa the next day. I was tired from the trip, tense and upset about what was to begin the next day. Zach was in a crib in the room with us, and I could hear his sleep sounds. I was angry with Joe for not thinking to move Zach to the study carrel, which was right across from our room, for the only night we'd have together for five weeks.

I thought of other times, before Zach was born, when Joe and I had been separated and our passionate reunions: when I was at college and Joe was in graduate school only a few hours away. On weekends I'd take the bus to see Joe, and we'd go back to his apartment: long kisses through the corridor before we even got in the door, later eating dinner, ravenous at one in the morning. Or, after we were married, me waiting up in bed, listening for the car to pull in the driveway after Joe had gone to give a paper at some conference, hearing him bound up the stairs, his joy at being home filling up the room. I would ask him how the conference went, but even before he could answer, I'd take him into our warm bed, loosen his tie, and cover his face with welcoming kisses. Later, after we had made love, I would lie in bed watching him unpack while he told me all about the meetings with those immodest declarations

("Oh, I was the best one, honey") that could only be shared with one who unequivocally loves you.

In Virginia, lying alone in a single bed across the room from Joe after he'd gone to his own cot, I could see Zach in the portable crib as moonlight flooded through the dormitory windows. Naked, I tiptoed across the cool linoleum and watched him sleep, his head resting on one pudgy arm. He was in a pale-yellow kimono and his hair looked white in the soft glow. I felt lonely and scared, and longed to hold Zach in my arms to comfort me for the loss of passion and desire.

4

When I look back now, I realize I was so angry at this terrible thing that happened to us and so frightened. I was terrified that I wouldn't be able to cope and determined, on the other hand, to be a super-mother. I was going to do it all! I was going to make Tim achieve the absolute most that he could if it killed me. I had this idea that if he didn't learn by the time he was three, all was lost (an early-childhoodintervention theory passed on to me by our first social worker. I latched on to it because it reaffirmed all my frantic feelings and need to do something—not just sit there, love him, and watch him become retarded!).

Michael and Colette turned three and four the August we brought Tim, still sickly, home from the hospital. For the next three years I don't think I heard a single thing they said to me, and I can only remember them in those years in terms of what was happening to Tim —a fact that still makes me want to sob.

—Donna Lee

The neurodevelopmental therapy program took place at a small private college set in *Sound of Music* hills just outside

Washington, D.C. Two floors of the dormitory were rented out to physical therapists and special-education teachers who came to take the course and to parents and their handicapped children who were the "subjects"; the idea being that the therapists and teachers would learn developmental approaches and therapy techniques, and the kids would receive the benefits of being continually worked with. Some parents, the "locals," did not stay in the dorm but brought their children in for each day's sessions, sometimes driving back at night for lectures and seminars.

The dorm group came from all over—from the Midwest to Mexico. Three of us were from around Iowa, and I knew Gail and Sandy well because they were part of a parent support group I had gone to that winter, started by a handicapped preschool teacher. We had even seen each other outside the group during the winter and spring and had become friends, drawn together by a common pain that opened a field of sympathy and understanding.

Really, we were an unlikely trio. Gail, gentle Gail, whom I had seen cry, but who had no bitter tears, no angry questions. Gail was a born-again Christian, not a Bible thumper, but a woman whose faith surrounded her like sunlight. Her relationship with Jesus was so enduring, so vital, that sometimes she'd talk about "the Lord" as if he were in the room. (She'd say, "He wants me to . . ." I'd say "Who?") Gail's boy, Scott, was a year older than Zach. Gail knew that he was severely brain-damaged right after he was born. Something to do with her hypoglycemia and the doctors not controlling his blood-sugar level or not giving oxygen— there were a number of mistakes. The damage could have been prevented. The doctors told Gail to institutionalize Scott, but she would not hear of it. So she took home her first child, and started looking for special programs, for therapy. At age two, Scott, a pretty, dusky blond with his mother's delicate softness, spent the day smacking his hands together, mouthing toys. He could sit up, but he did not move. Often he had grand mal seizures. He could not see.

Sandy was in her early twenties and had three children right after high school—boom, boom, boom. The last child, Russ, was normal at birth, but at three months he had had a severe reaction to a DPT shot, a high fever, convulsions, blindness, and severe brain damage. He was about eighteen months during the Virginia summer, a chubby baby, tight-fisted, with an arched back. Hard to carry, harder to feed, even his tongue arched. Sandy was a tough, small-town scrapper whose marriage seemed to be falling apart under the strain. In Virginia she chain-smoked and read movie magazines as Russ fussed through most of the night. One time Sandy borrowed a teacher's car to drive to the shopping center to get Pampers. She parked in the handicapped parking zone so she could run in carrying Russ, and when she came out, a woman was standing by the car. "Excuse me, but isn't this space for handicapped people?" the woman asked.

Sandy thrust Russ in front of the woman. "He's got cerebral palsy, he's blind, and he's retarded. That enough for ya?"

Most of the children in the program that summer had cerebral palsy, which is really more an administrative than a medical term. It describes brain damage that can be only motor, but about 50 percent of the children who have cerebral palsy are also mentally retarded. Zach, Scott, and Russ seemed to me to be the worst off of any of the kids, but they were also the youngest. Zach was better off than either Scott or Russ by virtue of the fact that he could see. He could also smile appropriately, and he could anticipate and respond when we played peek-a-boo. He seemed a lot more with it than the other two.

At fourteen months old, lying on his back to be diapered, Zach did not look abnormal in any way. But he had to be picked up carefully, his head cradled like a newborn.

I wheeled him along in a stroller, where he sat slack against the canvas.

All our meals were taken in a cafeteria in another building, up a rather steep hill. The children (only a few could walk) were pushed in wheelchairs and strollers up the hill, down a flight of steps, three times a day. The campus was not ideal for the handicapped.

After breakfast and lunch "work" began in the student union, which was set up with mats and physical-therapy equipment. Sometimes the parents stayed, helping the kids out, watching the therapists positioning them. Sometimes we went to our own group meeting on "Dressing Your Handicapped Child" or "Play for the Disabled."

Joe had told me a little about the lectures and the seminars over the phone. He was taking notes, planning to teach me all that he could in the weekend that we'd spend together. Mostly our long-distance calls were just gossip, small talk about people he'd met; I'd tell him stories about school, what Gabi said. Joe never did tell me how hard it was in Virginia—not then, during those phone calls. Maybe he thought I wouldn't come if he told me how he was counting the days until it was over.

I dreaded going, being the "only one." At home Joe and I had a morning routine worked out—one of us scrambling the eggs, getting the prunes and bran ready, while the other held and walked Zach, who woke up crying and starving. Gabi milled about, waiting until we were through to get her breakfast, or to get buttoned or combed.

Joe said that in Virginia he kept a banana and some cereal and prunes in the room "to get Zach started" and got dressed himself between bites. Then Joe wheeled Zach in the stroller down the hall to the bathroom, pushing and rocking him while Joe toileted, shaved, and washed. On top of the problem of trying to get ready and "out" with a fourteen-month-old who was continually fussing, was the tension that in these early-morning hours in the dorm, you might be disturbing someone else. Zach often fussed all through a meal, alternately crying because the food wasn't coming in quickly enough or because he didn't like it, or because he had gas, or who knew?

Dividing up the Virginia summer was both easier and

harder. Being the "only one" was physically and emotionally draining, but then, while Joe and I didn't have each other's support for taking care of Zach, we also didn't have the tension between us that his presence created.

Zach cried all the time—it was *my* decision to hold him or not hold him. No one said "Will you hurry" as I mashed Zach's banana and prunes; no one stomped around, slamming doors. While I felt I had to keep Zach quiet so as not to disturb the other mothers, I knew that his fussiness did not have the same effect on them as it did on me and Joe.

I made my own notes in the notebook that Joe left for me, recording what Zach ate, his fussiness during a meal, what times of day he seemed most alert, what specific exercises helped him build up his tone without making him too stiff. I ended up writing a lot about how *I* felt, how frustrating it was to watch Zach crying as different people handled him. Fix him up. Heal him. Help him. Oh, help me.

I found some notes Joe had written—folded up in the back of the book. I don't know if they were meant for me or not but they helped more than any suggestions about Zachy-care, for it made me feel closer to Joe than I had in a long time. He wrote:

Today I am buried alive in the blues. The whole week in fact has been low for me, maybe because the summer winds remind me of last summer's cancer inflamed. My mother and Zach hold me tight in their grips; the one strong and dead, the other soft and alive. I am filled with such a mixture of rejection and acceptance—both total. I reject much of my mother's way and struggle to accept her person totally. I hate and adore Zach. Never was such a burden so light to take, but today he was flabby, unmuscled, and I hated him for not being able to cooperate with my efforts to exercise him. I was frustrated in the project. When will I learn that not every day can go according to plan, that the world will not be tailored to my taste or need. So, it is my own need that sent me deeper today. My need to work with

Zach and feel him tense and do, not his lapse or ineffectualness. I am not brought down so much by him missing a day or not being consistently improving, but more by not having my need satisfied: my need to see him use his body.

I had thought that my "long trial" would take some dramatic shape such as alone wandering America for a couple of years. I now see this for the melodrama it is. I have a cheap romantic imagination bound to comic book images. My test began last summer; it continues amidst work and family and friends. It continues within daily life and that is what makes it so awful. Am I to be like my mother—dramatically great but fairly mediocre in the long haul of meals, dishes, lawns, cars, tiredness, mischance, misalliance, and disorder? Given a circumscribed time filled with definite destructive substance, my mother could and did rise to noble bearing. The true test, the tougher test, is found in indeterminate burden. It wears me away like a strong wind, rain, sun or it must become a moving earth upon which I am to waltz.

Zach seems to me to symbolize the abortive attempt to resemble normal families—families unlike my own only-childed family. Gabi becomes an only child, but a sister, too.

On the bright side, I think he has increased social awareness; he smiles more than he used to, and his bowels have become more regular. Since keeping him on a bran-and-fruit (especially prunes) diet, we've used but one suppository in the last four weeks. This has been due in part also to his increased physical activity. The standing, sitting, rolling, hanging, and prone workouts no doubt increase the peristaltic action. His gassiness also has decreased dramatically.

Coming to Virginia has been the biggest step for Zachy and us. For the first time clear-cut activities were laid out and this enables me to feel a sense of control, minimal to be sure, but a sense of direction that depends upon our efforts. Of course, this is a little scary since now we are also directly responsible for specific routines and progress or its lack. But I'd prefer the risk with the chance to take matters quite literally into my own hands.

We have some key things to be thankful for: Zach eats and drinks nicely—he is using his lips and tongue and teeth fairly well; his appetite is good (thank God, he likes bran and prunes); and unlike the two other babies in his handi- capped group, Zach is not blind.

I hope to find out what else we can do for Zach and where he can go from here. But I must remember to relax. I must remember to enjoy him as much as possible. I must remem- ber to laugh at him and me—his so-serious father.

Although other fathers came to the nighttime sessions and occasionally would visit the dorms (if they lived close by), Joe was the only father in residence. (Lena, one of the women from Mexico, took me aside the day I arrived in Virginia, and told me, "Ees good that you finally come. Eef that man walked out of the bathroom in a towel one more time . . ." and she grinned wickedly.)

Joe's presence, living in a dorm with dozens of women (all except one of the therapists and teachers were also female), profoundly affected a lot of the people there. The first few days I was in Virginia, women kept coming up to me, exclaiming how wonderful Joe was.

"Every day in that cafeteria, feeding that baby, every night, rocking that baby to sleep," Carmen said to me with awe.

Also at the college that summer was a group of nuns going to summer school. They slept on another floor in the dorm, and we'd see them in the cafeteria or walking in groups about the campus, and they would smile dreamily at the children. The second day I was there alone, two nuns came up to me and asked if I was Joe's wife. "Well," said the perkier one, eyes glistening behind wire-rimmed glasses, "I would just like to tell you that we've seen your husband every day taking care of Zach, and your husband

has been an inspiration to us. Just an inspiration. I hope
you don't mind. I know you are not of our faith, but we've
been praying for Zach."

"Oh no, Sister," I said, "we'll take all the help we can
get."

Joe was special—an inspiration even to women of God.
After a while I grew tired of everyone telling me how terrific
Joe was. Once I said to another mother, "You know you're
doing the same thing. You're giving up a summer away
from home to get help for your child. How come no one
tells *you* how terrific you are?"

"Oh," she said, open-mouthed, "I never even thought of
that."

(I have a friend whose husband left her one snowy winter's evening, a note on the kitchen table: "Forgive me, I
need to be free. . . ." The next morning she had to teach
a class at eight, so she shoveled the walk while the kids ate
their Cheerios in sleepy silence and then she bundled the
baby off to day care, came home from a meeting at three
to take her older son to flute lessons after she put the roast
in the oven.

That same year, a woman in town, in the pre–*Kramer vs.
Kramer* days, left her husband and small son to fly off to the
West Coast to find herself, without giving so much as a
week's notice. "Oh, Oh," said everyone in town, and offered baby-sitting and hot casseroles. "Of course, he won't
be able to come to work so early," said the sympathetic
boss of this now-single father. "Of course, we have room
in the day-care center," said the director. Oh, oh, a man
alone taking care of his child! Provision must be made.)

I don't think I felt jealous of all the attention Joe got. I
loved his nurturing qualities and felt bad that he was seen
as someone so "special," the good father as exception to
the rule.

What the experience in Virginia made clearer was how
Joe and I worked in our parental roles, how we were viewed
in them. Joe, as a father, was not seen as intimately con-

nected with the "being" of Zach as I; thus the lavish praise for all his input toward Zach's care.

I saw all the mothers there, some with older children, mothers who had spent years going from doctors to programs to treatments, always home with a child who doesn't go out to play, arranging time, directing activities for the afternoon, this weekend, forever. Seeing mothers who had older kids in wheelchairs, children who could not feed themselves or take themselves to the bathroom, brought home to me what being the mother of a handicapped child really meant—the paradigm for all that motherhood represents: selfless devotion, unlimited patience, endless sacrifice. The fear I felt in Virginia was for the loss of control I had about my own life, as if someone had sent my name in for the priesthood without my permission.

It was meeting Ruby McKnight that really turned me around. Ruby was the parent liaison for the NDT Program, and I had talked with her for more than an hour on the phone before Joe and I had actually planned to fly down. She had a quick-paced southern drawl and a personality that even over long distance could only be described as "bubbly."

"I am so enthusiastic about this program," she said. "My boy is fourteen, and he is *very involved,* but I do think that I am seeing improvement."

Ruby used the word *involved,* a cerebral palsy term meaning "he's got it bad." Joe and I first heard the word when Zach was a year old and we had a therapist come to the house to look at him. After about a half hour of getting him to try to hold a rattle or to place his hands together, she concluded, "Well, he *is* involved." I thought that sounded good. To "be involved" had such a positive connotation. Like being an "exceptional" child. Cruel euphemisms.

Ruby talked about the small progress her son, Johnny, had made. "He's holding his head a lot better." She encouraged us to "start early" with programs and therapy.

I was impressed. Here was a woman who, after fourteen

years of struggle, was still optimistic. Zach was only fourteen months old. Who knew what he would be able to do?

My first morning in Virginia, Joe said, "Oh, wait until you
meet Ruby, Fernie. She's really something else!" And before breakfast we met Ruby and Johnny waiting out in the
corridor.

Few people look like their telephone personality, but
Ruby did—short, perky, small-featured, and freckled. She
was the kind of person who looked as if she were always
wearing tennis shoes. Ruby welcomed me warmly and
made snappy jokes about my leaving a handsome husband
in a dorm full of women for three weeks.

Johnny was next to her in his wheelchair, enjoying his
mother's lively humor. He could not talk, but Ruby included him in the conversation, saying "Johnny thinks this
. . . Johnny feels that . . ." Johnny, who was not retarded,
was a cerebral palsy athetoid, which meant that he had little
voluntary control over his movements and, unless secured
by straps in his chair, his arms would fly unexpectedly from
his sides, his legs would jerk spasmodically. At fourteen
Johnny was matchstick thin; elbows, collarbone, knees,
stuck out in sharp adolescent gawkiness; but his face,
framed by brown curls, was soft and freckled like his
mother's. There was an English schoolboy look about
Johnny, a mixture of mischief and innocence. I thought, He
would've been some kid. Then felt guilty as if this Johnny,
who had joined our small circle, smiling and bright, were
not a kid at all. Yet this thought came to me frequently that
summer in my fantasies, a desperate wish to rearrange,
reconstruct, and rectify the damage—and always, even
years later, to watch Zachy as he slept, looking so normal
and right and in a brief moment, a fantasy, which later I
refused to encourage and nurse because it was not healthy
for me, to think of that "some kid" Zachy would have been.

In order to communicate, Johnny used a language board
that fit over his wheelchair tray. Arranged crisscrossed
across the board were words: various parts of speech,

proper nouns familiar to Johnny (names of family members), and frequently simple sentences about eating or using the bathroom. The columns were color-differentiated, and Johnny, since he did not have the physical control to point, found the words with his eyes as the person to whom he was "talking" followed. For those not trained to use the board, it was an imprecise, tedious process. Johnny, who followed baseball statistics and knew old rock and roll and laughed at Joe's dirty jokes, had so much more to say than that board allowed.

But Ruby seemed to read his thoughts, so attuned was she to the intimacies of her son's mind and body. Only once, in fourteen years, had he been away from her—one summer, when the McKnights had sent Johnny for a week to a camp for handicapped children. It was a disaster. Not being able to walk or talk or use his hands, Johnny was by far the most seriously disabled child. No one there understood what he wanted and he was frightened and lonely.

Johnny was totally dependent on Ruby, and she came through for him as his voice, his legs. I watched in the cafeteria as Ruby fed him, chatting about the day and how hot it was, scooping clean the sides of Johnny's mouth, wiping his nose, patting him on the back and holding his head down when he choked, all the time coolly, efficiently taking small bites from her own plate. It took Johnny a long time to eat, all that choking and gagging; my own food sat growing cold in front of me. Ruby had eaten her meals that way for fourteen years.

Nan, the therapist from Woodward, had lived with the McKnights the previous summer, when she had taken the NDT course, and Nan then learned from the inside what it was like to be a "handicapped family." She said, "It takes more than an hour just to feed Johnny; you're finished with breakfast and it's almost time to think about lunch." While Nan was there, Ruby, who apparently was never sick, was struck down for two days with a particularly incapacitating flu. Nan recalled Ruby lying on the couch, and Johnny, next to her in his wheelchair, unable to eat or smile, moaning and crying until his mother got better.

Nan had told me these stories out of admiration and reverence for a singularly dedicated woman: Look what a human being can do, look at the strength of a mother's love. But to me the image of Johnny's strangulating dependence as his mother lay sick was so frightening that I started to put up guards against that fierce need. I rationalized that there were others who could care for Zach as well as I—maybe better because they were not so painfully connected. I knew that others could find that special way to hold him, to soothe his cries. (Later, when Joe and I began to look for a place for Zach, I'd yell at him, "I'm not Ruby McKnight. I don't want to *be* Ruby McKnight!")

Certain pictures from that Virginia summer are etched indelibly in my mind: Ruby and Johnny on the patio in back of the dorm, Johnny signaling that he has to go to the bathroom by looking down at his pants. Ruby loosens the straps from his chair and, with a strength and surety that I thought impossible in such a tiny woman, heaves Johnny over her shoulder to go down the steps toward the bathroom.

A year later I remember this scene, looking at my nude body in the mirror before a bath and noticing that my arms have small, but actually well-defined biceps; my breasts are firm and tight—"good pecs" as the weight-lifters say. It's from "working out," by lifting and carrying and rocking Zach. I can see it now—a national body-building competition for mothers of handicapped children. We could make it a part of the Special Olympics!

After Joe left for Ames, I moved Zach across the hall to one of the unused rooms. With Zach in the room I knew that sleep would be impossible, for even with him across the hall it took many hours for my mind to stop racing, and even in sleep I was aware how my hands stayed fisted, how stiff my body was—just like some of the kids, spastic and rigid. (Sometimes I would lie like that on purpose, head flopped, back arched in a tight cerebral palsy thrust, to try to imagine how the world looked from the kids' point of view.)

In the morning I would wake in a panic, sweating, my heart like a hummingbird's. I'd wait for Zach's first cry. "Oh, God, I don't want this day to begin." I thought of the hours of chokey meals, of therapy, of Zach's continuous crying.

I understood in Virginia that I could not take care of Zach for the next fifteen, ten, even five years. I realized it because of what my body was telling me. In Virginia, without baby-sitters, without Joe to relieve me, it was just me and Zach. The physical manifestations of the stress I had felt since Zach's birth were more prominently revealed. I couldn't sleep. I also could not seem to eat—or at least I was aware that eating was something that was a chore. I remember sitting in the cafeteria at a table with Sandy and Gail and the boys. The food looked good to me, but I just couldn't get it down. Chew, chew, chew—till the food mixed with my own saliva. I'd get that watery feeling you have in your mouth right before you're going to throw up. The food just wouldn't seem to go down.

When I was a kid, I was as skinny as a pencil. Before I went to sleep each night, my mother made me drink a "guggle-muggle," a malted milk with raw eggs in it. This was in the preblender era and I dreaded getting to the bottom of that drink because of the "slime" of the egg. Sometimes my throat would close even before I half-finished the glass. "I can't drink any more," I begged my mother. "It won't go down."

So here I was again, twenty-five years later, with the same complaint.

Sandy and I had just come from a lecture, "Toys for the Handicapped Child." Sandy was very bitter. "Yeah, okay if a child *can* play, but for our kids? This all seems so ridiculous. Some of these kids are such a mess."

Sandy looked through her purse for a tissue, and, finding
a candy bar as well, unwrapped it and began to eat. "And,"
she went on, "I'm a mess, too. I must have gained twenty
pounds since I'm here; I can't stop eating." She looked
down at her thighs, which emerged substantially from her
jean cutoffs. "I eat when I'm upset," she explained.

Then, glaring at me in my shorts, she demanded, "And
how do you stay so thin?"

"I can't eat when I'm upset," I told her.

We sat on the hill, crying and laughing; in my mind's eye
I pictured us as old ladies: Sandy, all buttocks and thighs
ballooning out of sight; me, slowly disappearing as I shriv-
eled to the bone.

I felt good talking to Sandy, because my misery needed
company, because I found some solace and companionship
in her pain. We had stopped talking about what the kids
could do, or how to get them to do what they couldn't do.
We talked about us. We dared for those moments to be
utterly miserable, to curse our fate.

Later, alone, away from the specialists, the therapists, the
teachers, we mothers were sometimes totally honest. We
talked about our pregnancies, of "when I first knew," and
the stories were hauntingly similar. "I wish I had five
bucks," said Sandy, "for every time a doctor told a woman
that she was 'just being a neurotic mother' when she suspected that something was the matter with her baby—and
then there really was!"

Zach was the youngest child in the whole program, and
so I was the parent with the least experience with "learning
to accept it." Continuously I felt open and raw, often breaking down when I saw an older child in therapy who was
working so hard at something that comes so easily to everyone else. I cried about Zach. I cried about the other kids.
Oh, I was embarrassed at being such a crybaby, but sometimes I couldn't believe how accepting some of the others
seemed to be.

A few months before, I had started reading a magazine
called *The Exceptional Parent,* which was for parents of chil-

dren who had different physical and mental disabilities. Many of the articles were practical and "how to" essays— sort of a Hints from Heloise for the handicapped. In retrospect I'm sure the magazine serves a valuable purpose— parents are concerned with the nitty-gritty daily care of handicapped children and are interested in any tips that make feeding, dressing, transporting them easier. But at the time, I was not ready for such a commonsensical, positive commitment to going on with life.

In a letter a woman wrote something like, "I have two nonambulatory children . . ." and, in what I took to be a cheery tone, went on to share some method of pushing wheelchairs and shopping carts simultaneously.

After I read this, I swooned. This woman had *two* children who could not walk? Why was she talking about grocery shopping? Why was she not in bed under the covers? Or sipping gin from a flask in her closet?

For me part of learning "to accept it" was recognizing and articulating the horror. Later I could talk about going shopping.

One woman in Virginia whom I particularly liked was Beatrice, whose low-key sardonic wit I appreciated in a place where almost all of the therapists and teachers were as bubbly as counselors at a summer camp. Beatrice was in her early thirties; she had thick, waist-length dark hair and a strong-jawed, Indian-pretty face. She also had wide hips, and later, when she told me how difficult her labor had been with Niki, it was hard for me to imagine this to be so: her body looked so sturdy, so maternal. Beatrice was a potter and once took me to her house (she lived an hour away from the college) and showed me beautiful, big, bold platters and bowls into which she had delicately inserted bits of stained glass; the effect of the rough clay and the shimmering glass together was lovely. Beatrice's husband, Albert, was a scientist and their eight-year-old daughter, Niki, who had cerebral palsy and could not walk, was their only child.

Beatrice and Albert had suspected Niki's damage following the difficult delivery, and she was a nervous, fretful baby who needed to be constantly rocked or she would tighten spasmodically and scream. They started the trips to the doctors, to therapists, early. By the time Niki was two, they'd started her in a program called Doman-Delacato, which uses specific patterning techniques to encourage "normal" progressive movement to crawling and walking. Every day, women (neighbors) would come to Beatrice's house to "pattern" Niki—moving her head, arms, legs, to simulate crawling. The theory is that if the body is moved, eventually the brain "catches on," and the child can move herself voluntarily. One of the problems with the program, whether it works for some or not, is that it puts virtually all the responsibility for physical therapy on the parents— really the mother, since she's the one who's home leading the patterning session—so there is a tremendous emotional investment with regard to the child's progress and an almost exclusive focus on the child's problems. Beatrice told me that she worked patterning Niki seven days a week and followed a strict schedule that left only short periods of time for just "hanging around."

"If I weren't doing something to make Niki better," Beatrice said, "I'd feel guilty. Most of my day was spent doing something therapeutic for Niki. We had a kiddie pool that we used indoors in an upstairs bedroom and Niki would spend hours crawling around in the water because it was supposed to build strength. We had a whole downstairs 'therapy room' with prone boards and ladders and ropes and a patterning table."

The strict schedule included Albert taking over Niki's early-morning routine and breakfast and, when he came home from work, supper and bedtime. This gave Beatrice a few hours to go down to the basement, where she had a pottery studio set up, and do her own work; but it didn't leave any time for Beatrice and Albert to be together. They rarely went out because they wouldn't leave Niki. Niki's physical progress was the most important thing in their lives; Beatrice, who was a bright, perceptive woman, said that she knew that they had an emotionally unhealthy atmosphere, with their total concentration on Niki's progress, but, Beatrice said only half-jokingly, "We thought we'd work out Niki's physical problems, and then, when she could walk, we'd send her to an analyst to straighten out her mind."

Beatrice and Albert spent years doing Doman-Delacato. Early, a strange thing happened that perhaps even fanned their dedication: At three and a half Niki was "almost walking"; she had made rapid strides. Of course, excitedly, they continued with the program. But then Niki leveled off and eventually, even with the continued therapy, regressed. No one knew why.

Of course, any program like that is so difficult to evaluate because there are no controls. There are cerebral palsied children who have been through the patterning program and who walk, but how do we know what they would have done without it?

Beatrice had heard about the neurodevelopmental therapy approach and decided, after a last discouraging year doing patterning, to try to come this summer to Virginia and try the NDT Program. I was at once fascinated and repelled by Beatrice's dogged determination to help Niki no matter what the cost to her own life. One time, when Beatrice was describing for me a typical day when she was home with Niki doing her patterning and exercising, I said that I didn't know how she could live like that for years, with so little contact with the outside world. I told her how I needed baby-sitters all of the time to help with Zach, that I only felt good when I left the house to go to teach or see friends. I confessed a favorite fantasy of mine, which was to take out half the money in our savings account and run away, telling no one where I was going (I thought that California was appropriate) to start a new life. "Why not clean out the entire savings account," Beatrice suggested. "After all, it's your fantasy."

Beatrice said that we were just dealing with the pain differently but with an equally unbalanced response. "Your way of handling the problem is to run away. I immerse myself in it." She added, "We're both a little crazy."

I liked talking to Beatrice, but Niki made most social interaction difficult. She had grown up in a world where she had Beatrice's undivided attention for years, and she was not about to let go.

Niki continuously stopped conversations with comments or demands. Sometimes Beatrice attempted to talk "over" her, while Niki grasped Beatrice's arm, saying "ma ma, ma ma, ma" until she was spoken to. You could see Beatrice was annoyed but never did she say, "Quiet. Don't interrupt me while I'm talking." Niki's speech was also difficult to understand, so she used Beatrice to translate for her rather than try to make it on her own. I think that Beatrice was hurt that Niki was not seen more positively by the other mothers and the children, but the fact was that Niki was a pest. She would whine and call ma-ma-ma if Beatrice so much as went to brush her teeth without her. Niki consumed her.

One day after a parents' meeting I was particularly depressed. Beatrice said to me, "I know that when I get too down, and I really can't take it anymore, that I always have suicide as an option, that at least I have a choice about that. Of course," she added, "I'll probably have to take Niki with me."

I looked at Beatrice with astonishment. She seemed composed and objective. Funny, in the past year I had thought so often about Zach's death, about an "accident," about his never waking up from a nap, about a discovery of a tumor that would end it all; but never in my loneliest, deepest depression did I think about taking my own life.

In my dorm room late one night, all the kids were sleeping; Beatrice was keeping vigil at Niki's door "in case she calls." Someone had gone out and bought a bottle of cheap

Chablis, and we all drank it warm, out of Dixie bathroom cups. I was talking to Lena and Eliza, a black woman from Baltimore. Eliza said that when she first found out that Cammie had cerebral palsy, she was so depressed she didn't leave her house for a year. Lena's daughter, Christina, was nine, and she was bent, tiny as a sparrow, as she scooted about the floor, pushing off on skinny arms. Lena was pretty and vivacious; in the mornings she sang in Spanish in the bathroom. At home, in Mexico, she gave lavish dinners to entertain her husband's many business clients. "Oh, I go to parties; I still like to see people, to dance; but in here," she pounded her chest with an open palm, long mauve nails flashing, "something ees broke. I am never the same."

I first saw Jan the second night I was in Virginia, sitting in front of me at a lecture on "Advocacy and Estate Planning for Your Handicapped Child."

In her early thirties, wearing a jean skirt and a purple T-shirt, Jan was appealing in a goofy, kid-cute kind of way: red frizzy hair, light freckles scattered across a tiny nose, a toothy smile. Next to her sat Roger, dark-haired, bespectacled, a familiar stability—a look that bespoke law school and sensible cars and racquetball on the weekends.

The lecturer was talking about "when you are gone." Who could think that far ahead? Most of the parents in the room were in their thirties. Maybe it *wasn't* that far ahead. I wondered about the longevity statistics for parents of "special" children. I already knew about the divorce statistics.

One of the things that struck me as I looked around at a room filled with people whose children were all "abnormal" in some way, was how normal *we* all looked as a group —ordinary, middle-class. No one was drooling or sitting in a wheelchair. What did I think? That we should all be handicapped as well? One time I'd seen a child at Woodward who was grotesque, sitting bent, twisted, biting on his fingers. "Oh, your mom's here, John," said one of the careworkers as a woman with blond, swingy hair, smart in herringbone trousers and a brown wool blazer, came walking briskly down the hall. My mouth flew open. I don't know what I expected. I just didn't think she would look "like that." I suppose on a very unconscious level I did expect the mother to reflect the image of her child. And if Zach, as he grew older and lost his baby cuteness, were to become grotesque, a baby in the shape of an adolescent boy, with the beginnings of a beard, wearing adult-sized Pampers, how would I feel about being his mother then?

I looked at Jan and Roger. They whispered to each other, a smile, a shrug, sharing a joke of the very married, Roger's arm resting along the back of her chair, a light touch on her shoulder. A nice couple.

Later we met. They both came over to me. "Joe talked so much about you," Jan said.

I knew I would be friends with Jan. Warm and bright, Jan was intensely analytic, with a caustic humor. She had a daughter, Amanda, who was just Gabi's age, and a little boy, Eddie, who was some months older than Zach. Eddie was the reason that Jan came to Virginia from her home in a Chicago suburb. Roger was visiting for the weekend. I thought Eddie was the second cutest child in the program (Jan would probably just reverse the order). Eddie had tight white curls, a muckle-mouth, and porcelain skin. At two he could sit but could not walk, and he uttered not a peep but sat happily in his stroller or in a playpen, munching whatever object, edible or not, happened to be nearest at the time. He smiled away at nothing in particular, looking here and there and up and down and never quite connecting in any human way. Unlike Zach, who physically was gravid and floppy, Eddie was a coiled *boinng-boinng* spring, skinny, bouncy, light-bodied and light-headed, always in a purposeless motion. The therapists in the program thought that Eddie was overstimulated by the environment, and one of the things they did was to make him leather bands that fit over both hands, which, they felt, would cut down on the sensory overload that Eddie seemed to receive from the world. I don't know how much good they did him, but he looked adorable with these bands on his tiny hands, like a manic little archer.

Jan and I spent a lot of time together. After the boys' therapy sessions we'd go out for walks, or shopping, or sometimes we'd just hang around and talk.

Jan was a painter; one time she brought me a brochure announcing a show at a small Chicago gallery. At home the top floor was her studio; "I'm over the hill for the aspiring young artist role," she said, "but I'm still aspiring."

Jan was seeing a psychiatrist three times a week—she thought if she could deal with her feelings and find out who she was, she could deal with having a child like Eddie. I didn't really agree. I had seen a therapist that winter but stopped going after just a few visits. Joe was very angry with me for that. I guess what he wanted was for me to stop being so depressed and angry all the time. Maybe it was too early in the game, but I felt I had a *right* to be depressed and angry all the time. Well, I didn't want to be that way all my life, but in that first year, when we first found out about Zach, I felt I *should* be angry and depressed. "What do I have to see a therapist about?" I'd say to Joe. "I'm upset because there's something wrong with my baby. There may be something *very* wrong with my baby. To be well adjusted in this situation is absolutely crazy!"

Jan would tell me what she and her shrink talked about. Sometimes Jan and I would be depressed and angry together. For both of us the relationship was good therapy. And for me it was very cheap.

The group of handicaps in Virginia was not a very homogeneous one. Some of the older children merely "walked funny," and that was it. I don't know how it affected their lives, but it seemed so incredibly minor to me. Of course, everything gets so skewed in view of more severe limitations. Jan once was talking about twelve-year-old Jenny, a beautiful child with wide blue eyes and long, blond hair. Jenny was bright and sensitive, and she painted pretty, dreamy watercolors. She could not walk at all, and I saw her in therapy once being lifted out of her chair, her long thin legs crossing scissor-patterned over each other. She reminded me of that beautiful mermaid in the fairy tale, the one who falls in love with a prince and longs for legs instead of her fish tail.

Jan looked at lovely Jenny in her chair, a child who could tell jokes and paint pictures and braid her own hair and said, "So what if she doesn't go dancing."

She echoed my thoughts. Years ago I would have looked so sorrowfully at a child like Jenny. But being a beautiful, bright child who could not walk, who would grow up into a beautiful, bright woman who could not walk, did not seem so terrible. It was a difficulty and an inconvenience, but it was not a tragedy.

But the disparity that glared at me throughout our Virginia summer was this: Although *all* the children were physically handicapped in some way, not one of the older children was retarded.

Now Zach was still very young at this point, and his mental capacities were undetermined. Did he do so little physically because he *couldn't,* or because he was so brain-damaged that he didn't know enough to try? Joe and I felt a lot more comfortable with the words *cerebral palsy*—which somehow seemed like a disease that could be "cured," or at least "helped"—than the label "retarded." For a while we thought he would be "only physically handicapped." Then, after I met Johnny, I realized how impossible it was to say "only" in that context. In fact after meeting Johnny and seeing that lively mind trapped in a body with only eyes to communicate with, I secretly hoped that Zach would be too retarded to ever know the pain that Johnny must feel.

I confessed this to Joe, asking him, "If Zach were going to be as bad off as Johnny, wouldn't you rather Zach were retarded as well?"

Joe thought. "No, I could never want Zach to be retarded. I want him to be all he could be—I could never wish that on him."

The emphasis that summer was so on the *physical* part, the physical therapy, that no one thought to acknowledge (at least not aloud) the difference between Andy, who had cerebral palsy and who read Kafka, and Scott, who had cerebral palsy and sucked his fingers all day and who had no idea who his mother was among the crowd of women in the room.

One day we saw a film on institutions and the handicapped. It was a scare show. Beds and beds and rows of bodies in beds. Semiclothed people nodding off in corners, sitting in wheelchairs that faced walls. In contrast, there were scenes that depicted just how much handicapped people could do if given proper training and the right chances. The end of the film showed a man in a wheelchair boarding a handicapped-accessible bus, going to his job as a computer programmer in a handicapped-accessible office. The message was that institutions were terrible, inhumane places in which to live. The message was that handicapped people can become more self-sufficient if society helps to provide the options. Fine. What was the matter? Why did the film leave such a bad taste in my mouth? I looked across the room at Gail. She must know, I thought, that Scott will never board a bus to go to work, no matter how many options he has. The film intimated, in a subtle and insidious way, that institutions *themselves* were the reason these people looked and behaved so bizarrely, that given proper programs and therapy *all* handicapped people could lead productive lives. "Don't put them away" was the message. (A year later, when Joe and I were looking for a place for Zach, a social worker, trying to encourage us to keep him home, asked, "Have you ever seen a child who's been institutionalized all his life?" I was too wounded to reply. Later, only to myself, I asked, "Have you ever seen a mother who's cared for a severely retarded child at home for twenty years?")

The film ended and we had a parent-group meeting; everyone felt moved to action by the film's message: our kids are getting help; our kids are in good programs; no, no, we won't give up on them. Fight! Fight! Fight!

I was, as the counselors say, in a no-win situation. To criticize the film would be in some way to defend the institutions themselves. I remembered Geraldo Rivera's exposé of Willowbrook, a New York State institution for the retarded. Rivera and a film crew came in to show the world a human tragedy. In the sixties, when we were sending men to the moon and beautifying our highways, retarded people were warehoused in wards where beds were so close you could not put your hand between them, tied in chairs in medicated reveries, manacled to posts along walls, sitting in their own shit.

In those days doctors said to parents of children who were diagnosed early, "Put them away . . . forget these kids like a bad dream . . . go on with your lives." The Willowbrooks of this nation are the product of those forgotten children. Much as I wanted to go on with my life—to what my life used to be—I can't defend the institutions.

But something's not being said. The ultimate message, that "home" is the place for every child, a "normalized environment," doesn't entirely wash. Normal for whom?

I walked out with Jan, and we decided to pick up the boys at therapy and go have a Coke. As I entered the therapy room, I heard Zach's wails, and my stomach tightened. He was on the floor with Chris, his therapist for the week (they changed every week so therapists could experience children with different disabilities), and she was holding him in a sitting position, getting him to put weight on his hands.

He was not aware of me as I stood by the mat looking down at him. "We're almost finished," Chris said, looking up, smiling. She was a big woman, with broad shoulders and large, capable hands; the T-shirt she was wearing read "If it's physical, it must be therapy." She didn't talk to the parents that much, but she was serious and loving with the children. Some of the therapists seemed younger, less committed than others, but Chris meant business. I had heard others talking about how hard she studied.

I picked Zach up and held him in his favorite sitting position, rocking him and walking him around the room; soon he stopped crying. As long as he was being held or moved, he didn't cry.

Eddie was being held, ankles up, over a giant beachball, as a therapist rolled him across a mat. He was happily slapping the side of the beachball with a wet, sticky hand. Jan said, "Hi, Eddie," but he seemed to be looking either beyond her face toward the walls of the room or out the window.

Jan and I placed the boys in identical blue strollers and toddled off to the snack bar in the student union to get our Cokes, like two happy suburban mothers. In the strollers the boys looked normal enough, both of them adorable with their blond curls.

In the booth at the union Jan and I talked while I pushed Zach back and forth in front of me so he would not cry. Eddie never cried and was happily eating the strap to the stroller seat. Jan said she could leave him in a playpen alone for hours, and he would never cry. And when she came back in the room, he didn't even acknowledge her presence. He was so retarded that he didn't seem to know when he was alone or when there were people in the room. The only thing that seemed to motivate him in any way was food—more specifically, something that he wanted to put in his mouth. Jan said that he would crawl over her as if she were a piece of furniture to get something he saw at the other side of the room.

"But at least he never cries," I said, thinking how much easier it would be if I didn't have to hold Zach all the time, walking him about.

"But at least Zach knows you," Jan said. "He smiles when he sees you. You know I've left Eddie in the playpen alone and driven Amanda to school? I've felt terribly guilty about it, but when I'm gone and he sees me open the front door and come back in, it doesn't even register with him. So what's the difference? They keep telling us to talk to these kids, but it's so hard to remember to do that when there's no response. Yesterday, I realized after diapering and dressing Eddie that I hadn't said a single word to him the whole time. It's like dressing a mannequin."

I brought up the subject of the film and the feelings that it aroused in me. I asked Jan about the distinction between the older kids and the little ones. Did she notice that none of the older children was mentally retarded?

"I guess I hadn't really thought about it like that. I knew the kids were in all different places, but you know, you're right. The older kids are all just physically handicapped." (There's that "just" again.) I looked with her at our two little boys.

"So where are the older children who are physically *and* mentally handicapped?" I asked.

Both of us answered at once: "In institutions."

I learned a lot about handling neurologically damaged children that summer in Virginia, about building tone and loosening spasticity, about proper positioning, about rotational chewing. Zach was as floppy as ever, and he still cried if he wasn't moved.

At the airport to go back to Iowa people smiled at Sandy, Gail, and me—three young mothers with babies on their laps. Sometimes someone would glance back, puzzled at Russ, who looked a little odd, unfocused, his eyes swimming in his head.

I asked if they thought that the trip was worthwhile. Gail was very encouraged, planning to work with Scott every afternoon that he was home from preschool. She was going to have another baby in October, and I wondered how in the world she would manage. Sandy just shrugged: "Russ don't look no better to me." Next week she was going back to work the night shift at a factory in her town while her husband stayed with the kids.

Back in Iowa, Gail, Sandy, and I were going to continue to see each other. I suggested that we all do some writing, that we keep journals for the following year.

"It'll help us see where the kids are at, and it'll help us see something about our own lives," I told them.

Sandy said, "Honey, I'm not sure I *want* to see something more about my life. Anyways, between my girls and Russ and workin' every night, I might just have enough energy to write my name on some checks to pay the bills."

Gail was hesitant but willing. "Well, I guess I could try —but I can't promise. I'm sure not much of a writer."

"Hey listen." Sandy brightened. *"You* write and read it to me and Gail." Then, serious: "Are *you* glad you went to Virginia?"

"Yeah," I said. "I learned a lot about me."

Part 3

JOURNAL OF THE SECOND YEAR

1

I don't know how I got through those first two years. We lived in a small town and—this is some years back—there were no programs then. What I did was, I cut myself off from all my friends, especially those that had babies my son's age. Stuart was severely retarded and he also looked very abnormal. It's part of the syndrome he has— his head, his ears, are misshapen. I just couldn't bring myself to go to any of the young mothers' groups and see kids Stuart's age toddling about.

One time, I did bring him to a natural childbirth class when I was pregnant with our second child. We couldn't get a sitter that night and I didn't want to miss the class. And Stuart would just lie there. He wouldn't do anything to disrupt.

One of the women came up to me after the class and asked if I would please leave Stuart home the next time because it upset her a lot to look at him. I didn't go to another class after that.

—Alicia

Fall in Iowa. Along the road the tractors and combines ride through dark fields; they are painted bright red and yellow —like kids' toys. The farmers make the interminable ride up and down the earthy rows, eyes under their John Deere caps; squinting squarely against the dusty glare, slashing and turning the rich soil, up and down, back and forth across the acres, hour after hour under the autumn sun: midwestern Zen.

We've lived a decade in Iowa. I still don't know a soybean from a rutabaga and I have not made the effort to make distinctions. Our own backyard farming ventures have been half-assed but plenitudinous. A few tomato plants out behind the garage when the neighbors remind us it is time. In the summer and fall tomatoes line up along the window-sills, in bags on the back porch, finally excessed into juice and spaghetti sauce. Over the perennials, rhubarb and raspberries, we have no control. They spring up untended and guiltlessly; we eat these gifts.

There is something good and healthy about living in the midst of growth and reproduction. Even if I do not myself have a yen to go milking or digging or baling, I like the agricultural landscape.

People from the coasts complain about Iowa, about the stretches of flat cornfields. "There is nothing to see," they lament, "no mountains, no ocean, nothing startling or provocative in view, nothing to take your breath away."

That's true, I guess. But for me the ride home from school on a sunny autumn day is a small pleasure; the farmland has a bountiful beauty, undramatic but dependable.

I remember the time, our first fall in Iowa, that we saw a TV commercial for "Boar Power": two pigs spot each other across a grassy meadow and, as Tchaikovsky swells in the background, they race toward each other, desire in their chubby loins. Fade out before the consummation. Then a voice-over to describe how you, too, can raise these sexy pick-of-the-litters "if you use . . ."

Oh, we laughed then. Campy, yes. But something so touching about that porky passion.

That first fall in Iowa, Joe's first teaching job, me pregnant with our firstborn. Oh, then we were the real rubes. How little we knew about life.

This fall I am in a quiet panic. We have settled into a routine with teaching, Gabi in kindergarten, Millie to care for Zach three days a week, Zach's therapy, and his handicapped preschool sessions.

Joe wants Zach to be as normal as he *can* be. What I really want, I fear, is a normal child—therefore, my pessimism, my inability to cheer Zach on with good heart as the therapists try to sit him up, his little shoulders in their hands as his head flops back again.

They say, "Good boy, let's try that again." Then to me, "He's holding his head for nearly a minute!"

My enthusiasm is not fake as I smile and clap my hands in a patter of approval.

If Zach is not crying, if he smiles, if he looks at me and

connects, as he manages to sit by the therapist's supporting arms for that minute or so—then I feel filled up by the praise.

But the other voices, mocking and mean, won't give credit. They ask, "What's so good about holding his head up for a minute? He's eighteen months old. He should be dancing around the sunbeams in our living room. He should be piling blocks up toward the ceiling. He should be licking the honey from off his plate and picking sticky Play-Doh from off his fingers."

There is a part of me that unequivocally rejects Zach, rejects who and what he is, a part that turns from him, even as I hold him in my arms, delighted to feel his breath against my neck, to kiss his face.

As I do the therapy routines, I force myself to mechanize the activity or I feel engulfed by despair. If Zach cries and whines while we work with him, I sometimes feel irritated to the point of hysteria. Joe feels a sense of control by doing exercises with Zach, but I would prefer that my own care be more custodial.

Joe and I taught Millie some of the positioning techniques we learned in Virginia: how to get Zach to put weight on his hands, how to reduce the spasticity in his legs when we dress him. A lot of this is really common sense; there are no magical therapy tricks. It's bad for Zach to be flat on his back for too long as it is not a position that encourages normal movement. Also Zach shouldn't be in an overly supported position (i.e., being carried like a newborn) because then he doesn't work at holding up his own head.

Twice a week Gail, Sandy, and I drive to Des Moines so Nan can work with the boys. In addition to her job at Woodward, Nan has started a therapy program in the basement of a downtown church. She works with the boys for a half hour each, no charge. Nan is so dedicated, so enthusiastic, that I feel lousy when I consider that the trip to Virginia was really a waste of time.

Here in Ames, Zach is enrolled in a handicapped preschool—also with Russ and Scott, his crowd, also in a church basement. The teachers here know less about physical therapy, so it's mostly infant stimulation: eye-tracking exercises, peek-a-boo games. One of the teachers gave me a book called *Teach Your Child to Talk,* whose first chapter suggests that you pick up the baby "slowly and gently, making soft . . . gentle sounds to him." My impulse is to be snotty, to say, "Oh, really? I didn't know you were supposed to do that with babies. Well, no wonder Zach is such a little mess. It's all my fault; I never made any soft, gentle sounds to him." Of course, I say no such thing. The teachers mean well. Everyone means well.

The program lasts only an hour. That's all the handling the boys could take. Zach still cries most of the time, so it's probably all the teachers can take as well.

Gail and Sandy usually stay and watch, but I go upstairs in the church to try to find a place to read for the hour. Zach's wails follow me, meandering through conference rooms, up and down the pews.

Perhaps more than our despair at Zach's handicaps is the strain caused by his almost constant whining and crying.

In the morning Joe snaps at me as Zach fusses through breakfast. "Can't you see he doesn't like what you made him? Why do you have to be forcing him all the time?"

Later I yell at Joe for giving Zach a second suppository that day. Zach's constipation is an endless source of conversation and friction for us. We interrogate and accuse: Did you forget the prunes? Did you try the new medicine? Did you make him eat the bran?

Finally, is Zach crying because he is constipated? Joe always says yes. There is a reason for his crying. He is hungry. He is thirsty. He is constipated. (Joe never says Zach is crying because he is severely brain-damaged.)

We know this: Zach never cries when we hold him and walk him. Joe and I fight about that, too. I am spoiling Zach. I should put him down. But I can't stand the constant crying.

Sometimes during dinner, after Zach is fed and still whining on the floor by us as we eat, Joe, teeth clenched, scoops him up and puts him upstairs in his crib. Then Zach really howls. Joe stomps down the stairs, puts on a record, and we eat as the Rolling Stones are blasting, overpowering Zach's wails.

Zach's whining and crying—I feel it eating into me, making tears into my gut, etching lines across my face.

Yesterday I had been with Zach all afternoon. He cried every waking minute.

I was in the kitchen, cutting up a salad for dinner, and he was in an infant seat that could just barely hold him at sixteen months. I opened the kitchen cabinets so he could see inside from his place on the floor. Sometimes that catches his eye for a few minutes. I turned on his music box and placed it on his lap; he could watch the pictures go around. I tried to feed him, gave him a drink, holding his chin cupped in my hand between two fingers. Nothing pleased him; he continued to cry.

I felt something slip in me; come loose, unhinge. In a fury, I picked him out of the infant seat, kicked it across the floor, and started hitting Zach's behind as he lay floppily over my shoulder. "STOP THE FUCKING CRYING!" I screamed.

Zach cried hysterically then and I, feeling sick and ashamed, stood in the kitchen, holding him and rocking him and telling him over and over that I was sorry while he continued to wail. Gabi came in and looked scornfully at me. "Well," she said, "that may have made *you* feel a little better, but it certainly didn't do him any good, did it?" Zach had just started to settle down, his crying turning to little hiccupping sobs. "No," I said, "it did him no good at all. I won't do that again."

Can Joe and I blame Zach for what we've become? There is such a meanness in our house now, such a lack of caring. We have no additional reserve of energy for each other.

Our lives are taut with maintaining the balance to get through each day. There are no favors given.

We both feel the failure in ourselves and are so saddened by it. We thought ours was a pretty good marriage, but then everything was running smoothly before Zach. I liked going back to school, Joe loved teaching, and, of course, Gabi. . . . But tested, when push came to shove, when better became worse, we really didn't fare so well at all. How disappointed we are in one another.

When Joe's mother died last year, her last words were, prophetically, "Love Zach as much as you can, but do not let him destroy your family." Joe was the strong one, the one who accepted whatever would be. I didn't give him the time to mourn, not his mother's savage, cancerous death, not the loss of a son he could have had. I was so clutching and desperate that winter. We didn't really know how bad Zach would be, but I always had cold twinges of fear, inklings of dread, plaguing Joe all the time with my dark predictions. After a while he would turn from my weeping.

Meanwhile I feel as if time is running out. It's been a year since we've "suspected," and each day has intensified the fear, confirmed my most morbid intuitions. Shouldn't Zach be doing *something* if his development is merely "slow"?

Zach is, I know, far more damaged than we both ever thought possible as we looked at a Penney's Pixy Pic of him at six months, chubby and smiley. (Oh, but how long and hard the photographer worked getting him to smile, arranging him so his head would not flop forward; the line of impatient young mothers behind me with their carefully combed and primped infants.)

I don't want the credit for the more accurate prognosis. The point is that Joe and I have been emotionally out of sync for some time. We have some spotty times of tenderness and care. But mostly—I don't even know if it's *mostly*, it sure feels like it tonight—tolerance is low, and we are so quick to criticize. The other day Joe came into the living room eating a peanut butter sandwich without asking me if

I wanted one, and I actually hated him for that moment, for the statement that made to me: "I feed my own needs."

We are more physically estranged from each other than we have ever been—no kisses in the kitchen, no quick gropes before the kids awake. I fear I have lost not only passion but a capacity for sexual playfulness, intimate games.

Joe is angry at me for my lack of response. "How can you turn away from me when I need you now even more? We should be comforting and supporting each other."

There was a time, so recently, when I understood sex as a comfort. When Joe's mom was sick and he spent his vacation going back and forth to the hospital, I would wait for him at night, reading by a soft light.

"How was she today? How did she look?"

"She pulled the tubes out of her nose herself. She said she couldn't stand it anymore. The nurses were very angry with her and she said, 'They can kiss my ass!' "

We both smiled—Muriel's familiar bravado.

"Oh, honey, can I get you something to eat?"

"Afterwards," Joe would say, kisses on my neck, my breasts, and I would soothe him with my touch and ride away the pain.

But for me it hasn't worked. My own grief is so deep that I will not be wooed out of my despair. And I take umbrage at Joe's attempts. At night he pulls me to him, and feeling him immediately hard against me—I recoil at how easily he is aroused. Uncomplicated.

At four in the morning when I rise in a sweat-drenched panic (an institution dream, drooling adult retardates sitting on the floor of a big room, crying), Joe is sleeping peacefully next to me, his feet jutting out confidently beyond the covers.

In the morning he'll fix himself toast and cereal and wolf it down while he reads the sports section.

Joe's world is still working, sleeping, eating, making love. Why do I resent him for this—and, at the same time, feel a supercilious superiority? A feminist. *Tsk, tsk.* Well, he's a *man,* and don't we women all know how differently *we* feel? How more *deeply* we feel?

I didn't want to have sex the last time, but I went along, guilty about being so rejecting lately. Tracing Joe's muscled chest with my fingertips, I tried to get into it: a few kisses here, a tongue there, stroke, rub, hold.

When did this start, this empty, disconnected feeling? When was it last good?

As Joe entered me, I thought of Zach sleeping in his crib. *We made him doing this.* The words just come to me, a tone of fire-and-brimstone in the severe proclamation. Tears, hot and silent, leak sideways toward the pillow.

"Fern, are you crying?" Joe asked as his lips brushed against my wet cheeks.

Now it was getting difficult to breathe; my nose was all snuffly.

"Oh, honey," Joe said tenderly, mistaking the reason for my tears as an expression of sexual ecstasy.

"I was just thinking of Zach," I said.

Joe quickly turned from me, kicked up the covers, and wrapped himself in a cocoon of blanket on the far side of the bed.

"Well, why don't you start thinking about *me* for a change?"

Later, cutting through the silent dark: "You feel so goddamn sorry for yourself, don't you? You think you're the first person in the world that something like this ever happened to? You better get a hold of yourself. I'm not going to live this way."

It was Joe's idea to see a marriage counselor. He offered it as an offhand suggestion and I made the calls and set up the appointment.

"How about the third Tuesday of next month?" the receptionist asked. "That's about as soon as I can fit you in."

"Well, we both might be remarried by then," I said.

"Oh, is this a crisis? If you consider your situation a

crisis, then I might be able to get you an earlier appointment."

Her voice indicated that she indeed would be put out by a crisis. I didn't want to appear pushy. There were wives out there, battered black and blue, who deserved a place ahead of us in line. Our marriage was not in a state of emergency. I saw only a slow, increasing deterioration—like the erosion of topsoil. We could go another season or so.

"No, the third Tuesday of next month will be fine," I assured her.

We saw the marriage counselor twice. The first time he gave a little transactional analysis spiel: about getting your Adult to meet your spouse's Child, about marital trading stamps. I was put off by the jargon.

Then he asked us why we were there. I spoke first. I said that we were living with a great deal of tension and pain. Our second child was seriously handicapped. He cried all the time and needed to be held. Even though we had a lot of baby-sitting help, we were both exhausted taking care of him. Mostly we took turns so we rarely did anything as a family. When Joe and I were together, we were snappy with each other and often unkind.

I went on: I said that I understood how difficult I was to live with, but that I felt powerless; that I was worn out by depression and always on the verge of tears and yet, I said, I felt I had a right. I felt that what had happened to us— to have had a child who is so damaged—was truly devastating; on a scale of "bad things that can happen in your lifetime," it was a "10." Joe couldn't seem to admit that. I didn't like who I had become, weepy and full of self-pity. And yet somehow I felt I was more well adjusted to this situation; that I, not Joe, was behaving more normally.

Joe simply said, "I have to believe things will get better with Zach. I lash out at Fern because I feel her trying to bring me down with her. Sometimes she is more of a burden to me than Zach is."

The counselor's face was expressionless. He acknowledged that we were going through a very difficult time, that so often a relationship was irreparably damaged by a tragic circumstance. "Sounds as if you two aren't giving each other too many strokes," he said.

I thought, A master of understatement.

Later, Joe and I held hands as we walked together toward the car. I said, "Well, he uses all the right words, but I don't know how really bright he is."

Joe said, "You are a snob. You can learn a lot from people who are not as smart as you."

I said, "I don't see how a man who wears a plaid polyester suit can really understand who I am."

Joe said, "You are a bigger snob than I thought you were."

The second time, Joe and I fought in front of the counselor.

I was complaining of Joe's vocal abrasiveness, how he often had a nasty tone to his voice, venting his anger on me even if I was not the cause of the anger. How he never was angry *at* Zach but how hard he often was on Gabi and me *because* of Zach. He had a mercurial temperament: manic and "up" one minute; mean and hostile the next. I went on to catalogue examples of his deficiencies.

Joe's mouth was almost curled in contempt. "Do you really know what it's like to live with you? You're wallowing in depression—you won't even try to help yourself, to see anything positive in Zach. You think you are so sensitive, so feeling. You're a shallow little bitch; you're a princess, angry because your life didn't turn out the way you want it." Now Joe was caught up in the drama of the moment—I even saw something on his face, a hint of a smirk, as if to say, "Okay, I'll let go—let's put on a show."

I stopped him. "I don't see how this kind of attack is reasonable or helpful. I don't want to listen to it anymore."

The counselor turned to me. "You seem to be a very controlling person. You don't like the messages Joe is sending out. Why do you think he is so angry?"

Joe was actually smiling now. Clearly he felt vindicated.

During that session the counselor taught us something called "Bitch Time." It sounds gimmicky, but it's something we still use today and it really does work. It goes like this: One partner has either a major complaint that involves a complicated explanation or a series of grievances accumulated over a period of time. The partner requests a "Bitch Time" when he/she can let loose all sorts of denunciations and vituperations. The other partner (who has given *permission* for this Bitch Time) is silent. No excuses, no explanations, no defense. The issues may be talked about *at a later time* but the listening partner must not immediately respond, but take in what the other partner is saying.

It's a pretty clever technique. For one thing, because neither of the partners are rushing to defend themselves, they tend both to articulate the complaints more clearly and listen better. I liked it for us because I could hold forth without being interrupted (I must really be a controlling person) and, since there was no dialogue, there was no dispute—no rages or slamming doors. Also we took turns (not on the same night), so it seemed reasonable and democratic.

I was happy the counselor taught us that, but I didn't give him credit for much else. He was cold, too "professional." I wanted someone filled with sympathy for our sad situation, a Marcus Welby type who would pat my shoulder encouragingly and offer me hot Sanka.

This wasn't exactly fair, I know. At the same time that I accused the counselor of male chauvinism ("he wouldn't call *you* 'controlling,'" I said to Joe. "Oh, no, a man is *supposed* to take charge"), I wanted a kind of benevolent paternalism.

I told Joe that I didn't want to go back.

He balked. I was copping out, he said. But it was a weak protest. Both of us saw that if we went ahead with this counseling, it would demand a commitment and energy that we both didn't seem to have. Just arranging the appointments around our teaching schedules, Gabi's dance lessons, Zach's therapy times, was an enormous task. Besides, I felt guilty about asking Millie to stay the extra time. I felt guilty about paying her a baby-sitter's wages for what she did for our family. Joe and I would try and make it on our own.

Zach had a cold this weekend. He can't seem to shake it, get the congestion up out of his chest, cough, spit up. So he wheezed his way through the weekend, looking floppier and more pathetic than usual. No smiles.

At night I go in for a weary last night kiss and find Gabi turned to the wall, curled coldly against me.

"What's the matter, Goosie," I say, rubbing a bare, skinny shoulder peeking out from the covers.

"I'm just feeling very hostile toward Zach," Gabi says without facing me. "I think he gets entirely too much attention around here. He's all you ever talk about."

In the dark I smile sympathetically. Hostile is certainly what she's feeling, though I've never heard her use that grown-up word. Joe and I must use it a lot. We've been feeling it a lot. (Was it yesterday I woke up to a sinkful of Joe's dishes left from a late-night spaghetti repast? "This makes me really hostile," I say, pointing to the sauce-spattered stove.)

"I know, Gabs. He just takes up so much energy and time. What could we do about it?"

"Well, sometimes," Gabi said, not as angry now, but still talking toward the wall, "sometimes I just feel like yelling at him, 'You dumb baby, you stupid-liar-dumb baby.' "

"We could do that," I said. "We could do that tomorrow morning when Zachy wakes up. It won't hurt his feelings any to have you yell those things at him because he won't understand them, and it just might make you feel a lot better."

Gabi turned toward me, her eyes wide in the dark.

"I really could? You wouldn't get mad?"

I nodded and kissed her hard.

The next morning, before I got up, Gabi was already in Zach's room trying to comfort him, to hush his morning cries. Always this was a frustration for her—Zach never stopped crying when he was merely talked to. He needed to be picked up. Dead weight, he was much too heavy for her.

I put on my quilted robe and looked under the bed for slippers.

"Mommy, come. He needs you," Gabi called, worry growing in her voice.

As soon as I lifted him from the crib, the crying stopped. Some shutoff valve. Gabi held one chubby leg and kissed his thigh.

"Wasn't there something you wanted to yell at Zach?" I said as we started downstairs.

"No, I don't feel like that anymore." Then thoughtfully, "Maybe just telling you was enough."

Gabi is watching Saturday-morning cartoons. Joe disapproves. He tells her he doesn't want her watching all that crap. Alone, she asks me, "Is baseball crap?" because she sees Joe glued to the set during all the games. I tell her that I think it is. Joe and I have had this discussion before. He has a two-part argument: He is an adult and can set his own rules, the old do-as-I-say-not-as-I-do routine; and baseball and football and basketball have an aesthetic dimension that apparently Saturday-morning cartoons do *not* have. Joe has written a few articles on philosophy and sport and feels justified in this position.

Actually Gabi does not really like Saturday-morning cartoons. She tells me that they're "for boys," which means that there's a lot of action and noise: monsters, outer space, car sounds. Not her cup of tea at all.

It's a beautiful morning. Our neighbor's cat is stretched out in the sunny driveway, giving her side an occasional lick. From the front porch I can see kids whizzing by on bicycles, their raucous teasing carrying up the street.

Joe orders Gabi outside to "go play." Before she leaves,

she turns to me, offended. "I can't believe I am getting kicked out of my own house." In a few minutes I look out the kitchen window to see her balancing along the edge of the sandbox, singing her heart out to the imaginary audience beyond the backyard hedge. Her friend, Ann, comes out to join her, barefoot and still in her yellow pajamas.

I don't see Gabi again until noon when she comes in breathless, joyful. "Can I eat lunch over at Ann's? They're having tacos!"

Just in the past year has Gabi been eating over at friends' houses. I hear her sometimes after kindergarten making luncheon arrangements. The kids always say, "What are you having?" before the invitation is accepted. I tried to explain to Gabi why that's rude, that honest inquiry. It didn't make sense to her. I think I'll try that the next time Joe and I are invited to someone's house for dinner. "What are you having? Oh, lasagna? Sorry, we just ate that tonight."

Saturday. It will be a long day. Zach is not ready for an afternoon nap.

I walk him around the living room and dining room. I must be making tracks in the rug by now.

I could take him to the shopping mall, but I have nothing to buy. A walk around the neighborhood will only use up a half hour or so.

I hold him and rock him, listening to Phoebe Snow.

I think of all the Saturdays stretching ahead. We will never be able to tell Zach to "go outside and play." He will never have friends who come over to invite him for lunch. Is this what they mean when they talk about "least restrictive environment"? Least restrictive for whom?

Later, walking up the block, I see Lisa playing in the front of her house with her big brother. Lisa is exactly Zach's age —almost eighteen months. I remember sitting across from her mother at a neighbor's house, facing big belly to belly, some year and a half ago.

Lisa is very busy getting on and off her Tyke-Byke. She yells "hi" to me when I pass. Every part of her worked so well, and it seemed so damned easy.

Later, in an effort to get me to "accept Zach as he is," without comparing him to other children and feeling the pain of what he *can't* do, Joe asked, "Suppose there were three kinds of children instead of two: little girls, little boys, and little cuddlies. Cuddlies," he said, "were rare and special and very unique. No one ever knew how they'd turn out. And no one ever expected anything from them—they were accepted unconditionally as is. No one waited for the first steps at a year; no one listened for the first word."

Joe pretends he is the nurse in the hospital, placing Zach in my arms. "Oh, Mrs. Kupfer, you have an eight-pound three-ounce cuddly . . . and he's very, very beautiful."

I am a little nervous about losing weight. I haven't weighed myself since Virginia, but I think I might be under a hundred pounds. All my last year's jeans are swimmy in the ass.

Because I can't eat when Zach is up, I've been making a concerted effort to make myself a big meal when he goes down for naps. Lately, though, I've been so sleepy that I go to bed rather than eat.

I was telling Mary Beth this the other day after she was telling me how lousy I looked. She didn't say exactly that. She said, "I've seen you look better."

Then last night Joe was at a meeting, and Mary Beth called. "I'm coming over late with supper. Don't eat anything."

About nine she pulled in. I was upstairs in bed, reading, and Mary Beth yelled up the stairs, "Don't come down, I'm coming up."

I laughed, bewildered, as she started unfurling a tablecloth, silver, a huge pot of steaming crab legs with melted butter and crusty, still-warm French bread. "You eat, I'll watch," she said, pouring the wine.

We sat in bed among the claws, getting very drunk, me licking butter off my fingers. Then she uncovered the chocolate cake.

I guess that's what I want—people to feed me.

A social worker from United Cerebral Palsy came to see me the other day before I left for school. She is the fourth in what I fear will be a continuing long line. What can she do for me? Her name is Tammy.

Most of the social workers I've met look like sweet young girls who are waiting to get married so they can stop working. Or they are married and waiting for their husbands to finish school so they can move to wherever he gets a job. Or they are waiting for their husbands to find a better job so they can have children. The social workers seem like nice young girls. Of course, they took these jobs because they were "interested in people" and I think that they genuinely are. But there is this air of bland impermanence about them, the silent admission that they have no real impact on the world. I don't expect answers or insight from these girls, who seem themselves as removed from human suffering as homecoming-game cheerleaders.

I let them all come and see me. I have this pragmatic view that the more people I know in this handicapped business, the more information I can have, the more connections I can make, the more help I can get for Zach. "Take advantage" is my motto.

I'm not sure that anything we've done for Zach has really helped him—I know it hasn't in any significant way. What has helped me more than anything else has been talking to other women who have handicapped children, a cruel common denominator that cuts across the divisions of economics, of education, of social class.

Rose Kennedy must have felt as much pain when she found out her daughter was retarded as did any factory worker's wife. Rose Kennedy must have felt the same grief for what could have been, the same sense of loss. Okay, her life was easier. She had a lot of household help. That still doesn't make the hurt go away.

I have this sense, this spiritual camaraderie with women, that I have never had before: not when I solemnly recited the Sigma Delta Chi oath and received my powder-blue and white sorority sweater; not when I marched shoulder-to-shoulder amidst a throng of women for the ERA.

I have this sense of camaraderie—maybe first felt in Virginia during those late-night meetings in our dorm rooms —with Lena, the Mexican woman who was very rich and who had asked how the washing machines worked (for she had never done her own wash), and Eliza from Baltimore's ghetto, and Gail, reading the Bible in her room. I thought of these women of disparate views and persuasions and realized: *We are more alike than we are different.*

I realized because of who we were before we were so touched, that we will deal differently with the experience, but the same sharp blade has pierced us all. I do not think that a woman who does not have an abnormal child can understand this. Josh Greenfield, in his book *A Place for Noah,* among others, writes about this kind of shared knowledge and says that all that we can do for each other is to "offer neither comfort nor inspiration but the testimony of a companionship."

So Gail, Sandy, and I, our intimacy evolving from the painful connection with our children, have offered each other this special witness.

At Sandy's house I can drink pop and bum her cigarettes. She is not unnerved as I walk Zach up and down the faded linoleum in her kitchen as we talk about the deteriorating states of our marriages.

"Steven didn't come home last night," she says. Deep circles around her eyes testify to her vigil. This interests me. I never had a friend whose husband didn't come home at night, who went out with the boys to drink away his domestic despair, to go to work the very next day after sleeping in the back of the pickup.

I suggest to Sandy the middle-class panacea for all marital woe.

"Why can't you two try counseling?"

Sandy smirks, raising a questioning eyebrow. "Why, it doin' you and Joe any good?"

Gail and Ron do not seem angry with each other, although sometimes Gail says, "We can get tense. Especially if Scott is up screaming for half the night."

Gail's whole life revolves about her commitment to God, and she believes that God gave her Scott for a purpose. Her devotion makes acceptance easier. I told her that I'm not even sure that I believe in God, that for sure I do not believe that these children are "planned" by any higher being. They are accidents, terrible and tragic accidents, resulting from genetic misfortune or medical incompetence, or unexplainable injury. Anyway, I told her that if God did plan Zach for my life, I think He made a mistake. He must have meant this baby for a woman down the block and confused the addresses.

I could always get a smile out of Gail. "Oh, Fern." She would shake her head, still pious, but tolerant of my irreverence.

One time I asked Gail and Sandy out for breakfast during the boys' therapy hour, and as we sat over coffee and fast-food Danish, Sandy talked about the coming years.

"I guess we'll have to put on an addition to the house so Russ can sleep downstairs. And we'll have to make the doorways bigger for a wheelchair. It'll get too hard to carry him up and down the stairs." She says this distractedly, lighting another cigarette.

I say that suppose Russ does not change. That he just gets bigger, but remains a severely retarded child who cannot walk or talk or see. Then what will she do?

"I don't know. What choices are you givin' me?" Sandy asks sarcastically.

I don't know the choices myself.

Gail says that she knows Scott will not be able to live at

home eventually. "And I'm hoping that the Lord will help us make that decision when it is time."

When is it time? I know we three are getting through the afternoons, the weekends. We have gotten through this year. Does life become something to "get through"?

Gail thinks it was in God's plan for her to have a child like Scott, but she said that ultimately Scott is not hers alone to worry about, since she saw him as God's child. Her first responsibility was to Ron, to her marriage.

When she talks like that, I am jealous of her faith and her commitment.

Gail talked about caring for Scott as a baby. "I *willed* myself to love him. But there was no joy."

I can't say that is exactly true for Zachy. There is lots of pain and resentment, but when I come and get him after therapy, when I sneak up close to him and put my arms out in a welcoming hello and he smiles in recognition at me, his mother—well, there is pleasure also.

Scott and Russ don't whimper and cry all the time the way Zach does, but because they have no vision, they are so much less "there."

Gail once was describing Scott to someone who had never seen him; explaining how handicapped he was—that he doesn't walk or talk or see or understand anything you say to him.

"Oh," said the woman, "he's like a vegetable, then."

Gail asks me why was she so surprised and hurt at that remark. "Surely the woman was right. That is the word we use to describe people who don't do anything."

I think of Scott's sweet, pale, fine-boned beauty so like his mother's.

"Well, he may be a vegetable," Gail concludes. "But he's *my* vegetable."

Joe and I are supposed to go to Iowa City for Zach's eighteenth-month checkup. Zach is pretty much the same physically as he was a year ago, a fact that is outstanding only when you realize how dramatically children change during the first year and a half of life.

Joe would say I am not being entirely fair. I'm not. There *is* a difference in alertness and receptive communication. His physical tone might be slightly better qualitatively: he has a bit more head control than he did as an infant. But there are no skills that could be checked off that he has now that he didn't have last year. In fact one thing that he doesn't do anymore is turn over, and he did that quite a few times as a young baby. Nan says those were "accidental," those turnovers, a reflex rather than a skill. I do think Zach looks more alert; he seems to focus a bit better as we stand in the doorway of his room and wave to him in his crib.

But his life is moving in slow motion and sometimes I think there's no progress made at all. When I think of Zach's development the past year, I feel a suffocating thickness surrounding me. There is no moving on.

I both dread and anticipate going back to the doctors. Maybe now there is something they can tell us. I resolve to be firm but pleasant. That my own heart is breaking is of no consequence to medical diagnosis.

Always with me is the knowledge that I am not behaving very well, furious with the doctors who are only guilty, after all, of having lousy bedside manners.

Last year on one visit to Iowa City I remember a young resident, the second in what was to be a long series that day, as he came into the examination room, red-nosed, runny-eyed, a crumbled tissue in his hand: he had a bad cold. Without a word of acknowledgment or introduction he sat down at the table and began uninterestedly flipping through pages of Zach's thick file, pausing to sneeze and blow his nose, searching through his white lab coat for another tissue.

"Who are you?" I demanded, my voice filling up the little room.

"Oh—*heh, heh*—sorry"—more nose blowing—"I'm Dr. Bruner. I'm looking at . . ."—head-scratching, searching the paper in front of him—". . . Zachary's case."

"That's Zach-ar-*i*-ah," I said archly.

Why, because the man did not introduce himself, because he mispronounced a difficult name from the file, why because the man had a cold, did I wish to draw my nails along his smooth cheek, to draw blood?

Another time I was with a foreign doctor, a small, dark man who spit out words in clipped English. He approached me in the waiting room. Standing very straight, at attention, he pointed to Zach with a long index finger: "He is your son?"

(No, asshole—he is my husband.)

It's not their fault. They are healers who cannot heal. They hate the reality of children like Zachariah, who make mockery of years of studying, test-taking, sacrifice.

All the parents of retarded children have doctor stories. We get a perverse enjoyment out of swapping stories about who had the most insensitive doctor, the doctor who made the stupidest predictions. It is necessary for our own survival to dump the anger someplace. We're mostly angry because our children are not whole.

This time we are going to Iowa City Hospital *School* to be seen by a "developmental team," similar to Woodward's staff in that they work with children who are clearly developmentally disfunctional rather than "sick."

In the morning we see a doctor who rubs his brow as he reads through Zach's long file.

We go back over the pregnancy, the delivery, as Zach whines in my arms.

The doctor looks confused, helpless even, and I feel bad for him. He is a kind man who sighs as he jiggles one of Zachy's little arms.

Then he takes Zach from me and sits him on a table. Zach, unsupported, lurches backward as the doctor, a little shaken, catches him and holds his head.

"Oh, so he doesn't sit at all," the doctor says softly.

Joe and I stand by quietly. What is there to say?

Another doctor appears. They talk together as the first doctor holds Zachy awkwardly in his arms.

"Is there another child at home?" No. 2 questions not us, but No. 1.

"Yes. "

"A girl, five years old," I offer.

"And she appears normal?" says No. 2.

(*Appears* normal. Oh, you bastard.)

Later we go into a separate building labeled "Hospital School." In the corridors are kids in wheelchairs coming and going and some just hanging around. Off the corridors are a couple of classrooms. A social worker meets us in the hall and brings us in to "meet the team," all women who seem cheerful and competent.

We are in a room that I suppose is used for therapy. There is a mirrored wall, a large gym mat spread out in the middle of the room, and a few toys. The social worker sits in a chair by the door, taking notes. The rest of us sit around Zach, who has been plopped down in the middle of the mat, screaming.

He is impossible. Of course he has a right to be impossible, having been awakened at six for a long car trip, prodded and poked at by doctors all morning, missing his morning nap.

The occupational therapist tries to interest Zach in some toys, but it is to no avail. He cries inconsolably. The physical therapist picks him up and his body tone is worse than ever—he folds almost in half, like a cooked noodle. She puts him back down on the mat.

I can't stand it. I pick Zach up and rock him, taking him out in the hall to soothe him. There's a red wagon there, propped with pillows, and as Zach's sobs subside, I place him in the wagon and push it back and forth.

Joe comes out of the room, hissing at me. "What the hell are you doing? What good will it do if they see Zach asleep?"

I hiss back, "What good will it do for all of us to sit around watching a crying baby?"

"Well, this was pretty stupid of you to plan this session

for the afternoon, when he's too exhausted to do anything."

"*Do* anything? *Do* anything!" I spit out at him. "Just what
exactly are they missing?"

I turn, pull the wagon back into the room, Zach in the
wagon, drifting off to sleep under the fluorescent lights.

I sit on a straight chair, pushing out the wagon with my
knee, back with its handle; Joe enters, stony-faced, and sits
by my side.

"Maybe," one of the therapists suggests uneasily, "we
can just ask you some questions and then you can go to the
cafeteria to get something to eat. Leave Zach here with us
—then we'll all look at him when he wakes up."

I am thankful. It is always a relief when anyone offers to
stay with Zach.

The speech therapist asks, "Does Zach ever make the
same sounds for something he wants, even if it isn't the
right word for the object?"

"No." We shake our heads.

The physical therapist asks, "Does Zach ever try to reach
a toy even if he cannot? If you place him on his stomach and
place a toy in front, will he make an attempt to reach toward
it?"

"No." We shake our heads.

They ask us questions about what we did in Virginia and
about our home routines. We tell them about the bolsters
we use to prop Zach, about the special chair we had built,
about the giant beachball we exercise Zach on, about the
infant-stimulation class Zach was in.

"You've been doing all this the past year?" asks the
nurse. (And I read in, "Well, he certainly hasn't improved
much, given all that.")

Later, after a quick and silent lunch from the vending
machine, Joe and I walk back to the room.

Zach is up. He isn't exactly crying, just pouting and whining a little. When we come in, he does not look up.

One therapist is holding him, balancing him in a sitting

position on the mat; another is offering a toy, a pull-string doggie whose tail springs out wildly behind.

Zach, looking petulant and uncomfortable, pays it no mind.

Placed down on the mat on his stomach, he begins to wail.

"He's probably hungry," Joe says. I pick Zach up and rock him quiet.

Then they begin to talk. Everyone, therapists, social worker, nurse, offers something. They are clear and honest. They say that Zach's problems are probably just as much mental as they are physical—or at least they are so inter-related that they can't speak about them apart from each other. In a young child one sign of mental retardation is developmental delay. Zach at eighteen months is severely developmentally delayed, but, in fact, "delay" here might not be the appropriate term at all. They are not optimistic about what Zach will ever be able to do. They are not sure whether or not Zach will ever sit up, let alone walk and talk. That given the careful and intelligent care Zach has had, and seeing the scant progress he has made (I am right about reading into that remark), they are unwilling to sug-gest that we devote ourselves so intensely to making him "better."

They seem sad as they speak their difficult truth. I feel grateful, for all along I really knew, oh, this is very bad. Turning toward Joe, I see his face blazing with pain, a dazzling tenderness as he reaches for Zach and takes him from my arms.

He is defending Zach. "How can you say that after only seeing him for one afternoon?" His voice is tense, tight.

They say that brain-damaged children were virtually all they did see, that after years of seeing these children they are pretty good at evaluating them.

Joe says, "Yes, but you can make mistakes. He's still very young. He really had a lousy afternoon."

I ask the practical questions. (Part of the report written up by the team after that afternoon visit reads, "The mother is more realistic in regard to the extent of the child's disability.") "What would *our* future be like living with a child like Zach?"

The social worker replies, "Well, Zach will be in school when he is three. That will give you some relief. You might be able to manage with that. . . ."

It was dusk by the time we came into Ames. Joe had been crying off and on during the trip.

"You must think I'm such a fool," he said. "I never, ever believed it would be so bad."

"I'm sorry," I said weakly into his shoulder.

Driving home, I suddenly was surprised at seeing the trees so bare along the windy road. It was a winter landscape—yet I had thought we were still in autumn.

Change comes so sneakily and swiftly—behind our backs, but right under our noses.

Is that how it is to grow old? We say "grow" old, as if it is a slow process of evolution. I think that really is not so, that perhaps one day we just look in the mirror and say, "God, I'm old . . . actually old." And the recognition is shocking.

There doesn't seem to be any change in Zach. Will I look at him one day soon, shocked that he is no longer a baby, but a little boy?

I'm waiting, just going through one day at a time. Oh, it will be a long winter. . . .

2

Sometimes it takes a specific crisis to turn things around. We had been living in what I would consider a crisis situation for almost five years.

Kirk is severely retarded but very mobile. He is not toilet trained and is (forgive me—I don't know any other way to put this) a shit-spreader. I don't know how many times my husband has come home from work and found me on my hands and knees, crying, trying to Spic-and-Span ground-in B.M. out of the living-room rug. It's a wonder that he ever came home at all!

I was always nervous; I never wanted to go out and see people. My doctor kept prescribing more Valium.

I think that I would still be scrubbing and crying today, if Todd, our older boy, had not been in a serious bicycle accident. For two days he was in a coma. For two days all I could think of was the irony that he might die, and Kirk would live.

I was bitterly angry at Kirk, who was still blissfully spreading shit on the walls, at my doctor, who was sedating me so that I could put up with it, at myself, for refusing to take control of my own life.

When Todd was home recuperating, I pleaded insanity to a sympathetic social worker, and she worked to get Kirk placed in a resident school for the retarded. The school balked at first because they didn't think that Kirk would "fit in" with the rest of their clientele. (Damn it, if he "fit in" anywhere, I would have kept him home.) I stayed stoned on Valium and remained cool but incoherent, an obviously unfit mother for such a child.

Todd is completely recovered, thank God. Sometimes I feel guilty because I am grateful for his accident, for the sympathy we received from the tragedy, from the realization I gleaned from it.

—Cynthia

It is winter. Joe comes limping through the door, his face a doughy white.

I am at the stove, holding Zach, stirring vegetable soup.

"I went up for a lay-up, and I came down on someone's foot. Oh, God, the pain. Like someone shot me. Look at my foot, how it just flops back and forth; it feels all mushy," Joe says, holding onto the edge of the kitchen counter.

The flame under the soup goes off; our coats go on. I pack a jar of baby food for Zach. Who knows how long we'll be kept waiting in the doctor's office? Gabi wants to take a special doll.

We all go in when the nurse calls, like a gypsy family, still in our coats, the kids with blankets, seating ourselves snugly in the little room.

The doctor *tsks* and shakes his head as he cradles Joe's leg in his lap.

"You've torn your Achilles tendon." He goes on to explain the healing process, the options.

"The first month, a cast up to your thigh, your leg bent to facilitate . . ." he goes on. I hear "crutches . . . then a shorter cast . . . no weight on the foot for three months."

The doctor leaves to make ready the preparations while Joe rails and pounds the examination table. "A lousy lay-up. And I knew I shouldn't have played that third game."

I am already planning out the next few months: Joe will not be able to drive our shift car, he will not be able to carry a cup of coffee from room to room. Oh, God, he will not be able to carry Zach, to walk him to soothe his cries.

And instead of rising to the occasion, I feel the strength ebbing from me as I sit with Zach, now whimpering in my arms, on the stiff office chair.

At home I stand staring over reheated vegetable soup. Should we have grilled cheese sandwiches with it? I look into the refrigerator for a long time at the cheddar cheese. We have no processed slices all ready to go. Should I take out the block of cheese and cut it up? I can't decide, and the refrigerator is not giving me any answers.

I am still holding Zach because if I put him down he will start to cry, and that is more painful to me now than the ache in my arms. I don't know how to start going about making the sandwiches. A salad seems out of the question —all the chopping and shredding. How about eggs and vegetable soup?

I go into the living room where Joe, his newly casted leg up on the coffee table, is drinking a shot of V.O.

"I think I am having a little breakdown," I tell him.

I feel sleepy and very passive and soft. If someone will only tell me what to do, I could be okay. But I can't think of what to do by myself. I am in bed by eight o'clock, not asleep, but curled up and clutching through the night.

The next morning Joe is on the phone with a social worker from Woodward, sounding very firm and take-charge, and I rock Zach in the next room, humming, "Oh, my man I love him so." Joe is talking about respite care, and I hear the words "medical emergency . . . necessary . . . immediate. . . ."

Then he comes swinging into the living room, already so graceful and adept on his crutches, a natural athlete. "Come on, pack him up. We're taking Zach to Woodward until I'm out of this cast. He'll be there during the week and you'll pick him up and bring him home on weekends. We should be able to handle that."

Even though I did the packing and am doing the driving along the slippery roads to Woodward, I feel like a little girl, small behind the wheel, grateful that Joe is in command.

"Do you think this is a medical emergency?" I ask meekly.

"You know if *you* were on crutches and couldn't carry Zach, and *I* was the one who was falling apart, you wouldn't even ask that question," Joe says.

Zach is in a different ward at Woodward from the one he stayed in for his evaluation. But he will be "worked over" by the same people.

I spoke to Nan, and she personally (not a therapy assistant) will see Zach every day. She feels committed to us for going to Virginia at her suggestion. I honestly don't know how she can stay so up, working with the kids she sees every day.

The ostensible reason that Zach was accepted for this short-term program was *not* because *we* need help, but because *they* (the institution) feel that they can help Zach. This is not totally true. We know that; the social worker who arranged for Zach to be there knows that; even Nan must know it. But I think they have to justify it to themselves: that they are not merely giving custodial care; that they are truly making a difference.

We speak to a psychologist who starts talking to us about toileting programs. Joe listens politely, but I look at the man with mocking disbelief, "Hey, Zach is twenty months old. He would not be ready to be toilet-trained if he were *normal,* maybe not if he were gifted. Do you have any kids?" I ask with suspicion.

He backs off. He was talking about toileting programs in a more "theoretical" sense, about what they could do with even very retarded kids, he explains.

The staff feels a sense of success with these toileting programs and they spend a lot of time with them. All over Woodward there are kids sitting on toilet bowls. Many of them are not actually toilet-trained as much as they are toilet-timed, conditioned, like so many Pavlovian dogs, to release when they are set down on the cool rim every few hours.

Zach will sleep not in a ward, really, but in a double room, separated by bright blue partitions. His roommate, Kelly, has hair the color of a lipstick I had once in high school: orange poppy. When we see Zach's room, Kelly is on the bed, being changed, and he gives us an *"ahh"* greeting when we enter. He has a palsied body, very stiff, but there is something "in there."

In the unit is also a handsome black boy, about ten years old, very retarded. He does not speak or walk, but the top half of him seems perfectly developed, and he scoots about the floor pushing himself with muscled arms, in a little wooden cart—like Gershwin's sad Porgy.

I see one of the therapists playing ball with him, and it surprises me that he throws so well, with such natural coordination. Do the stereotypes prevail? Even in the institutions do the black kids make the teams?

I look at him for a long time. He has a truly lovely face —taut dark skin, high proud cheekbones. I think of him as "normal" for a while. Then someone tells me that he is an identical twin. His brother is perfectly normal; he, the second twin, was severely brain-damaged at birth.

Joe hobbles along behind me as we go to the social worker's office to sign some forms.

He still has his blue winter coat and by now, exhausted from all the walking around through the ward, a line of perspiration is rimming his hairline.

"You're going to get sick if you don't take that coat off," I tell him.

Joe smiles. "And you don't want to take care of me any more than you have to."

I remember that Millie is supposed to come tomorrow; I have to call her. What if she wants to get another baby-sitting job while Zach is at Woodward? I panic at the thought. Joe must have seen my face, for he says, "Oh, I called Millie this morning before we left and told her what happened. She just said, 'Oh, dear me.' "

"What if she leaves us, Joe?"

"She won't. She said for us to call when Zach is home on the weekend. She wants to come over to see him."

On the ride home I think of the last time we left Zach at Woodward for the evaluation.

"You know what I really hate? I hate telling people that Zach is at Woodward."

"It will be good for you," Joe says. "Humility was never your long suit."

Patterns of family living weave themselves in an intricate design, a too-tight double knit. We all live with a certain kind of craziness, some more than others, I suppose. It's easy to become so trapped that we see neither alternative nor possibility. With Zach gone during the week we are coming to realize just how much tension there is in the house when he's here, just how much of a daily giving-up there is to care for him. I hear a phrase, repeating in my ears, pounding with each heart beat. It has become my mantra as I go about the ordinary activities of the day, as I water the plants, as I type up a new syllabus, as I shop with

Gabi for new blue mittens: I want my life back . . . I want my life back . . . I want my life back.

This afternoon Joe calls from the office. The students in his seminar have handed in their first paper and feel like celebrating; they want to go out drinking with him after class.

"Oh, go ahead, honey. Gabi and I will eat without you. I'll save you something," I say charitably.

Charity begins at home. But not in a home where there's nothing left to give. I know if Zach had been home and Joe called with that request that I would have played sergeant. The pass would have been denied. *Unless,* of course, *unless,* he would give me some time the next day. Then maybe we could negotiate. Tit for tat. We add up the points, precise as calculators. Although both of us continually strive to even the score, both of us feel taken advantage of and unappreciated.

Later I wash dishes as Gabi pulls up a stool next to the sink and tells me about a child in her kindergarten class who doesn't yet know his colors.

"Not even red or blue, Mom."

I *tsk* along with her. Hard to believe such cultural deprivation. Gabi knows the subtlest shades—beige and silver, even tricky turquoise, maroon, navy blue. Who taught her these? Not me. When Joe and I divide the time, when Millie comes and I run away from Zach, I run away from Gabi as well.

Joe comes in, swinging the back door open with his crutch, looking rakish, his coat draped over his shoulders. He is flushed and voluble after three beers.

"How's my girls! How's my girls! Oh, I haven't seen you both all day!"

He comes over to the sink with wet, sloppy kisses, still frosty from the winter night. Now he is whistling, rummaging around in the kitchen drawers, looking for an extra-large plastic garbage bag to put his leg in so the cast doesn't get wet as he bathes.

"Who wants to help me wash my hair?" He needs someone to soap and rinse—it's hard for him to balance with one leg hanging out of the tub.

"I do I do!" Gabi says breathlessly as she climbs off the stool, as excited as if she'd been invited to Disneyland.

I build a fire and make myself a pot of herb tea with honey and sit down to read Sunday's *New York Times,* which we don't get delivered in Iowa till Wednesday. That's okay. Old news is good news as far as I'm concerned, because whatever it was—earthquake, union strike, assassination—we have survived long enough to see it in three-day-old retrospect. There's a kind of power in that view.

After Gabi is in bed, Joe comes down spanky clean, the bar-smells of smoke and beer all washed away, to sit by the fire. He takes one of my feet, which is hanging over the edge of the Barcalounger, and rubs the arch.

"I love Zachy so. Sometimes I think I love him more than I love Gabi because it is a pure love, just sacrifice and need. But it's been better for us with him at Woodward. It's better when he's not in the house. I see what he does to you. When he's home, your face seems all pinched and worn to me. You don't stand up straight when he's home."

I do not understand Joe's uncomplicated love for Zach; my own feelings are so confused. I know that people do not love their children equally. Joe and I love our unequal children with unbalanced fervor. Sometimes Gabi will ask that archetypal sibling question: "Who do you love more, Zachy or me?"

I say, "I love you both in different ways." I don't say, The truth is, Gabi, that I would give you the only lamb chop from my plate some hungry day, the only blanket from my bed some freezing night. The truth is, Gabi, that I would die for you. I love you more. It is Zachariah who is my Heart's Needle, whose being fills me with pain and rage as his soft smile catches my breath.

There are certain risks with having a child, and even the normal ones don't come out just the way you want them. They have big ears or stringy hair, they don't share their toys, they pick their noses in front of company, they're rude to your friends on the telephone. Only occasionally do you wish they were not here. You never seriously consider not having them live with you.

But now, with Zach away, I look with a certain clarity at who we were before we had him. There is a self-consciousness about everything I do now that he is not here. I recognize the lightness, the ease with which I go about the mundane tasks of living, seeing again who I was before I had Zachariah. There is no going back, I know. But I see what we could become and I know we must take control.

Joe thinks that when Zach is home for the weekends now, he cries less. I don't know. He does seem awfully happy to be home, especially sitting in the car as we pull up, and I say, "Do you want to see Daddy?" I'm sure he understands, for he tightens and smiles so wide, showing his teeth like so many tiny Chiclets.

The next hour or so is very good. I walk Zach around the house, showing him his toys, his room, holding him in my arms as I answer the phone, twirling the cord for him to make a lasso.

Joe sits in the rocker, his casted leg raised up on pillows across the coffee table, and holds Zach while I mash up some banana for a snack. The first hour or so Zach never cries but looks alert, pleased to be here in the bosom of his family.

Gabi refuses invitations to play at her friends' houses. "My brother is home," she explains, as if a big college man has blown into town for the weekend.

Sometimes the dinner times are okay, the blended food goes down easily. Other times the crying begins after two gulps, then the choking starts. Between spoonfuls I walk Zach around the dining room, just as I did when he was a tiny infant.

Saturday night we keep Zach up late, rocking him as we watch TV. Joe makes Zach laugh by loudly rustling the newspapers over his face. Later I give Zach a bath, using Ivory to wash the newsprint off his nose and forehead.

But Sunday is too long, especially if Zach is up before seven. He seems to cry more. Has the novelty of being home worn off, so that he is no longer excited and grateful? Is he too brain-damaged to feel gratitude, and that first-day rush is just some primordial recognition?

Sunday afternoon, Gabi takes the ride with me to Woodward to bring Zach back for the week. So this has become a part of our lives, taking him home, bringing him back to the institution. We drive through the trees, the quiet on a frosty day, toward the neat brick buildings.

Everyone says how awful institutions are. But it's not "the institution" but the children I see in Zach's ward who fill me with despair. The rooms are nice: Big Bird, and Charlie Brown, and Mickey Mouse on clean walls; sunlight filters over tables of Fisher-Price villages, music boxes.

But, oh, the children. Gabi does not like to be touched by the children who grab sometimes with sticky hands as we pass. She says they are "a little yukky." She is being kind. They are a lot yukky. A young girl with the beginnings of breasts is sitting, floppy-headed, on a mat, her tongue lolling, stiff hands, holding a pink baby rattle.

The institution will be depressing no matter how many gay cartoon plaques line the walls. The reality of a severely brain-damaged girl-woman is awful. Even if we get rid of institutions, as the "progressives" want to do, that reality will not go away.

Society does the same thing when we play up the horrors of nursing homes. We say how it is a national disgrace how we care for our old people, how nursing homes are understaffed, how they afford little privacy, how abused the patients are, how little dignity they are left with, as if the nursing homes themselves *alone* were the scandal and the tragedy. What is left unsaid? Why are we afraid to face our own debilitation? What's really crummy is being old and sick and not being able to take care of yourself, or spending a lifetime planning for tomorrow and now not remembering what day it is. That's the real indignity.

How we must hang on at all costs. We are a culture that controls nature, whose technological ethos must extend to our own nature as we simply refuse to accept decrepitude. In a perversion of the Hippocratic oath, we extend life at all costs—including the psychological ones.

This might be forgivable were we also a culture who revered the aged and the infirm, but the irony, of course, is that we do not. There is little respect given to the graceless old.

We blame nursing homes for the pain as if they are the cause for senility, for invalidism, and we romanticize about other cultures who "care for their own," not seeing the gnashing of teeth caused by two generations of women in a shared kitchen.

Later, riding home with Gabi, Zach's car seat empty in the back, I suggest we go to the movies: *Freaky Friday* is at the mall.

The crowd lines up for the four o'clock show; inside, row after row of noisy kids wave and call to each other, sitting so sure and straight. It is hard to switch gears, adjust to the mass of normality after the institution.

But I get totally into the movie. Barbara Harris is adorable as the mother who unwittingly switches bodies (and therefore roles) with her young daughter. I whisper to Gabi, would she like to trade places with me, have to cook meals, teach classes. I do not mention Zach. "No way," she says. "I like my own life."

The lights flash on. For the first time that weekend I am feeling relaxed, my stomach is not tight.

A few rows ahead of us a boy takes another boy's jacket and races pell-mell up the crowded aisle. The jacketless boy bellows, "Hey, retard! Get over here with that jacket, you retard."

Why should I feel such a pain at a young child's meanness? Gabi sees my eyes fill with tears, and she rubs my arm. "They're only dumb, rough boys, Mom. They don't know any better."

I have to drive Joe everywhere and this has become another source of friction. He must comment about my driving—even for the lousy six blocks it takes to get him to school. And why do I feel so insecure being in the driver's seat with him? (Should I take that metaphorically as well?)

This has been a cold, snowy winter, and I'm the one who drives the twenty-five miles to my school; I'm the one who drives the county roads every weekend to pick up Zach at Woodward. But driving with Joe in the car is something else again. I stop too short or grind the gears—only because he makes me nervous.

Yesterday, after the third remark (he was even telling me when to shift), I pulled over to the side of the road and let him have it. I was so angry, I felt like smacking him with his crutch.

"Look, I don't give a damn how you'll get to school, but I'm telling you this once—one more comment from you about my driving and I don't take you *anywhere*. This chauffeur will quit. Got it? If I drive, you be quiet. Just stifle it."

A quick flash: Joe at nineteen, me sitting so close beside him, before bucket seats, my hand on his thigh. The speedometer reaching toward seventy. Me, meekly: "Don't you think you're going a little fast, honey?"

"Who's doing the driving here, anyway?"

Oh, tough, oh, cool, as we raced along the left-hand lane of the Long Island Expressway, cars jumping out of our way like scared rabbits.

A year, three speeding tickets later, Joe's license is revoked for three months. Joe claims that the speedometer on the car was broken (it *was* about four miles off). The judge says, "Didn't you notice you were passing everyone else on the road?"

Joe answers, "Well, sir, I've been passing people all my life."

Now, years later, Joe sits sweetly next to me. "I'm sorry, Fernie. That's terrible. I won't criticize anymore."

But that night after I pick him up and we head into our driveway, he says, "Good turn, honey. You didn't hit the curb."

I turn off the car, sitting for a moment with the keys in my hand. "And I don't want your patronizing appreciation, either. *No* comments about my driving."

"Boy," Joe says as he limps into the house. "Boy, are you tough!"

Woodward has been adapting a wheelchair for Zach. Zach seems much too little for a wheelchair, but the therapists say the positioning is better for him than just lying flat, and the stroller is too supportive.

I cried the first time I saw the wheelchair. Then I overheard Joe telling someone about how well made the corner seat adaptation was with its straps and boards, about how "lucky" we were that we could get it on loan from Easter Seals since it cost almost eight hundred dollars. There was no room left in me for gratitude. I was too sad and angry seeing that little chair sitting in the dining room.

When it first came, Gabi was excited and immediately jumped in and wheeled herself through the house. Joe came downstairs, and seeing Gabi in the chair, he yanked her out with such ferocity I thought he was going to slam her against the wall. He thundered, "Don't you ever play in this chair. It is not a toy. Don't you ever let me see you in it!"

And Gabi, frightened, started to sob and buried her face in my belly. I said, coldly, that this eight-hundred-dollar well-made chair can certainly hold a forty-pound little girl. Joe looked murderously at me.

But, of course, another part of me understood. We both had this flash—that terrible image of our healthy child in that chair, her skinny legs dangling. We reacted differently —me, slowly and silently gasping. Joe, exploding.

When I picked up Zach this weekend at Woodward, he was lying in a playpen, surrounded by colorful toys and *not crying.* He was not being held and still not crying. I was so pleased. They're trying to do behavior modification to eliminate some of the crying behavior. I feel a bit apprehensive about that since crying is the only thing Zach can really *do* to get what he wants. What he usually *wants* is to be held and walked around, which seems pretty reasonable to me if he can't do anything for himself. But I really was pleased to see him there, not exactly "happy," but peaceful maybe, and not crying.

When I stood over the playpen and said, "How's my boy?" he gave me the biggest, warmest smile, and I loved him to pieces.

Even this weekend at home he has been in good spirits.

After dinner we sat around, and I rocked Zach while Joe played Go-Fish with Gabi.

I looked at Joe's crutches alongside the coffee table and Zach's wheelchair by the window. I asked Joe, did he think America was ready for a new family situation comedy: *The Handicapped Family.*

Gabi and her friends, Teri and Ann, are upstairs coloring; on the way to the bathroom I hear their conversation.

ANN: My sister is so mean; she teases me and makes me cry and then slams the door in my face.

TERI: Well, *my* brother once messed up my room and smashed my toys and hit me.

GABI: Yeah, but *my* brother is retarded and handicapped and brain-damaged.

TERI: I know. My mom said for me not to talk about it.

GABI: Why? We talk about it all the time around here.

I have been thinking a lot about the women I met in Virginia, especially Jan. Tonight I told Joe that I really wanted to find out how she was doing, that I was thinking of calling her. Joe frowned, looking over at our last phone bill sitting by the toaster. He pushed a book of stamps across the kitchen counter: "Why don't you *write* her a letter?"

Dear Jan:

I think of you so often; I've started so many letters in my head. Then, when I finally did decide to write, I had to rummage through so many collected papers in the dresser junk drawer to find that sheet with the addresses on it. The whole "Virginia summer" (as Joe and I refer to it) has a surreal quality to it, distorted by my emotional craziness and the intense intimacy with people whom I'll never see again. I hope you're doing well. I liked you a lot.

Here's what has been happening in my life. Coming back from Virginia . . . back to my real life, I fell apart. I guess, somewhere in the back of my mind, never articulated, was the feeling that the five weeks of physical therapy was somehow going to be the "end of it all." A cure for Zach? I don't know. Anyway, I realized it was not even the beginning. I saw my life stretched out—the next few months, the next few years—and I panicked. Joe and I were getting along miserably. He was impatient with me—for myself, my pity, my anger, my negativism. I loathed his optimism and his air of bravado toward our family and friends. Alone, he was often hostile and angry about trivial incidents—the car not working, dishes in the sink—but never about confronting what I took to be of monumental significance: Life's Shittiest Deal. We saw a marriage counselor for a while. I didn't like him much, since I thought he exemplified all the male workings I was rejecting in Joe—that toughness.

Anyway, Joe and I kept bumbling along. I am teaching part-time in a community college in another town. I have a wonderful woman caring for Zach but still spend a great deal of time driving him around to stimulative sessions, therapy, etc. Zach continued to grow, not do much, and cry.

Then, sometime in the beginning of winter, Joe tore his Achilles tendon while playing basketball and was to be in

a cast and on crutches (a month of which was a thigh-high
L-shaped cast that made movement of any sort very difficult). I thought very seriously of leaving the pack of them.
Joe could not help out with what Zach needed the most: to
be carried and walked about. Joe could not even bring
Zach, after a nap, down our winding staircase. (If a house
was ever designed to thwart the handicapped, ours was it.)

Realizing my tenuous hold on stability, Joe called Woodward and made arrangements for respite care for Zach,
since I could not possibly manage the house, my job, and
the group we endearingly called "The Handicapped Family." Oh, Joe could also not *drive,* and so I also had to
chauffeur him back and forth to school, meetings, etc.

Well, Jan, life without Zach seemed so normal and so
easy that it was downright sinful. We were able to eat a meal
together without tension. I was able to read a story to Gabi
without rocking a baby simultaneously. I was able to have
sex and enjoy it (well, at least Joe and I weren't always
fighting).

The difference between Zach here and Zach at Woodward was so much more startling to us this time than last
year when he was at Woodward for five days. Last year I saw
the separation as a respite from a very demanding baby. In
that sense it was a good break for us.

I view this separation differently. Zach is almost two and
still is like a very young baby. I realize how increasingly
abnormal our lives are becoming as he becomes more difficult to care for. I realize the strain we are under, taking care
of him. (The weekends are especially bad.) And I don't see
the end in sight.

But let me backtrack. Right before Joe's accident, we
took Zach back to Iowa City Hospitals for another evaluation. It involved a team of therapists, education "specialists." They were not optimistic. In fact it was the first time
that I felt I was being told the truth about the severity of
Zach's condition, and frankly I was relieved. In essence, but
not in these words, they said, "This kid is going nowhere,

slowly—given all the work you've put into him." This was the message. Not that he had a "little cerebral palsy" or that he might be a little slow or might walk funny, but that there was a significant possibility (probability) that he would not talk or walk or even sit up. We pressed them on that, and while I sort of thought he eventually *would*, they were more cautious. The news was absolutely devastating to Joe, into whose accepting mind these horror fantasies never came. I, on the other hand, felt the comfort of having my worst fears confirmed and facing them head-on was easier than the haunting possibilities. Also, I felt far tenderer and more loving toward Joe, who was in need and acting for once the way I felt a human being in pain should act. He cried and did not yell. In short, we switched roles —not permanently, but effectively, for the short transition period.

Last year, a friend of ours asked me if I ever thought about institutionalizing Zach. I was appalled and angry. This year, of course, the question does not seem particularly outrageous at all.

We are now talking about looking for "places" for Zach. He is in a program at Woodward where he gets therapy daily and is worked with by all sorts of special-education people. We take him home weekends. It has worked out okay, I think. Next month we will take him home, and I'll try and make it through the spring and summer. We hope soon that he'll get into a residential facility. They have a few good private places in Iowa. Zach won't be in an "institution" per se.

Unfortunately there is nothing really appropriate *here* in central Iowa (although there are long-range plans for a children's convalescent home in Des Moines). We have some group homes here in Ames, but the kids are older and more functional.

This decision did not come easily. For a while I wished that he would remain very handicapped so my guilt would be alleviated by the justification that "we just couldn't man-

age him" but I've worked through that. I want him to be as
good as he can, to learn as much as he can. I also know that
he can't live with us and, very frankly, I don't think the
sacrifice would be worth it (for him or us) if he did.

The past month of phone calls has been incredibly trying. I think a lot of people (women) keep children like this
at home for years and years because working this all out is
such a difficult task.

A friend at work has a neighbor who has a severely retarded boy who is in a small residential school in northwest
Iowa. I called her this week just to ask about the place, how
old her boy was, when was he placed, etc. She was very
encouraging. When I protested, saying that Zach was very
young, not even two, that I was looking for "maybe sometime in the future," she said, "It's not too soon to look
now." And then, "I spent five years of my life on the floor."

I called the place and asked for the director, but when I
started my story, "I have a little boy who . . ." I just burst
into tears.

The director said, "You just cry, dear. I'm holding on."

Gail Sander (Scott's mother, remember?) had a beautiful
normal little girl in October. I am so happy for her. She is
so busy now, but she is a very tough, together lady.

I have gone on. This was a very confessional letter and
I hope you don't think I'm using you as a shrink. What I
really want, I think, is your approval. (I picture you now in
a chair, nodding, and replying, "So, Fern, what do you
think?" Are you, by the way, still seeing your shrink?)

When I was visiting my parents, I met some people who
had just put their twenty-three-year-old cerebral-palsied
son (not retarded) in a nursing home. They were shattered.
All I could think of was—all those years to come to that.

Gabi is in kindergarten now. She loves the idea of "real
school," of rules and regulations—she always has been a
sweet goody-goody.

Joe went out and bought Chinese Checkers tonight and
whipped us both shamelessly. How that man loves to win!

My regards to Roger. I hope you're both doing okay. (A bland statement, I know.) Are you doing much painting? Please do write.

Love,
Fern

And Jan replied:

Dear Fern:

I've read your letter several times since it came—so much of what you say is very familiar.

This has been a very trying winter for us, too. Eddie has been in a new preschool, all-day program this fall. He gets intensive therapy, has wonderful teachers.

I think our disillusionment with Eddie has been slower and stretched out over a longer period of time—I attribute this to all the good programs. There was always another one to try something that made the existing experience only a stepping-stone to the next program. Anyway, however you slice it, reality is creeping in. Eddie is in one of the lowest-functioning classes at the center. In the fall when he started, he was taking tentative walking steps if you held his hands. Well, he's over three and still there. He also only knows his name and "no." He cannot complete any cognitive task.

Eddie's teachers have been very supportive and extremely observant, which leads to our present situation. Since Christmas especially, but probably way before, Eddie has been having petit mal seizures. They are very subtle: head nods, blinks, stares, rolling of the eyes, but continuous. He's been having as many as thirty-five in a half-hour period. Well, last month after he fell over a few times, we had an emergency EEG done. There is something scary about the thought of having an "emergency" anything. Well, his EEG is extremely abnormal and his neurologist (one more specialist we now see regularly) told me he was amazed "the child was conscious with such an irregular

EEG." In the next breath he tells us that if he can control the seizures, we ought to see an improvement in Eddie. Well, Eddie is now on a new drug called sodium valproate, which the FDA just approved, and we're waiting and watching. I feel like we're playing Russian roulette. Okay, he'll be better (what's "better," by the way?) if we can control the seizures, but what if we can't? It seems they never had success with this particular type of seizure pattern before this drug, and only some of the patients respond favorably. The waiting and adjusting can take months—in the meantime he has had his share of winter illnesses, which wipes him out and panics us.

My state of mind is extremely mercurial. Either I'm "handling" things, painting a lot, seeing friends, etc., or I'm in the depths of depression. I don't know how much is Eddie and how much is me. I'm seeing my analyst four times a week—it's "true analysis" at this point, couch and all. I'm for the most part pleased with him although there are times that progress is too slow. I want answers now. I want to know what's going to be with Eddie. Can we keep him home? For how long? And if he'll eventually be in residential care, why wait, why fall in love with him more just to have him taken away?

I have a lot of conflicting feelings of love and hate. To top it off, he has gotten cuter. Why is he so beautiful? Sometimes it seems like a taunt. I share your feelings of wanting him (at times) to lose ground or be *too* anything to keep him home. I'm afraid, though, that once we put him in a residential facility I couldn't be able to see him or have him for weekends. I want a clean break. I don't know if I could handle seeing him once we give him up.

The therapy helps here—I don't have to throw it all on Roger. Sometimes, I use Eddie as an excuse, though. He's a built-in crisis. I can avoid facing a lot of things by bringing him up.

We looked at the institution near us at Thanksgiving. In some ways we know it's inevitable, and it makes day-to-day living easier to know that when it gets too rough we have an out. Realistically, I don't think he'll be living home with us for more than a few years. He's getting mobile but has no controls; he eats everything—bills, newspapers, books. He still is good-natured, though, and a very lovable little boy.

I have been doing a lot of work and recently sold two paintings. I think I use the painting to pull myself away from Eddie. When he's home, I don't spend that much time with him. When I do, I find his lack of abilities a bit overwhelming.

Eddie had a psychological assessment done at school, another in the great series. This one, however, had him come out at an eight-month level. The upsetting thing about that was that's exactly (with small variations) where he was last year. He has a few scattered skills above this level—spoon-feeding with assistance, and crawling, but he has essentially not grown. That's devastating!! If left to his own devices, he would spend much of the day pulling his hair and eating it. He used to venture out to pick up a toy and eat it. Now he doesn't need the world.

Last Thursday we went to a genetic clinic for a full-day evaluation on Eddie. There will be more tests, including a CAT scan, a chromosome study. Everyone seemed concerned about the seizures. I think there is some possibility that it's degenerative. Part of me hopes so, and the other part of me gets scared that I could think that way.

Fern, I don't feel as if I've given you a picture of where we are. I find letter-writing difficult. I'd much rather have an afternoon or a week and while we're wishing, just us— no kids.

Roger seems more accepting of Eddie than I am; sometimes it seems so because he's not with him as much. I wish my painting were elsewhere. I'm always squeezing in time; I rarely have large blocks of time except at night.

It's hard to figure out what's Eddie and what's the rest.

Maybe, if I didn't have Eddie, I'd have to make more of a "statement" with my art or make more money. Sometimes it feels good to have a reason to do or not to do a lot. I find it frustrating that I put in a lot of time, but the monetary gains are small. Roger doesn't push me here. But I feel the need to make money. Somehow money and success are all tied up together, and how can I really be good and yet not make much. . . .

Sometimes I wish I could see the future—know what will be and relax, knowing we only have to fill in the middle. But what if I don't like the ending!

I guess it's going to get harder as Eddie gets older. I fantasize about running away and leaving it all. When we fight, I fantasize that Roger will take up my fantasy and leave *me* with it all. I think, I know, we have this silent pact (sometimes not so silent) that we're in this together and no one goes anywhere unless you take Eddie with you. The latter part is our suicide pact—we half kid, but there is a lot of truth and fear behind it, i.e., all sloppy driving is to be done with Eddie. . . .

Take care. I have to stop and do my morning errands while Eddie's in school.

Love to all,
Jan

3

Who we are doesn't seem to change. After a few years of a good therapist I am beyond the anger and anxiety attacks and am cruising along nicely with chronic depression and a return of childhood asthma—the rest of the world cannot fathom the suffocation of this life, but I think it's terribly appropriate that I have trouble breathing!

Our Emily will be six in April. A beautiful, normal-looking child who was perfect in every way at birth, but forever lost to an un-detected, diagnosed-too-late, treated-too-little case of hypothyroidism. She functions at about fourteen to twenty-two months and is essen-tially nonverbal. Most disappointing is the rate of development, which, to my chagrin, is slowing. The gap between Emily and normal grows with every hour. No one will speculate on her future, but it is not, in a word, rosy.

In the beginning I was labeled an "anxious first-time mother" who was "expecting too much" when at five months Emily was lethargic and passive. After two years of dealing with the medical world I was beginning to have recurring thoughts of punching a pediatric neurologist in the face. These days I save my fantasy vio-lence for "multidisciplinary teams" and social workers. Words like intake and appropriate have been known to drive me to antisocial behavior.

Recently we came home from a five-day California respite and I found that twenty minutes after walking in the front door, my an-ger/frustration quotient was just as high as before I left. My emo-tional battery, I fear, is no longer rechargeable.

What do I do? I love Emily, but living with her is making me a bad mother. I think I could love her more if I didn't have her here, if there were a light at the end of this tunnel.

I have made the initial contacts, and I see what's down the road: resistance. The head social worker proceeded to dump the guilt load of the decade on me. She intimated that if, and it would be a big if, we were found eligible for a grant, that most likely Emily would be placed with another family "who could handle a handicapped child." She hinted that Emily didn't sound bad enough and that I wasn't crazy enough. Maybe if I go on drugs and become psychotic, I could call her up for an intake that would meet her criteria.

I read with a chuckle in this morning's paper of Senator Hayakawa's latest suggestion that the handicapped should be drafted. Who knows, if no place else will accept us, perhaps we can turn Emily into a WAC! As the social worker said to me, "You've got to remember, ma'am, that we are dealing here with public funds."

Our family life is nonexistent. Nothing we do is normal. Worse, nothing we do is happy.

—Denise

A Dialogue

ME: Daddy and I are going to start looking for a special place for Zachy to live, a place where a lot of people can help take care of him.

GABI: Millie can help us take care of Zach.

ME: Yes, but we need even more help than that. You know Zach is getting bigger and bigger.

GABI: Well, that's what happens to children. No one gets *smaller*. That's dumb.

ME: We might take some trips and see some of the special schools, and we'll all go together.

GABI: Will a special school teach Zach how to walk and talk?

ME: I don't think so, but you never know.

GABI: Well, if you never know, I think Zach should stay here with us. He belongs to us.

ME: He will always belong to us. But taking care of him every day will get too hard.

GABI: So what if I don't like the places and I don't want him to stay there?

ME: It's my decision and Daddy's. We make that choice.

GABI: I think it's a lousy choice to make.

ME: So do I.

We've had a few days of Iowa spring: cathedral-blue skies, frantic chorusing birds, noble tulips—and wet basements.

This morning I asked Gabi what she thought of Zach not living with us anymore. This idea, of course, is not new to her; she's heard us talking about it for months. She went with us to visit the first residential facility, a trip combining both business and pleasure. We were going to a friend's wedding in western Iowa (Gabi was excited about being a flower girl, lovely in blue velvet), and we were going to look at the Tommy Dale Developmental Center in Sioux City. We went to Tommy Dale first.

I don't know why I was so ill prepared for what I saw there. I had seen severely handicapped children with their parents at the therapy program in Virginia; I had seen Woodward. Maybe it was acknowledging the permanence of such a condition. While the kids at Woodward's respite unit were eventually going home and in Virginia the kids were there to become "better," Tommy Dale was a last stop. Joe asked me before we left, "What kind of a name is 'Tommy Dale'?" I said that probably the facility was started by some rich people who had a retarded kid named Tommy Dale.

I remember going to visit Joe's grandma in a nursing home in Florida years ago. I had to be psychologically braced, set, before I could handle going in. Us, young and tan, coming in from all that sunshine to the gray; the smell of cafeteria lunches, urine, medicines, disinfectant. The smell of death. When I knew what to expect, after we were there a few times, I could deal with it. The first visit, though, sent me reeling. I clutched Joe's hand as we walked past the row of wheelchairs lined up in front of a giant color TV.

And so Gabi clutched my hand as we walked into Tommy Dale and walked past children in wheelchairs, children lying spastic and twitching on the floor, children sitting, rocking themselves in self-stimulated reverie. The social worker spoke about therapy and programs as we toured. Joe responded intelligently with questions, peeking into rooms and corridors as if he were inspecting a summer camp. In one room, a hydrocephalic child, her (his?) head big as a beachball, lay on a beanbag chair. I heard Gabi gasp. I don't remember the rest of the day, except that when we left, Gabi couldn't wait to tell me on the steps outside that she certainly didn't think that place was for Zachy.

Again I pictured Zachy big. It's one thing to be carted around like a baby when you're only two years old, and cute. It's quite another to be a baby in the shape of an adolescent boy with pimples, with man-sized hands.

We left Sioux City in silence. In the car Joe jauntily asked what I thought. I looked at him with tears streaming down my face as if he were crazy. He appeared calm, in a good mood, but I knew that in a half hour he'd cut off another driver, cursing him, or snap at a waitress in the restaurant. Gabi, in the backseat, was drawing pictures of monsters with her new markers.

So I asked Gabi this morning what she thought of Zach not living with us anymore. She said that although she really liked it better when there was just the three of us (i.e., before Zach was born), she was upset that strangers would see the three of us together and think that that's all there was, that she didn't have a brother at all. This deception was a betrayal of Zach. I feel it, too, Gabi. "Well, if someone asks, you tell them that you have a brother," I responded. "But how do I explain why he doesn't live with us?" she asked. I think of that, too. It makes more complicated the innocent question "And how many children do you have?" I picture myself at cocktail parties for the next decade, "Well, I have one child at home, and one in an institution."

Today Zach is two years old. It's been a long two years. He got cards from Great-Grandma Ethel and my aunt Anna. I put them under the pile of bills. I'm not able to overcome the pain, ignore the bitter cruelty of those gay "Now-that-you're-two" cards with pictures of little boys who sail boats and race toy cars. There's something bizarre about all those pretenses of normality.

My mom sent him some shorts and shirts in a package with no note. No mention of a birthday. I understood that. Later she told me that in the store she started to cry while she was paying for them.

We had no parties here. I suppose that Zach has a right to birthdays. He's been here two years on this day and he's a person. But to make this day special, to celebrate his birth and growth and life would only be, for me, a lie. What would it do but perhaps assuage some of my guilt, to show what a good mother I am? I look at him objectively and see what he can do at two. Not much. It's easier to list what he cannot do. He can't say *mommy.* He can't crawl. He can't feed himself. He can't sit up. Yet he connects with his eyes, searching my face when it is close. I know he understands some of what we say to him. I know that he has a little self deep in there, struggling to make connections with the world. He's *there.* Often I wish he weren't because that would make less complicated my feelings, my decisions about the future. He pulls me toward him with his cry, his eyes searching mine, the smell of his soft neck, the room spins. . . .

Jan's therapist says that depression is anger turned inward—or anger is depression turned outward; I forget which. But I notice as my mopey, teary-eyed days are less frequent that I am becoming more and more angry. At whom? Good question. Sometimes at Zach, poor thing, who through no fault of his own was born retarded. I feel most ugly when it is Zach to whom the anger is directed. Here I am, capable, strong, furious at this little boy who lies on the green dining-room rug. More often, of course, Joe and I are angry with each other. *Testy* is a good word for it. We are "testy" with each other and our voices have a taut edge, throats tight. Dinner time is especially bad, even though we have canned the concept of "traditional family dinner" because Zach's feeding demands one's complete attention and because cooking a family "meal" properly balanced and attractively served is too much for any of us. Still, unstructured as it is, what with Gabi going to the refrigerator for yogurt and us feeding Zach bananas (his favorite), it still is a lousy time of day. Yesterday Zach was particularly whiney. (Did he want a drink? Did he have gas?)

Joe exploded at Gabi for "not sitting properly in her chair."
I laugh—as if we are at some formal dinner party instead
of at a table still piled with toys and newspapers, getting up
and down for Zach (What does he want? More banana?
Another drink?), facing his wheelchair to the wall as they
taught us at Woodward, these fancy behavior mod tricks to
teach him that he cannot get what he wants by whining,
while Gabi is crying into her yogurt, her little butt firmly
planted on the chair. I am angry at Joe for not being aware
of the real reasons for his hostility, aware of just how tense
we all really are. But how can Zach take the whole rap for
a bad dinner scene? In other homes parents are yelling at
children who didn't wash their hands well, who spill their
milk after careless reaches. In "normal" homes dinner time
tensions run high. Okay, we'll blame Zach for *some* of it
then. How much?

Often I'm angry at strangers. Dull, sloppy women in
supermarkets blithely wheeling their normal kids. Sometimes any woman with normal kids seems to me carelessly
unaware of her good fortune. Last summer in Virginia I was
sitting with Jan, Eddie and Zach in their strollers, waiting
to go into the therapy room. Across the room a woman was
chasing a toddler who looked teasingly over his shoulder as
he ran, shrieking with delight. But she meant business.
When she caught him, she smacked his behind several
times until his giggles turned to tears. "Stay put," she com-
manded, putting him down in a chair, "and don't move.
Don't you ever move." Jan and I sat looking at our children.
Jan turned to me with clenched teeth: "I feel like shaking
her," she said.

Dear Jan:

This was a difficult weekend. (What? I should write to
you after a fun weekend, when I am feeling stable, without
depression or self-pity? Too boring.) Zach is home, the end
of his "three-month short-term program" at Woodward
State Hospital. How do I feel about that? Ambivalent as

usual. (I don't think I've had any one strong feeling in the past year and a half that wasn't complicated by other strong feelings; it makes me dizzy sometimes.) It is much easier without him home. The physical burden of being with him —carrying him around, changing his positions, placing toys in accessible places—is, of course, absent, but more important, the emotional strain is so diluted when he's gone. I felt a dull sadness, but not the tearing pain when I see him lying on the floor like this giant infant.

We enjoyed the weekends when he was home. No, that was a false word. We enjoy movies, outdoor barbecues, *not* the weekends. I meant to say there is a *positive* feeling; it was often *good* when he was home for the weekend. The time was condensed and precious. We knew the weekends were devoted to Zach. He's warm and affectionate—so we did a lot of holding and hugging and kissing.

But you're right about handling these weekend scenes. It was so hard. I think: Better if he were *away for good,* and we could stabilize and go on with our lives. And yet Zach is my son (I don't usually use that word easily or well, though Joe does), and I want to see him. And, of course, I feel responsible for him. I don't know how to find the balance. Having him home all the time is physically and emotionally impossible for me. The "visits" make me a little crazy—like an intense affair you know should end, no future in it. Why prolong the pleasure and the pain? When I took Zach back to Woodward on Sunday night, I always felt awful. Sunday night—the careworkers looked tired, stoned, the place was very quiet and somehow more institutional than during the day. Still, my overwhelming feeling when I took him back to Woodward, the biggie feeling that washed over the regulars of anger and grief and guilt (my familiar triumvirate), was *relief.* And the realization of this is proof to me that for my own life I'll be "doing the right thing" by trying to get Zach into a residential facility, or "place," as soon as possible.

I want to know how *you* are, as a separate person but,

unfortunately, never apart from this circumstance and these children. The children. That word often floats into my head, unrequested, to describe the "clients" at Woodward State Hospital. Seeing the kids rolling on mats, twisted bodies, strange sounds—ahhhhh, like drowning old men, bizarre movements of self-stimulation—rocking to create their own reality, saliva bubbles . . . ridiculous.

Gabi will be home from kindergarten in a half hour. Seems like I barely have time for a cup of coffee, a little writing, a bath—there she is! I like her an awful lot.

We celebrate something in the Midwest called "Mayday" where children come with baskets filled with little tooth-rotting treats, ring your doorbell, and run like hell (lest they be kissed, the ritual goes). Anyway, this holiday rivals only Halloween for junkdom awards. In an effort to keep the stuff away from Gabi I've been nibbling all afternoon and now feel quite nauseated—the caramel-corn–jelly-bean–taffy combo now beginning to take hold.

It's finally spring here. We get it wet and late, but it finally comes, then turns into summer as you go out the back door.

Gabi stays out most of the afternoon with her friends. The neighborhood is clotted with children. Tuesday and Thursday I'm gone all day at work, and Millie is here to care for Zach.

I checked into the expense of Zach's residential care. It seems that this varies from state to state and Iowa apparently is a "good" state when it comes to social services. We would pay about seventy-five dollars a month; the rest comes from federal and state monies.

A friend of mine whose child is in a care facility says that she sometimes feels guilty that the government is paying for the care of her child, that it's a kind of welfare. I told her that parents of handicapped children have enough to feel guilty about without thinking they are social parasites. Hell, I told her, with all the money we gave to arm Iran under the Shah, we could care for all our handicapped people. (Maybe we could ask for our rusted-out fighter planes back and turn them into group homes.)

Zach will be up from his nap soon. I sometimes get so afraid. Afraid of the strangling responsibility once again. But also afraid of letting myself feel too much.

It makes me feel better to write—especially when I can be honest in trying to sort through all this mess. Also, I needed your letter because it verified my own un-uniqueness, and this was a comfort to me. Most of the time in Virginia I felt like a freak. Everyone was so concerned about *their kids, their kids, their kids.* (I still hear that woman—Colleen, the older nervous lady who chain-smoked—talk about how bologna and toasted cheese were her Bobby's favorite sandwiches and were these good for him if they didn't facilitate proper rotational chewing?)

Tonight is Joe's and my anniversary. Ten years. Seems like a hundred. Seems like one. We fight about the same things we fought about as teen-agers when we "went together": his authoritarianism, my carelessness, his nasty moodiness, my manipulation. I can't go on because it won't seem balanced—all I can think of is more of Joe's negative qualities. Oh, yeah, which leads me to my inability to respond favorably to and accept criticism and his inability to criticize helpfully. We're still together. (I don't know if I should feel proud or silly about it—it's so passé.) I often, but not consistently, love him. I often, but not consistently, would like to pack him in along with Zach and run away. Joe got a sitter for tonight—we're eating out—he wants to go dancing. I still love to be in his arms.

I'm having a friend who is a photographer do a "family portrait." (We have so few pictures of Zach, two albums filled with Gabi.) I'll send you one if they come out well.

Please be well and strong and please, please write . . .

Love, Fern

I feel good. Zach has been so warm and responsive. I need so little sometimes from him—a smile, his eating without choking, his waking up and not crying.

Yesterday I grew a little, came out of the closet as the mother of a handicapped child, as it were. Before, taking him out for a walk or shopping with him in the stroller, I always felt an uneasiness. He can still "pass" as normal unless there is a direct and then uncomfortable encounter: a salesgirl hands him a lollipop—he doesn't reach; we stop for a hamburger, and the waitress asks if I'd like a booster chair—no, I say, he doesn't sit up; I'm holding him sitting in a doctor's office, his body slack against me. "Oh, is your little boy tired?" an old lady coos. (No, lady, he's retarded.)

The wheelchair helps in this respect. It sets everything straight. No doubt about it, there's something wrong with this kid! And the public admission makes me an honest woman.

Yesterday was bright and sunny, and Joe took the wheelchair outside and we puttered around, pruning some bushes, and then took Zach and Gabi for a walk around the block. My neighbors, who had been secreted by the Iowa winter, all burst forth and came out to see Zach. I was a little nervous at first; they were, too, I think. But then it just flowed. Doris, our across-the-street neighbor, told me how cute Zach was, what a good job Joe and I were doing. Hannah asked about the wheelchair and what the therapy programs were like. I felt their warmth and support.

Mrs. Truman, an elderly neighbor lady down the block, saw me wheeling Zach and called me up to her porch. With a shaking finger she told me not to worry, that Zach would "grow out of this handicap, just you wait and see." I smiled and told her that I didn't think that he would. I liked her for wanting to wish it so.

Relationships are a tricky business when one has such a child. Most people don't seem to be able to handle the problem very well. I feel mixed—I don't want people to feel sorry for me (I do enough of that on my own). On the other hand, I want some recognition of the most significant presence in my life. It's hard to get that balance with people you don't see very often. Some people react by doing the "invisible child" routine: continuing to make small talk (which seems so much smaller in Zach's presence) and pretending that he isn't there. Of course, adults do this with normal children, too, as they play in the periphery of conversation. But for me Zach is *very* there. And his existence must be recognized.

I am so absorbed by Zach and his deficiencies that I have to force myself into the give-and-take of ordinary friendship. It is as if everything else—all talk of books, movies, the affairs of the world, affairs of friends—all this is put up on a shelf somewhere.

At tea at Mary Beth's house one day we talk about Zach not living at home.

"For us to have to institutionalize Zach—that's the worst thing that can happen," I say, weeping into my cup of Constant Comment.

"No," says Mary Beth, matter-of-factly. "The worst thing that can happen is that Zach will not be bad enough to be institutionalized—but won't be good enough to live at home with you either."

Zach "comes alive" with a lot of extra stimulation or, as Joe says, "rough stuff." So he is just like a normal little boy in that respect.

Joe plays a game called "Captain Cuddley," where we put aviator goggles (swimming, really) on Zach and "blast off" by doing "wheelies" in his wheelchair.

Joe says (very animatedly), "Do *you* want to play Captain Cuddley?" (Finger pointing to Zach's chest.) "Ready for the countdown?"

Zach smiles and lets out an open-mouth gasp in anticipation as Joe begins, "Five, four, three, two, one . . . BLAST OFF!!!" and he zooms Zach around the first floor, crashing into walls ("Look out! It's a meteor shower!!! *Baboom, babooom, baboooom!!!*"), overturning the dining-room chairs on a trip through the galaxy.

It's a little rough on the house, but Zach loves it.

At night after supper we put on loud rock music, Bruce Springsteen or The Who, and Joe dances Zach around the room, Joe's manic energy trying to pump some life into Zach.

Later I hang Zach upside down by his ankles, turning him from side to side. The therapist says that this will build his tone, and Zach seems to like the jostling.

Oh, we work so hard for his smiles.

There are some families, I have heard, where the damaged child is the favored one, forever innocent, blameless. I can understand this, seeing Gabi play with her friends, running up and down the stairs, quick turns, skips, jumps, sure-fire talk. The contrast of her playing in front of Zach, she moving easily in and out of fantasy games, oblivious to Zach's great weight as he sits strapped and propped in his heavy chair, is overwhelming.

Indeed, her normality can seem shallow and careless.

It was suggested to us at Woodward that we continue the prompt feeding that they did with Zach this winter: We're supposed to hold the spoon with his hand around it, dip into his plate, guide it toward his mouth. I don't think he is near ready for this. He cries continually during the meal, his arm gets spastic, and his clutch reflex tightens. So then we have to remove the spoon, loosen up his arm, and move him around to stop the crying. There's food all over the rug, Gabi is tense and eats next to nothing, and I don't even try. Even Joe, brave soldier, is deflated by this dinner-time exhibition.

We did it for two weeks until I finally told Joe, "Screw it, we'll just feed him as we always did."

I think Joe was relieved.

Gabi asked me if we could bring Zach in for "Show and Tell" at her kindergarten—seems many children "share" their younger brothers and sisters. Gabi, in her wise and adult way, asked, "How do you feel about this, Mom?"

I told her that while I wouldn't choose to do it myself, if she wanted to, it was really okay with me. We picked a day (Monday), and she was excited all weekend. Gabi wanted to wear a little red plaid jumper that my cousin had given her because Zach had a matching red plaid jumpsuit and they could "be twins." We washed and fluffed out Zach's golden curls that morning. They both really did look super. We took him over to Crawford School, right around the corner, Gabi pushing the wheelchair. I wondered about her presentation—explaining the wheelchair, Zach's obvious defects. What words would she use—all those she heard us use around the house, in tearful telephone conversations to family and friends. "Retarded . . . brain damage . . . developmental delay"?

We wheeled Zach into a hushed circle of eager faces. Gabi went first, stood up proudly, and announced, "This is my brother, Zach. He's two years old, and we're wearing matching outfits today."

A particularly bad morning. Zach was up at six; all I could think of was the endless stretch of hours ahead. Joe is off to work, but he will be "on duty" here this afternoon.

Zach, whining and cranky (from being up too early?), needs to be moved, held, rocked endlessly. I simply don't know what he wants. If I knew that this was an infant colic, something that he would outgrow, then I could endure this. But this has been going on for more than two years.

Joe thinks that Zach's skills are improving. That is such bullshit. I hear Joe tell people on the phone how well Zach is doing in therapy. I gnash my teeth in the next room. Zach is going nowhere—slowly. I am going out of my mind. I am feeling so alone . . . making circles around the living room and dining room. What do I do with this child? I think of Iowa prairie women from another century—alone in the house with their children. Certainly some of them had handicapped kids. Women alone in midwestern farmhouses, never seeing another adult for weeks (months?), men gone, then coming in too bone-tired to be needful of their family's pain. I picture myself alone, day after endless day, with Zach, who never sits, never plays, and cries and cries and cries. Would I kill him?

Zach is whining in his wheelchair and I am standing at the sink, up to my elbows in suds. "What do you want?" I would feel better if I screamed; my stomach is so tight. I don't because it upsets Gabi. Later Joe and I will end up screaming at each other. I am so out of control.

My brother calls long distance from Tulsa, and I vent my directionless fury and blazing self-pity at him. "I can't stand it anymore," I cry. Ray cries with me, and I am only angered at this response. Nothing he does can please me. I hate him for having a normal, healthy two-year-old who is yelling in the background, "Daddy, look!"

We talk about finding a place for Zach. Ray calls it "institutionalizing" him, and I am further angered by his insensitivity for not using the appropriate euphemism: "residential facility." Ray asks me how I think I'll feel if we have to make that decision. I say, "I have already made it, buddy. I am through. I am trying to save my own life."

Our weekends are not like other families' weekends. Ours are charted, plotted: Who's on duty with Zach? We always take turns. This Saturday I'm up at seven, and Joe holds and walks Zach while I hurriedly blend up eggs, bran, and prunes. Joe straps Zach in his wheelchair and moves him around to get him to stop crying while I tie a bib around his neck. When things are under control, Joe goes back to bed. I don't rush feeding Zach because there's not much else to do with him, so these custodial chores—feeding, washing, dressing—make up how we spend the day with Zach. After breakfast I wipe Zach off and place a bowlful of marbles on his wheelchair tray. Now Zach can use his hands to palm some of them, and I think he likes the clatter they make as they roll off the tray and onto the floor. We spend about fifteen minutes like this—he drops them, I pick them up and place a full bowl again before him. I wheel Zach into the kitchen while I do the few breakfast dishes. By now he is beginning to fuss, wanting out from the confines of the chair. If I lay him down on the floor, he will cry. So I walk around, holding him in his favorite position, legs folded as if he is sitting in a little chair. We look out the dining-room windows, but I don't know if he can focus that far. "Look, Zachy, it's raining outside."

At eight I hear Gabi rustling upstairs, and I am thankful for the company. I think Zach smiles as he hears her coming down the stairs. For a while we all cuddle in the big rocking chair in the living room which is "Zach's chair," bought for that purpose; Gabi, her eyes still sleepy-soft, kisses Zach's shoulder. We turn on Saturday-morning cartoons, and I sit mesmerized by color and sound.

At nine Joe comes back down, makes some eggs and toast for Gabi and himself, then takes Zach upstairs to give him a suppository, waits for the bowel movement to come, then lays him down on the sponge to give him a bath. This is my time. I can read the paper, have a cup of coffee, eat breakfast.

Our whole day is segmented like this. I have an hour off to go to the library. Joe has an hour off to go to the gym. A college girl comes for a while in the afternoon to take Zach for a walk, but today she has a big test to study for and calls and says she cannot make it. Sometimes Joe and I meet on the stairs; I'm coming down from a nap, and Joe is going for one. We pass Zach from arms to arms: your turn. The other gets a brief respite. We don't ask, "How are you doing?" because if it's a bad time, we don't really want to hear about it.

At night as I am taking a bath, Joe comes in to talk. He's going to the movies by himself because I am too tired— besides, I'd really like to be alone. Sitting on the toilet bowl, with his coat on in the steamy bathroom, Joe turns to me with a sad, worn face. "Fern, do you want to separate? We can't go on like this, never being nice to each other. There's no love."

I am steeping in a tub of hot, hot water, trying to ease the tension in my neck and back.

I don't think about "us" or how we are getting along, or whether or not we love each other.

"Who will take care of Zach?" I say.

And right now that is all we can really think about. For even with baby-sitters and household help it really takes the two of us, plotting out the hours, full time, for a child who sucks up so much energy. Neither of us could do it alone, nor could we afford to maintain two households and keep as much child care as we need for Zach.

"I think we're both stuck in this marriage for a while, for better or for worse." I smile ruefully.

"Well, it can't get worse," Joe says before he leaves.

We cannot make it together living with Zach, but sometimes I feel we will not be able to endure even when Zach no longer lives here. Our emotional support blanket has worn that threadbare.

I went with a social worker from social services to look at a home for severely handicapped children in Forest City, Iowa, about an hour and a half from Ames. The social worker is a young girl in her twenties who has no children of her own and thinks Zach is just "so cute!" I don't want to alienate her because the social workers have some power; it is they who decide whether or not residential placement is "necessary."

On the ride up we make small talk, and she tells me that last night she saw a "terrific movie"—the latest Burt Reynolds flick. I think, Oh, my God—I'm placing my life in the hands of someone who thinks *Smokey and the Bandit* is a great film.

The director shows us around the different housing units. The rooms in the cottages themselves are bright with crocheted afghans from home; a poster of a little girl picking daisies which reads "I am somebody special"; and family pictures in traditional poses.

Connected to two of the units is a classroom for the profoundly handicapped. In one corner a young woman in a gray sweat suit is sitting cross-legged on a mat, holding a little girl in her lap. As the woman relaxes the child's stiffened limbs, I hear her saying, "Who did your hair today, Nancy? You look so pretty in that ponytail. That will be nice to have a ponytail in the summertime. You will be so cool, so pretty. . . ."

On another mat is a boy around fourteen whose spastic body is draped over a beanbag chair, a towel under his chin to catch the drool.

"John just came to us last year," the director says proudly.

"Oh, where was he before this?" I ask, slightly self-conscious at using third person, invisible.

"He was at home," the director replied.

I think: Who was his mother? A woman, old beyond her years. A woman with arms of steel. How did she do it? *Why* did she do it?

There is a poem in Anne Sexton's *Transformations* about mothers who turn "radishes into rubies" and "wear their martyrdom like a string of pearls." Looking at this boy here, thinking of Zach, my own little radish, in bed at home, I remembered the refrain:

When a child stays needy until he is fifty—
　Oh, mother-eye. Oh, mother-eye. Crush me in—
The parent is as strong as a telephone pole.

The director and the staff I met were very proud of the place. "But I'm afraid," the director said kindly, "our waiting list is long."

Joe and I keep talking about the places we've seen. It's no longer a question of *if* Zach will go to a "facility," as they say, but *when* he will go. I don't recall a specific time when we actually made this decision. I know there are waiting lists for the good places and other parents have told us to take a vacancy quickly or we could lose it.

I remember the social worker from Iowa City who said that when Zach would be in school, we could have "some relief."

That phrase stuck with me: "some relief." It seemed an odd way for a family to live their lives, dreading weekends, holidays and, oh, that long summer. The school would give "some relief."

In Josh Greenfield's book *A Place for Noah,* about his family's years of living with an autistic, retarded child, it seemed that so much of their energies were spent making up patchwork arrangements for day care after school, for weekend respite care. When I asked another mother of a severely retarded child if she'd read the book, she said, "I couldn't finish it. I thought, 'Enough already! Get rid of that kid!' "

Zach at eighteen months was still like an infant.

Zach at two years is still like an infant.

If he were ten years old, the social workers would say, "Poor woman, she just can't lift him up anymore."

But now I think the social workers think that it is "too soon" for residential placement, that our family can still remain together. The Family. The Family Together. Sacred as a religious shrine. It is "too soon" for residential placement for Zachariah, and I am not yet crazy enough (I haven't threatened suicide); our marriage is not yet bad enough (we haven't threatened divorce).

How long are we supposed to hold on? And who are we doing it for?

Joe would hold out longer than I, but then I do a lot more of the everyday care.

I asked Joe, if I died, would he try and keep Zach at home? He said, "Yes, I think I would. Of course, I'd have to marry someone pretty fast who would take care of him. It might be hard to find someone that desperately in love with me."

Zach sleeps well—I'm thankful for that. I spoke to many mothers whose brain-damaged kids could never quite get a hold on the difference between night and day, kids who kept the whole family up with screeches and yells, kids who walked around (if they could) all hours of the night, showing up in unusual places—a neighbor's unlocked car, an all-night supermarket. Of course, floppy, sweet Zach doesn't go anywhere. (Sometimes when I change his diaper, he cries as I go out of the room to get a washcloth. I say, "I'll be right back, you just stay there." And a mocking voice answers, "Well, where's he going to go?")

Sometimes, though, Zach awakens when we check him— an old house and the floorboards squeak—or when it's real hot and he wants a drink of water. I love these times. For one thing Zach is at his most charming, most alert, most smiley. Joe says it's because he knows that it's a forbidden time, and if he's not fun to be with, we'll dump him quickly back to bed. But there's something more mysterious going on. When Zach wakes in the night, his whole body tone seems stronger; he sits better and holds his head better than at any time during the day. Also his eyes are big (only the hall light is on outside his room) and well focused. I notice this in contrast to how he looks when he's *outside* during the day, a look Joe and I have described as "blurry." He does not look around then, but seems either inwardly focused or concerned only with those objects within one or two feet of his line of vision. In part I attribute that to overstimulation: there's just too much to take in—trees, cars, noises. Zach's deficient neurological system can't handle all the stimuli, so he just "blurs out." But it also might have something to do with light and dark. I don't think it's because his body has been at rest for a period of time, because I never notice an increased tone or alertness when Zach wakes up from a nap.

When I see him at night like this, I believe that's who he really is—a gentle and sweet little boy whose smile lights up

the night. At these times Zach is absolutely edible. Damp
curls stick to his head, his body is soft with the smell of
Pampers and talc and baby sweat—delicious! I nibble his
round shoulders, cover his face with kisses as I sing. He
looks lovingly in my eyes and reaches tentatively to touch
my face, cooing softly. Your mommy loves you, your
mommy's here, I say, rocking fiercely. Sometimes tears run
down my face onto his undershirts. (*Other voices:* "He's your
child. No one can have the feeling that you have, holding
him in the night like this. So life with him is tough. Your
problem is you can't handle adversity. You want a life of
ease. Grow up already. Learn to sacrifice. Become a better
person. Keep him.") We rock together in the chair in his
room, going through a medley of "Old MacDonald" (a
little too zippy for that time of night), "Moon River" (better), and "Good Night, Irene." For some reason this last
has come to be his good-night song since he was an infant.
It has an ironically appropriate stanza:

> Sometimes I live in the country,
> Sometimes I live in the town,
> Sometimes I take a great notion
> To jump into the river and drown.

4

*At least Zach is so bad that he'll always be in a protected environ-
ment. He won't know the cruelty, the social isolation of being different.*

　*Sometimes I try and sort out for myself what's hard about just
being with* kids *all weekend and what's hard about being with a*
handicapped *kid all weekend. Normal kids can drive you crazy. I
hate the summers of hearing the screen door slam a hundred times*

a day as the kids go in and out, in and out. I just finish the breakfast dishes, and they come in asking for lunch. There's a lot of that dependence and need with normal kids.

But if my friends complain about taking care of their normal kids, or ever compare their lives to how it is taking care of Nina, I feel like screaming at them—that they don't really know what it's like at all.

I think it's really harder as Nina gets older and I see kids her own age doing things that she'll never be included in. Last summer we were at the pool, and I saw all the preteen girls standing around with their friends, giggling and sharing secrets. Of course, none of them would be caught dead spending a day with their mothers.

Nina was in the pool, splashing and having fun. Only this year she learned how to put her face in the water, and she is very proud of that. I am sitting by the shallow edge of the pool with the mothers of toddlers as Nina shrieks excitedly each time she goes underwater. Every few minutes she yells, "Look, Mommy, look at me, Mommy. Watch this, Mommy!"

Like the young mothers beside me, I wave and pretend to smile. But, you know, after twelve years, I don't want to hear "Look at me, Mommy" anymore.

—Sara

Joe calls me from the kitchen: "Look, he's holding the spoon by himself." Actually Zach's managed this off and on for the past year, never with any consistency or regularity so that one could say, "He holds his own spoon." Yet Joe still gets excited over Zach each time he does it. Sometimes I can share that pleasure, but most of the time I feel numbed by the repetitive attempts and from mouthing the same words of encouragement.

Zach is sitting in the wheelchair with his bowl of mashed bananas, and Joe, Gabi, and I watch as he hits himself in the forehead with his spoon, like the spastic jokes we used to laugh at in high school. "Well," says Gabi thoughtfully, "not bad if his mouth was where his eyes are."

I think what has drained me more than anything this past year, maybe more than Zach's crying, is the lack of change.

The retarded are very boring. Now that's something I've never heard said (aloud at least—though it must be thunderously echoed in the minds of parents of retarded children), but it is a truism that makes the endless day-to-day job of caring for such children monotonous and grueling. They don't seem to change.

Yesterday Joe was giving Zach a bath and had him lying on the big yellow contoured sponge that we use so we don't have to lean over the tub and hold him. In the next room I heard Joe's enthusiastic prompting, "Come on, atta boy. Kick your feet. Kick your feet." I could hear Zachy giggling and splashing. Two years of saying "Kick your feet"—in Joe's mouth the words sounded new and fresh though he'd said it hundreds of times himself these past two years. How many more years will he be saying "Kick your feet" to a baby in a bathtub? I feel all used up. What I see stretched before me, if we ever keep Zach at home, is an eternity of babydom.

I took Zach to Woodward today to see Nan ("I'm bringing him in for a tune-up," I said), and we saw all the therapists, teachers, careworkers, who came to know and (apparently) love him. All of these women came out of offices, from classrooms, ohing and cooing (I told Joe that it was like showing up at a gala with Robert Redford). There Zach was, plump and pretty, his body tan from floating in our little backyard kiddie pool, his hair blonder and curlier than ever—the cutest kid in the institution. He really was. Being with him there at Woodward distorts my world. This crazy kid who's causing me so much pain and anguish and here he's Mr. Popularity. On the other hand I'm happy with all the fuss. He's my child and, however complicatedly, I love him.

The next day . . . Millie is home with Zach while I take Gabi to swimming lessons. I spot Beth sitting amidst the throng of mothers in the bleachers, watching her six-year-old in the pool. Beth and I greet each other like sorority sisters who have endured pledging and hazing together. Beth is active in our retarded citizens group and has a severely retarded daughter who is in a group home in northern Iowa.

I tell Beth about my apprehension about meeting with the social workers to discuss placement for Zach, about these girls making decisions about my life. They could not possibly understand how it *really* is. She nods sympathetically. "Some of them are not even parents of normal children," she says, "let alone *real* parents."

I told Beth about visiting Woodward with Zach yesterday and how strange it makes me feel. Beth says she feels the same when she gets a note from one of Carol's teachers asking permission to take Carol to her home for the weekend. Once she even got a thank-you note after a holiday saying what a fine time she (the teacher) had with Carol. "It makes me feel about this small," Beth said, holding up her thumb and forefinger together. "What does it say about *me* that they enjoy her so?"

I remember the second year Joe and I were married when I worked in a day-care center in Rochester, New York. The children there were described in the sixties social-welfare jargon as "culturally deprived." About half were black, about two thirds were from single-parent (read "mother") families. All were poor. The kids all seemed so needful. I loved taking them home on a weekend—a big treat was going out to a restaurant to eat (usually pizza), to the park the next day if it was nice out, or to a kiddie matinee, having them help me bake cookies to take home to share with their brothers and sisters—a special, sharing time—not like work at all.

So I was always a little surprised when I brought them home (some apartment project on the other side of town, windows with torn shades, teen-agers sitting on cars jiving each other, broken glass where kids rode their tricycles) and was greeted at the door by a mother, not exactly hostile, but cool, suspicious. I would chat away about what a fine time we all had, how well behaved her child was, how I had enjoyed it. The mother never thanked me, nor did she ever invite me in.

How young I was then. Shiny-faced weekend do-gooder. What did I know about living every day in a one-bedroom apartment with four kids, the baby with an ear infection most of the winter, crying, no man. Welfare came spying on you to make sure it stayed that way. What could I know about any of that? And me a honky to boot.

So often I am careful to say to all the handicap professionals—those who invented nifty terms like "mainstreaming," "normalization," those who close institutions before they open community residential placements, those who talk about "preserving the family" as if it were a religious shrine, those who give our children therapy and programs that make adaptive equipment, and those who want to take them home on weekends because they *do* really care—I say to those people, you have never lived day-to-day with a retarded child of your own. You do not know what it is like.

Gabi is playing in the plastic pool in the backyard with her friend, Ann—I hear squeals of little-girl giggles as they duck each other. I wheel Zach out in the chair, down the ramp we just finished building, and place him so he can watch the girls play. Looking from the kitchen window, I go back to making supper. A few minutes later the girls have left, are busy making pies in the sandbox, the grains sticking to their wet legs. Zach sits facing an empty swimming pool.

"Turn him around, Gabs, so he can look at you play," I yell from the window.

"Sure, Mom." Gabi walks carefully across the hot brick patio in her bare feet and turns Zach's wheelchair around to face the sandbox, kissing him, cooing, "You bored, baby boy? You want to watch us play?"

But five minutes later Gabi and Ann are back in the pool, and he's alone again.

Last night I had a dream . . . I was in a church, and next to me was a middle-aged man, balding, dressed in a black suit. He turns to me (during what was the service, I think) and whispers, "Your son is simply a delight! A very beautiful, special child." I tell him that our son is severely handicapped, that we are looking for residential placement. The man looks so surprised.

"Why, surely your son doesn't need that," the man says. "You must be making a mistake."

I am in a rage, screaming at this bewildered man. "You sanctimonious prick. You don't know what it's like at all . . . you don't know what my life is like at all!"

Everyone in the church turns around and stares disapprovingly. I run out crying.

This weekend I went with Beth to the Iowa Association for Retarded Citizens convention in Cedar Rapids. I think having Zach has tapped a hidden political bent: I go to all these meetings, speak out, make connections. It all has to do with power, I think. Being powerless and alone just adds to my depression, so I join things. At least I feel as if I'm doing something. If I gave in to how I really feel, I think I'd crawl back between the covers.

Three men ("professionals") were talking about "preventing residential placement." I was furious the whole time they were talking. How dare they talk about residential placement as if it were something that must be prevented, like tooth decay! Don't they realize what some of these children can do to families? The more the anti-institutional trend becomes the vogue, the more guilty parents are going to feel if they have their kids placed.

Beth nudges me in the side to speak up, and when I raise my hand, she whispers, "Good for you."

Later another woman comes up to me. She tells me that

her hyperactive, severely retarded son was in Woodward's short-term program.

"You know," she said, "after he was there, I stopped and took a deep breath and looked at my life for the first time in six years. My other children could play without locking themselves away. My husband and I could go out for dinner. At night we could just sit on the couch, watch TV with the kids, and eat popcorn. We were just like a regular family. When Woodward called me after three months and told me to pick Danny up, I told them, 'No, I won't.' Then I said, 'And if you bring him here, I won't let you in.' It took years and refills of hundreds of Valium prescriptions, but I know that Danny shouldn't live in our house."

Only a small percentage of retarded people are severely and profoundly afflicted. The general atmosphere of the convention is very positive: focusing on what the retarded people can do for the community, what good workers they are, what good citizens they can be. The stress is on how really little difference there is between retarded and nonretarded people.

Later, in the bathroom, I am talking with a group of women about some of the presentations. One says, "Maybe the theme of this convention should be, 'What's so bad about being retarded?' "

Another mother adds, "Retarded people *are* different, damn it. That's why we join organizations like this—to make sure they are protected and cared for, to fight for their place in the community. My daughter can work in a sheltered workshop, or maybe later she can get a job in a cafeteria, something like that; but my biggest hurt is *her* knowledge that she is different. She is so terribly lonely. On Saturday night she'll watch *Love Boat*. She says, 'Oh, Mommy, I like all that kissy-face stuff.' But she has no friends who come and call for her on Saturday night, no boyfriends to take her to the movies."

We go in for a banquet lunch and listen to a speaker talk about the "Future of Our Retarded Citizens." It sounds hopeful, grandiose even—like a graduation speech.

After the luncheon Beth and I file out with the crowd to go to the workshops. There are a few parents who have brought their retarded children along with them to the convention, and across the room I see an elderly woman with her Down's syndrome daughter. The girl, in a pretty pink-flowered sundress, gets up from the table, pushes in her chair, and places her napkin, neatly folded, at the side of her plate as she leaves with her mother. Walking through the crowd, behind her mother, the girl casually raises her sundress to her waist in order to adjust her pantyhose, flashing her voluminous buttocks as she continues through the crowd. It looks like a cut from a Fellini movie. Beth turns to me with a smile and whispers, "Normalization."

Dear Jan:

I really need someone to talk to now. Joe is disgusted with me, and going to friends continually with need is also disgusting to me. In fact, basically I think I'm disgusted with myself—*hmmm*—all very disgusting!

We saw this place, Hills and Dales Child Developmental Center. The physical facility was actually quite nice. The place was started by a woman who has a handicapped child (where she got the energy to care for such a child and start a place like this, too, is beyond me), and the design of the place looked very uninstitutional and bright. They have wonderful equipment—all sorts of adaptive devices, prone boards, toys. The staff ratio is excellent, and they have full-time therapists. The drawbacks are that there are too many kids—over fifty—and that makes the place less homey. Seen en masse as we did when school was out and all these children were in the "dayroom," the effect is jolting. None of the kids can walk. We passed the rows of different sized wheelchairs lined up along the side of the room. That's another negative: Most of the children there seemed so much worse off than Zach, more retarded. Unresponsive—lots had visual problems, seizures, etc. The staff went wild for Zach—ushered him away and played with him for the afternoon while we met with the social worker. They were thrilled with his responsiveness and overall cuteness. They said, "Boy, if he comes here, we're all going to really spoil him; he's such a doll." It felt good feeling proud of him.

All Zach can really do is smile, but somehow there, among all those other children, this seemed more than enough. What is that saying? "Among the blind, the one-eyed man is king."

Dubuque is very far—four hours by car on roads that will be bad in the winter. Too far to stop by just to see how he's doing. Still, it seems to be the only place with an opening within a year (that's because another facility is opening in Cedar Rapids and some of these kids will be moved), and I don't know if I could hold out longer than that. Eventually I think they'll build a place in Des Moines, but I don't like the idea of moving him around either.

He has some good days—when his tone seems improved, when he's holding his head better, when he seems happy. But these pass, and he's often as "blobby" as he was last year in Virginia, whining and crying continually. I just don't know what he wants.

Our equipment at home helps in some respects. We rigged up a porch swing with hammock netting and a Bobby Mac seat; the wheelchair with its tray makes him happy for a while (he can touch toys on the tray, and we have a sticky plastic mat that keeps them from sliding off).

I know we are doing the right thing by making this decision to place Zach. I know I shouldn't feel as if I have to give any justification. But it is, after all, a failure of sorts, isn't it?

Much love, Fern

When Joe and I talk about Zach not living at home, he makes sure to tell me that it is *our* decision, not mine, not his. But after we saw Hills and Dales, and I was complaining about how far away it was, how I didn't like what the other children looked like, etc., Joe started raging: "You can't stand him living at home. You can't stand him living there. What the hell do you want?"

I know that it is really better for Zach to be out of the everyday pattern of our lives, but I really have trouble letting him go. And even as I say this, I know that I am looking forward to it.

I wonder how our child will fit into our lives as a visitor?

I am careful of the language I use with regard to this decision, and I am careful to correct others who talk of "giving him up." We say that we will never give him up.

Years ago parents of severely retarded children did "put them away," for the institutions were so awful that so many parents could never bring themselves to go and see them. What happens to people who live with *that* skeleton in the closet?

When we told my parents that Hills and Dales would have a place for Zach this summer, my mother was relieved. She has been so worried about me, always asking "How are you?" not only emotionally, but physically as well. Every conversation she demands, "You're eating, aren't you?"

Perhaps I *have* been brought up in a protected environment. Right before Gabi was born, my mother asked, "How long is the nurse going to stay?"

"Ma," I said, "women who have babies in Iowa don't have nurses stay in their homes. They go back into the fields the next day."

My parents came out right after Gabi's birth and my mother thought I was brave but foolish to go food shopping two weeks after a cesarean section. She went with me, watching as I pushed the shopping cart. "Just tell me if you get dizzy."

Now she thought how much better it would be for me if Zach didn't live with us.

"I'm sad about him, but I care about *you* first," she said.

My father, the silent partner, was on the extension phone.

"What do you think, Daddy?" I asked.

"This summer? Well, it's kind of soon."

"You don't really approve, do you, Daddy?"

"Of course he does," my mother offered. "He wants what's best for you."

"We both want what's best for you," said my father.

I think I was more nervous about telling Millie.

"She loves Zachy so," I said to Joe.

"Do you think we should keep Zach at home because you don't want to break the news to our baby-sitter?" Joe asked.

So that afternoon, driving Millie home (Zach blank and peaceful in the backseat), I told her that Hills and Dales would have an opening for Zach by the end of the summer.

Millie just said, "Yes, it's very hard to take care of him," but I saw her blinking back the tears.

We have to meet with the social workers from Social Services, Zach's preschool handicapped teacher, the therapists, and a representative from Woodward to discuss Zach's placement at Hills and Dales. The social workers must approve because the government foots most of the bill. We will pay only seventy-five dollars a month even though Hills and Dales is a private facility.

There is something bizarre about us all sitting around the table, all the experts, the consultants, the advisers—so much energy and time—so many write-ups, referrals, reports. So much money. All for a little boy who lies there like a newborn and cries to be rocked.

Two different social workers have stressed to me how much Zach's care costs. They are wary. They will only recommend placement as the last resort.

(That week Joe showed me an article about how much it costs to incarcerate a criminal in the state of Iowa—almost eighteen thousand dollars a year. "Maybe we could get Zach to rob a gas station," Joe said. "Then there'd be no question about state-supported placement.")

I know that when the economic crunch comes, it will be social services that are cut. Now the Association for Retarded Citizens is talking about fund-raising. They are having a raffle and a skate-a-thon to raise money for their projects. Why doesn't the army have a skate-a-thon to buy new guns? Why doesn't the navy have a bake sale to get new ships? I hate this nickel-and-dime-skate-for-a-cripple approach to charity.

The social workers look at our family and think, Well, this is an unfortunate circumstance, but this family can really make it. I have to make a case for myself to convince them that I really can't.

There is another reason why the experts will recommend placement only as a last resort. It is humane and well intentioned, though misguided. It is their belief that the best place for every child is at home with his family. Even if that were true, it's not always the best place for the family.

Looking at the problem objectively, I know that the de-institutionalization trend is a good one. Looking at the families I know who have severely handicapped children, I fear this trend will do a great deal of damage if preventing institutionalization is the primary goal. Again, back to money—no one in these times is rushing around to put up new community facilities.

There was a lot of talk around the table about whether or not Hills and Dales was an "appropriate" placement. Someone noted that all the children at Hills and Dales were nonambulatory and perhaps it would be better for Zach to "see" children who could walk.

I said if we were talking about "appropriate" placement, then he should be with kids who couldn't do anything at all. Besides, I was afraid that Zach would be left behind in a place with mobile children, as the staff had to keep up with retarded youngsters who could get into things. And, I warned, other children who would move about could abuse Zach, who could do nothing to protect himself.

I saw nods of agreement around the table.

The social worker said that she wished there were a foster family available, that "a two-year-old boy needs a mother."

I sat tight-lipped while Joe replied, "Well, Zach's care has exhausted us for two years now and we have a lot of help. Zach needs to be continually repositioned; he takes a long time to feed, and he has to be held and walked a lot of the day. Do you have a family who could do all that?"

No, she admitted that she knew of no such family.

Tersely I added, "I would not approve of Zach living with another family."

The social worker noted that Dubuque was four hours away; it would be difficult for her to make the necessary visitations.

"It will be difficult for us, too," we told her.

Woodward, only a half-hour's drive from our house, would not take children under six. It was also an "institution." Even though I thought Zach was well cared for at Woodward, placement there wasn't something I really wanted to fight for. Not if a place like Hills and Dales was an option.

I suggested, "When we take Zach home for a visit—couldn't you see him then? Couldn't that satisfy the requirement?"

They said that could be looked into.

Then there was nothing else to say. Joe and I knew that Zachariah's placement at Hills and Dales would be approved (however resignedly), and we left feeling like the bright champions of a high school debate.

At home a letter from Jan was waiting for me. After asking for respite care at the institution near her home, Jan did a turnaround and applied for permanent placement.

Dear Fern:

I'm ready, I'm drained, I'm tired. Caring for him is just too much. I want out.

Unfortunately, I also love him. I feel like we're turning him into something of a Christ figure (except we're suffering and he's happy).

Well, the wheels have started. Unfortunately when you

deal with a state institution, the wait can be long. We do have our doctors and the school staff pushing for us. Hopefully, he'll get in soon. In a way it's like waiting for your kid to get into Harvard. Will he have the right recommendations, his grades—are they good enough—maybe there's a vegetable out there who physically needs it more. I don't want to prove to them I've had it! Can't they just take my word? I mean, I'm seeing my shrink four times a week to stay in touch.

I think Roger was thinking more in terms of placing him when he's five or six. Since he doesn't do the daily caring, it all seemed feasible. It's such a vulnerable position to be in, to be out in front saying "Let's do it" when you're not sure what the other guy's response will be.

Eddie's teacher finally told me at the end of school that Eddie is probably close to being profoundly retarded, but he has the motor skills of a higher-functioning child (with maybe a 30 IQ for motor skills; it is ridiculous to talk about IQ points at this level), making care for him harder. He is now into chewing on light-plug cords. I hit him so hard right before vacation when I caught him doing this that his nose began to bleed. He cried but went right back to the cord, as he couldn't get the cause and effect of crime and punishment.

What would ever become of us all if we keep him home?

I wish we could talk. I'll call later this week—after eleven.

Love always,
Jan

Joe and I are alone in the house with Zach because Gabi has gone with her friend Ann and her family to stay with their grandparents and celebrate July Fourth. The kids get to march down Main Street in the parade, and Gabi is all excited. She knows I think all that stuff is hokey, but I still can share her excitement. Also, I'm glad I got out of taking her to see the fireworks here in Ames. Joe usually doesn't make concessions for that kind of thing and won't take her to events that he doesn't enjoy himself.

Since Millie is off for the holiday, Joe and I planned yesterday to share this day. Joe has morning shift till twelve; I have a longer time, but included in that is Zach's nap.

Zach cooperatively didn't wake until 8:30, which gave Joe time to meditate, me to drink coffee and read the paper. We were actually both happy to hear him cooing when he awoke. I was in the bathroom, and I heard Joe in Zach's room, playing peek-a-boo, lifting Zach's shade, telling him it was raining outside, turning on the music box. Seconds later Joe, teary-eyed, appeared in the bathroom doorway, his arms filled with Zach. "Oh, God, Fernie, I miss him already."

Connie and Gayle, two women who have worked with Zach at Woodward, offered to take him for the weekend. Friday we took Gabi and her friend, Ann, to Adventure-land, and they had such a wonderful time that Joe and I, at first put off by commercial Americana (a puppet show was sponsored by McDonald's; a mini-Jeep ride sponsored by Standard Oil), got sucked in by their appreciative enthusiasm. I got sick to my stomach on The Scrambler, the very first ride I went on, but I wouldn't give in—especially after paying the eight-dollar admission fee. Two corn dogs and three roller coaster rides later, I was doing fine. Mind over stomach.

Driving home Friday night, I remarked to Joe how good it felt to go home and know that Zach would not be there, that we didn't have to come home and work. "Yeah," he said, "it sure seems easy."

Saturday morning we got up to go to visit friends in Coralville. I was finishing the breakfast dishes and preparing to make a picnic lunch. Joe was out mowing the lawn and came in shirtless and sweaty for a drink. "I wonder," he said, standing in the doorway with a glass of lemonade, "how long we'll feel this freedom when Zach is at Hills and Dales. I mean, this really isn't a vacation—we're doing what people do in ordinary life. You're doing dishes, I'm mowing the lawn. But we feel so free. Without him to move from room to room waiting for the next cry. It's an incredible difference." Incredible, yes. We both have to work on not feeling guilty for enjoying, relishing even, what is only, after all, a normal life. It is not as if we're good-time Charlies, irresponsible high-livers. We just want our lives back again.

Sunday afternoon we're driving back to Ames; Gabi is sleeping, hot and still sandy from a recent swim in Coralville Lake. We're all sunburned and rested.

"Did you miss him?" I ask Joe.

"Yes," he says, "but not as much as I thought. I missed him in a physical sense, holding him, smelling him. But really there's very little to miss."

We get in the house, unpack our few things, and take the leftover fruit out of the cooler. I want to call Connie and Gayle to tell them that we're home and we'll be by shortly to pick up Zach. Joe is already nervous and short-tempered. "Let's just go," he says abruptly. "Get in the car. You don't have to call."

I protest that I think it's more polite to call first; and, besides, I want them to have Zach ready.

"You're just stalling," Joe says nastily. "I want to go now."

I get in the car, angry and hurt, as Joe peels down the block like a hot-rodding teen-ager, violently shifting gears. Joe asks if I know their address.

"No," I reply coolly. "I was never there. *You* were when you picked up his wheelchair months before. Don't you remember where they live?"

Joe turns the car around, the tires squealing as we go (too fast) back to the house to look in the phone book. We race in silence to their apartment on the other side of town.

Connie and Gayle are welcoming and warm. They are nice people.

"He was just fine," they say. (Would they say anything else, I wonder?) Zach, sitting in his wheelchair, sees us and immediately begins to wail, a heartbreaking cry, his mouth open so wide that I see his little molars. Joe scoops him up out of the chair and his cries turn to sobs. My arms itch to hold him and give him comfort. I hug him in Joe's arms.

We pack the wheelchair, assorted toys, diapers, and clothes into the car. I thank Connie and Gayle, but it's hard to smile.

Later that night after Zach and Gabi are asleep, Joe and I are lying spent on the bed, watching TV. We both cannot stop hearing Zach's plaintive cry, picturing his face with its look of hurt abandonment.

"It's good that he's going soon," Joe says. "This will only get harder."

The date is set for August 17.

We are packing Zach off. He has been packed off quite a bit in his young life—always so we could catch our breath, some respite needed to survive. To Millie's for the day, to Woodward during the week. We've spent a lot of the past year just making arrangements not to be with him. That's a fact that will always make me sad.

But now we are packing Zach off for good. I tell Gabi that we will see Zach at his special "school," and we will take him home sometimes with us, that he will always be a part of our family, but I don't think she entirely believes it. Do I?

I made a list of all the clothes he needs, long pants and shirts for fall, some warm pajamas. In the boys' clothing section I look for plain T-shirts and jackets, ones that do not say "Football Star" or "Super Jogger."

I have to get a marking pen and labels, to print Zachariah Kupfer so his clothes don't get mixed up with the other children's. I can't find a marking pen and I won't ask a salesgirl because I am crying. Trying to pretend I'm packing him up to go to camp will not work. It's the end of summer, not the beginning. And, of course, Zach is too young for camp. He is two years and four months old, and he is leaving home for good.

Dear Fern,

What kind of world is it to have to fight to get a child into an institution? The staffing we recently had recommends that Eddie be home in the "least restrictive environment"; they expressed a desire for Eddie to spend time with his "peers" so he would not become "institutionalized." What a bunch of crap!

They did not question any of our finds—the accidents at home, our need for constant surveillance. In order for him to be in a less restrictive environment, everyone else has to be restricted. Eddie has no sense of danger—he climbs anywhere, eats everything. The institution's audiologist found that he did best in an environment without too much distraction, i.e., she got results with a white wall—add a toy and he couldn't always find the sound. As Roger pointed out, he never ate furniture in that room (there was none).

The staff kept referring to Eddie's great potential. He hasn't gone anywhere in two years—where's the potential? Besides which he doesn't know how to imitate. Why should he suddenly imitate institutional behavior? Also, who are his peers? He's not exactly material for your local nursery school—all his "peers" will always be severely retarded.

They talk about "normalization"—God, he doesn't have dyslexia!

Other reasons for rejection, left unsaid, but those I intuit, are:

1. He's too young. He should be home in his mother's arms. I have not put in enough time. The social worker said to me, "No one ever said having a handicapped child was easy."

2. He's too cute. Compared with the other children, he's magnificent. They must all want to protect him from this "fate worse than death."

Even Amanda is angry with me. She said, "You probably think that he is the dumbest of all babies, but I love him. If he goes away to a special school, I will run away, too." How is Gabi taking Zach's imminent departure? It's somewhat different because Amanda probably has more interaction with Eddie because he can sit and move around, and he never cries. For her it's like having a cute little puppy around to play with.

In the past month we have taken Eddie to emergency twice for eating marbles (I try to be careful, but Amanda left them in her room) and mothballs (Eddie climbed to the top of the closet).

There is a man (about thirty) in the institution who was just hospitalized for eating a package of nails. He had lived home with his parents until he was a teen-ager, had never been toilet-trained; he screeched through the night. (We've been sleeping with the fan on so we don't hear Eddie's yowls.) I saw this man, and my life (what it could be) flashed in front of me. I know Eddie shouldn't live at home, no matter how guilty they try to make me feel. Really, a woman has to have a very low opinion of herself to endure such a life.

We're in the process of appealing their decision. I'll keep in touch to let you know what's happening.

Love, Jan

I really can't believe this. The phone rang this morning. Joe answered it, and I could see his face fall. "Uh-huh. Oh, I see. Well, I guess so," he was saying. It was the social worker from Social Services: Did we think we could wait another two weeks to bring Zach? She was going on vacation soon, and she would not be able to comply with the state regulation that a foster-care child (that's what Zach was now) must be visited within fifteen days of placement.

Joe, looking stunned, held the mouthpiece of the telephone as he repeated her request, the dilemma, to me.

Without even thinking, I took the phone from him; something rose and surged within as I heard my voice sure and strong: No. Sorry, we couldn't take Zach to Hills and Dales even a *day* later than the assigned day. We, too, were taking a vacation and had airplane tickets for the very *next day* after Zach was safely deposited. No, we couldn't rearrange it—there was a tour leaving (for South America, Mozambique, who knows where). Sorry, but it was absolutely impossible. But *she* could get a waiver from some Social Service superior so that she could make her visit at a later date; or she could get another social worker to take her place or *she* could change her vacation and take it at a different time.

"Oh, well," she said, a bit cowed. "I didn't think of those alternatives."

Joe turned to me, whistling softly in admiration, as I hung up the phone.

"Whew, Wonder Woman."

As it turned out, a waiver was accepted. She could make the necessary visit a week later, the rule was stretched, and the system didn't break down.

Perhaps it would not be impossible to explain to a social worker who is so busy filling out forms in triplicate why postponement would be unacceptable when you have D-day (departure day) all planned and you are psychologically set, unable to put it off any longer. But we were set for August 17; our emotional baggage was packed, ready to have our son leave our home, to redefine our family structure. No, to postpone Zach's departure for even a day or two was a cruel stay of execution. I really felt I couldn't endure it. How was this innocent little social worker going to know all that? So I told her about the mythical airplane tickets. *That* she could understand.

Jan sent me a copy of the letter that she and Roger wrote as a plea to get Eddie a place in the institution. It was a masterpiece. Five single-spaced, typed pages, Roger's law firm on the letterhead, detailing what life with Eddie was like, and how impossible it was to continue to provide for his needs and maintain a certain quality of life (not to

mention sanity) for the rest of the family. The letter apparently convinced the board that made the decision. Eddie
will get residential placement.

There are two horrible realities here. One is to have to
make the extraordinary effort to record just how awful your
child is, to tell just how much he is ruining your life, and
to make the sad workings of your family life so graphically
explicit that you will "win over" the experts, browbeating
them into offering you residential care.

The other is that a five-page treatise, eloquently worded,
written by two people with graduate degrees, decided the
case. What about ordinary people with their own extraordinary Eddies and Zachariahs? What about those who cannot
articulate the pain? Who stands up for them?

The time has come.

It's the end of August, still hot and sultry, but there is a
different smell to the air. In the past few days I have noticed
the dark comes sooner now.

I pack a picnic cooler with egg-salad sandwiches, pickles
and chips, and grape lemonade. We are going to stop in a
pretty roadside park that we saw when we first went to
Dubuque to see Hills and Dales.

The night before, I packed up the car with Zachy things:
his new clothes (I never did sew in the labels), the quilt
blanket, a jack-in-the-box, a squeezy rubber duck, photographs of Joe, Gabi, and me to put on the walls behind his
crib.

The day is glorious, the sun slanting evenly over flat
farmlands, the trees so green and crisp in the distance.

Gabi sits in the back with Zach, who is propped and
belted in the infant car seat he is outgrowing.

Zach either doesn't know enough to look out the car
window to see that there is a whole other world out there,
or he doesn't see well enough to make it worth his while,
but he is content riding in the car, all movement soothing
him, easing some pain or irritation, filling some need we

can never understand. It's the *movement* of the car that he likes, the spinning wheels atop the road, for he whines in protest if we idle too long at red lights. We say, "Okay, okay, here we go," as it blinks green.

We ride for two hours and Zach doesn't sleep but stares contentedly at the back of my bucket seat. Gabi talks to him sometimes, touching his hand to her face, and he smiles.

Then we get to the rest stop, a "scenic overview," and park as close as we can to the picnic table. We get out of the car, carrying our stuff, Zach draped floppily over one of Joe's shoulders. I start pouring drinks and setting out paper plates that must be held down with sandwiches or they will blow away.

At the overview are Joe and Zach, looking very scenic themselves as Joe swings Zach in the air, down, around, as streaks of trees and sky flash by overhead, and Zach's soft laughter fills up the valley. How we all love to hear Zach laugh! It is not something that he will do readily on his own, but if we shake him or swing him or fly him around the room, we can usually get a few chuckles out of him.

After lunch we drive the last two hours. "I'll hold him," I tell Joe. "That way Gabi can stretch out in the back."

Zach falls asleep in my arms, and I press my lips against his forehead all the way to Dubuque, feeling peaceful and not really sad. "This is the end of something," I think, filled with relief at not having to face the next weekend, the next year, with the weight of this burden, my son.

As we drive into Hills and Dales, I see a young girl, a careworker, sitting out on the patio feeding ice cream to a teen-age boy in a wheelchair. As she wipes his drooling mouth with the tip of his bib, she leans over and kisses him on the cheek.

At that moment I feel inordinately grateful to her.

Past the glass door a large portrait of Jesus hangs, beatific and perhaps a little sad, watching over all the children as they are wheeled past him to be fed blended lunches or as they lie on mats on the dayroom floor.

Zach will be in a special room right by the nurse's station for the first two days where he'll be closely watched, monitored, "and loved a lot," says a brown-haired nurse as she smilingly holds Zach's chin in her hand.

We meet with the cook. "He likes bananas and ice cream," we tell her, and she assures us that he'll get plenty. We meet with the therapists. "This is the way he likes to be held . . . these are the songs he likes to hear."

In the director's office Joe and I are signing forms, permission slips, medical releases, while Gabi is off having a Coke with one of the nurses, and Zach is being wheeled around and shown off. I break down into hiccuping, indelicate sobs. Elaine, the director, comforts me. With an arm on mine she says, "We will take *very* good care of Zach." Then softly, "My own boy is here."

Joe was never one for long good-byes. In college after a weekend spent together, languorously lying in each other's arms, he would put me on the bus to go back to school with a fast kiss, and by the time I got to my seat he was gone, no waving good-bye in the distance as my bus turned out of the station. I used to think that he could just not bear to see me leave him, so he went off quickly to pine and sigh. Now, many years later, as I have seen him leave a party ("Okay. Good night.") as I linger and lounge at the door continuing shreds of conversation ("Let's just go," he says), I know that my romantic vision did not explain his preference for zippy departures.

We leave Zach's bag of new fall clothes; one of the nurses is holding Zach, and we give him three quick kisses from us all. Joe turns, without looking back, but I glance over my shoulder to see Zach lying limply in the nurse's arms, staring suspiciously into her face, unaware of our exit, but not quite at home.

We get in the car and have not even backed out of the lot before Gabi asks, "Now are we a three-person family?"

Part 4

AFTER ZACHARIAH

1

I will never forget the day we placed Justin. I cried for three weeks. I had enough people telling me I had to do it, but I was grief stricken, defeated, exhausted—well, you know. But the relief. *I was actually riding my bike leisurely around the neighborhood with no reason to go home. It was wonderful!*

It is hard for anyone who hasn't had a child like Justin to understand. For five years I could never *sit down. I could* never *relax. It was a twenty-four-hour surveillance. I was always so glad when he was hospitalized for any one of numerous reasons. It gave me some relief.*

I can remember one summer evening before Justin was placed. We were sitting in our backyard with our other boy, trying to eat a picnic dinner. We had locked Justin in his room so that we could eat in peace, just once, without having to chase him and keep him busy as we ate. Well, our neighbor came running through our house and burst out the back door, yelling that Justin was on the roof. He had punched out the screen of the window and climbed out. I understand why years ago retarded children were locked in back rooms.

What was hard at first, right after we placed Justin, was seeing that extra chair around the kitchen table . . . and the first summer we went camping, I felt as if I had to explain to strangers that there really were four *of us.*

But I knew right after Justin left that he could never come home again to live—no matter what. We see him often, but I am still—five years later—firm in this resolve. Even though he has calmed down tremendously, I can never risk it. I think if I had to live tied to the schedule of that little yellow bus for the rest of my life, I would come to know the true meaning of despair.

—Eleanor

Dear Jan:

It's late . . . I can't sleep . . . Iowa thunderstorms are making violent nights, and I feel ablaze with energy. It's been this way for the past few weeks. After two years of being depleted and drained, I feel this frenetic surge. I'm trying to direct it to creative ends, but I have not been writing at all. Teaching takes up enough time to give me some focus. Yesterday (I didn't teach) I cleaned out the basement and weeded between the bricks of our uneven patio. We have not yet eased into a pattern in the absence of Zach. I know superficially I am "doing well"—alive and enthusiastic in my teaching, involved in Gabi's life, seeing friends. Inside I ache. I keep closing the door to his room —too painful to see the crib, the diapers still in piles in the holder. Like going through a death, but not a death—thinking of him there, held and loved by strangers.

In the morning I still listen for Zach's whimpers. Gabi tells me that she heard his morning cries this week. "You were dreaming," I say. "You're just used to hearing them every day, that's all." Gabi cried yesterday. She said, "I can't get used to missing him." This is a new time—something to work through. It's so very hard. All my thoughts about Zach, all the remembrances, are positive. That's so crazy, when in reality I recall how we were all just "hanging on" those last few weeks, waiting for him to go, how taking care of him seemed so impossible. Missing him now takes on mostly a physical proportion. It is his beauty, his smell, the soft babyness that I miss—a physical craving. I long to hold him. I don't think of all the crying, his need, my desperation over what to "do" with him, walking through shopping malls without needing to buy anything, just to pass a Saturday afternoon, to keep him moving, keep him from whining.

Recently I went to a local Association for Retarded Citizens meeting, and the program there was so upbeat: talk of all they were doing in Ames, work programs for retarded citizens, teaching survival skills, etc. One of the ARC bulletins said, "Developing positive public attitudes about mentally retarded persons is an important part of what the Associations for Retarded Citizens are trying to accomplish."

And I thought of Zach, so small, so far away. It's hard to reconcile the personal hurt with the political aims. I don't feel positive at all.

A preschool handicapped teacher from the Area Education Agency called this morning and asked if I'd help her start a parent support group for Story County, and I thought of the irony of me as any kind of model. But I told her I would, and truthfully I think I have come very far and have a lot to contribute. I can't do it, though, unless I feel I can be totally honest—and that may be too rejecting for the kind of support group she has in mind.

The other day Joe was lamenting the fact that we didn't have a lot of money because then, he said, we could keep Zachy home. "If we were millionaires," he said, "we could have a big house and hire round-the-clock help, our own therapists, specialists, and see him whenever we wanted." When I told him that even if we were millionaires, I wasn't sure that I would want Zach to live with us, he was shocked. I told him that seeing Zach all the time (even if others were doing the carrying, the feeding, the dirty work) wore me out, that his efforts in the face of his enormous disabilities pained me. Joe really couldn't understand that. "Then you really don't accept what he is," he said. Maybe that's true. Strange how Joe and I are still learning about each other's reactions to Zach. Both of us have been disgustingly sentimental these past few weeks—we cry looking at two-year-olds on TV commercials. Joe sometimes goes into Zach's room to smell his blankets. He came out sadly tonight, holding them. "They're beginning to lose the smell," he said.

Yech! I am becoming sloppy, maudlin.

Gabi came home with a picture she drew at school of "what makes you happy." There was her drawing entitled "My Family": Joe, looming very big; me standing (actually floating, Chagall-like) subserviently next to him (armless, in a long, green gown); a long-haired Gabi with red bow lips on Joe's other side; and Zach, an infant lying flat on his back by our feet. We are, however, all smiling.

Yesterday Joe and I had a big blowup over whose turn it was to food-shop and do house chores, over consideration and appreciation, the same old rot. It's reassuring how we can fall back into the old pettiness after the worst of times. Is it possible that even during years of plagues and famines husbands and wives fought over "picking things up around here"? Our small ordinariness depresses me—I feel that given the tragedy of Zach, we should have seen new visions and acted accordingly, to appreciate our normal time together. That's not quite fair. You know how one fight colors everything, blocks off all the previous weeks of good time? Actually Joe and I have been fine. There is not that driving tension anymore, that force that unrelentingly sharpened both our edges. We are doing okay—though not quite as well as the Waltons.

We ate dinner at Gail and Ron Sanderses' the other night. I reminded Joe not to say "Jesus Christ" as a casual expletive and I was amused to hear him say "Oh, gosh" to a comment of Ron's. It sounded so corny and sweet. Their little girl is vivacious and bright and Gail adores her. Ron seemed interested when I talked about Hills and Dales, but Gail said she is "not ready yet."

Ron talked about how Scott's screaming fits drive him up the wall. He said, "The other night I told Scott, 'I am getting awful tired of you being retarded. When you going to snap out of it, boy?' "

Scott is now at school for almost five hours a day, so Gail will have it a little easier. She told me she stayed the first day of school and came home in tears. Scott is in the lowest-functioning class at the special ed. preschool, but she said the other children were walking around, playing, responding to at least some instruction. Scott, at three and a half, can sit by himself—and that's about it. He can't see—he really can *do* nothing at all. She said, "If the other children are low functioning, what's that make him?" I told her, *very* low functioning.

Zach, of course, is gone. And Russ is also no longer in that group. Sandy and the family moved to Missouri a few months ago. Sandy wrote and said they found a good place for Russ there and Social Services was really helpful in getting him in. But she also has not adjusted so well. She said, "I have a lot of time on my hands now, and I do too much thinking."

There's a big ISU football game and the whole town is taken over by spirit: the smells of autumn fire up the competition. I hear bugles and whistles and the cheers of the crowd from my bedroom window as I write this. Gabi is downstairs with two friends discussing the merits of Superstar Barbie vs. Ballerina Barbie.

Next week we're all driving up to Dubuque to visit Zach and attend school and staff meetings, which they arranged for Saturday. There's also some kind of parent picnic that was announced in a flyer we received that described "Fun and Games—Dancing"—*and* my perverse humor immediately conjured up pictures of the games we could play, like those old sick jokes ("Can I use Johnny as first base?"). Something in me reacted against the organized gaiety of adults who have only in common the despair of damaged children.

Gabi really is an only child now. That would be okay with me had we chosen it, but Zach's having been here and gone makes me feel like an emotional amputee—the twitching and pain in the invisible limb is still very real.

We are all anticipating seeing Zach. We don't know what his reaction will be, but I think he remembers, in some secret place in his blurry brain, and feels abandoned, and will cry when he sees us. I'm rehearsing that reunion in my mind, so I'll be prepared. Another part of me knows that I will never be prepared to see him there, my beauty, amidst the wreckage.

Take care,
Love, Fern

Hills and Dales Resident Evaluation:

Zachariah Kupfer

PROGNOSIS: As a result of his stable, nonprogressive neurological disorder Zachariah is significantly dependent on others for routine care. His general health is good.

PHYSICAL THERAPY
Zach exhibits general hypotonic muscle tone throughout with minimal fluctuation of tone. When he becomes excited or attempts voluntary movement, he exhibits spastic patterning especially evident in the lower extremities. His range of motion is within normal limits and he demonstrates symmetrical back posture with no evidence of scoliosis.

Zach was seen on a daily treatment program. His goals were: 1) increase head control, 2) increase weight bearing in kneeling position, and 3) increase trunk control. Zach is able to hold his head up for one minute when placed in a prone position; however, his average time is twenty-five seconds. He is able to tolerate knee-standing for thirty seconds at a time. The standing position has not been used in therapy sessions this quarter as the emphasis has been placed on knee-standing (kneeling) to improve trunk control, protective responses, and equilibrium responses. Because Zach exhibits hyperextension of both knees in standing, this was avoided to prevent undue stress on his knees.

FEEDING
Zach is involved in a therapeutic feeding program. The two objectives of the program are: 1) to facilitate lip closure, and 2) to facilitate chewing. Facilitation techniques are used when necessary to promote lip closure. He is now exhibiting a chewing motion instead of a sucking motion when food is placed in his mouth.

Zach has not been losing much liquid while drinking. The use of the tippee cup has helped diminish the loss of liquids. Zach seems to enjoy his liquids.

Zach is fed in his own wheelchair. The feeder sits in front of him. His feeding equipment consists of a regular dish, a tippee cup with a spout, and a youth spoon.

POSITIONING
Zach's positioning program was specifically designed for implementation by direct care staff. A one-man lift is used when lifting and transferring him. The recommended floor positions for Zach are prone on a floor mat, flexed sidelying on either side on a floor mat, and supported sitting in a U-shaped bolster while supervised. Specific procedures are also used when positioning Zach in the wheelchair. Small bolsters are used in the chair to keep his legs in straight alignment.

PSYCHOLOGICAL EVALUATION
Zach seems alert but just doesn't respond much to environmental stimulation. Vision and hearing seem adequate for present programming. Feeding and dressing are dependent at present.

Results of the El Paso Development Scale are as follows:

Gross Motor	18 weeks
Fine Motor	24 weeks
Receptive Language	34 weeks
Expressive Language	16 weeks
Cognitive Social Skills	44 weeks

RECREATION THERAPY SERVICES
Often during free time Zach was given a book or toys to play with while in his chair. Again, emphasis was on increasing Zach's use of both hands for manipulating objects.

On several occasions Zach was placed on a cage ball and rolled from side to side. He responded by smiling.

Zach participated in swimming, and a trip to the mall.

Presently, Zach has two Big Sisters and a Foster Grandparent.

EDUCATIONAL PROGRAM

Zach is able to hold head upright for forty-five seconds while in supported sitting.

Zach will grasp objects placed in his hands 20 percent of the time.

Zach has shown ability to prolong vowel sounds up to five seconds.

Zach will visually fixate on objects at any point within ninety degrees of midline.

Zachariah receives occupational therapy five days a week for one half-hour session each day. Zachariah receives speech therapy on a consultation basis. Many activities are provided to build muscle tone, to improve reaching, grasping, vocalizing, attending, and head control.

NURSING

Zach's general health is very good. He has a good appetite and has no difficulty sleeping nights. He takes a nap daily. Zach has had no seizure activity. We have used a suppository for bowel movement as needed.

We have noted some irritability.

We found that Zach was cutting teeth at this time. Two molars in the back of his mouth were starting to protrude through and were slightly reddened. We applied Numzit as needed and this seemed to help. He was also put on a blended diet at this time so the sensitive areas in his mouth would not be irritated.

Zach has had no other problems and is a delightful little boy.

FAMILY INTERACTION

The parents, Joe and Fern Kupfer, are expected to maintain a close involvement both with their son and with his program. These parents indicate a desire to take Zach home for visits and to participate in all program planning conferences for Zach. Every effort should be made to include these parents in all phases of their son's program.

Zach's placement at Hills and Dales is considered to be "long term." The parents indicate their desire to have Zach placed closer to their home. We would expect Zach to be transferred when and if a similar residential program becomes available closer to the parents' home.

Our first trip to Dubuque was one that I remember most clearly. It had been a month since we had seen Zach, and it seems strange, recalling it now, that the first thought that came to me when we pulled into Hills and Dales and saw him sitting out in his wheelchair under a big patio umbrella was "Oh, he is wearing matching clothes."

I had not thought when I picked out clothing for Zach over a month ago, teary-eyed behind dark glasses, choosing two shirts to go with each pair of pants ("outfits"), that somebody else would be dressing him. I didn't think of this when we left him at Hills and Dales; I didn't think to say "He is an impeccable dresser. Please make sure he continues in this tradition."

But now the fact that the careworkers had thought to put on his light blue denim pants with his powder blue and white polo shirt with the white collar made me feel that this was indeed a good place for Zach to be.

Perhaps that sounds trivial, comic even, that in the face of my son's severe handicaps and abnormalities I should be concerned with color coordination. I've thought about that some. One reason for the concern is merely practical: Zach is totally dependent on other people. For his whole life he will be. Therefore I want him always looking the best he can possibly look, to be as appealing as he possibly can be.

The other reason is symbolic: The careworkers, by not just taking out any old shirt and jeans from a drawer, by making a choice, are saying, "This child is important to me; this child is a whole person who demands a thoughtful putting-together."

So Zach, that little Beau Brummell, was sitting out when we pulled up and we stayed in the car for a while looking at him from the distance.

There were three or four kids in wheelchairs under that umbrella. The day was quite hot for the end of September and everything was very sharp and still. Zach sat resting his head against the corner seat of the back of his wheelchair, a Humpty-Dumpty plastic toy suction-cupped to the wheelchair tray. A girl in jean cutoffs was feeding the boy in the chair next to Zach and she turned and gave Humpty-Dumpty a few spins.

We all got out of the car and I held back, watching Joe and Gabi descend on Zach, who clicked in when they were about three feet away, his mouth softening into a smile.

Joe knelt down in front of the chair and drummed the tray with his fingers. "Hey, Zachy, look who's here. Daddy's here and Gabi and Mommy" (though I was not in view).

Zach's hands fisted in spastic excitement and I heard his sharp intake of breath, almost a squeal. Joe kissed his face as he began to undo the Velcro straps to lift Zach from the chair. Then Joe made him laugh out loud by jumping up and down with Zach in his arms. When he stopped, Zach was still cooing. Joe passed him to me.

I held his head in my palm: "Hi, Zachy, hi, hi," I said face-to-face.

Zach mouthed the voiceless *H* in response.

There were other families around, perfectly normal families who had come to visit their perfectly abnormal children. A few women were by themselves and some were older—grandmas? aunts? There was not a lot of interaction among families. The center for each group, the nucleus, was a child in a wheelchair, a child who would sometimes howl and thrust or drool, wetting a shirt front. Not pretty kids, most of them.

There are some children at Hills and Dales (and at virtually every institution in the country) who are "wards of the state," whose parents took a good look and said, "Goodbye . . . I'll see you later." (There are all kinds of stories: about death and divorce and alcohol and suicide—sometimes all of them together. If it weren't real life, it would

seem contrived.) At the very least I think it is a civic irre-
sponsibility to leave all the decisions about your child's life
to an institution or a state. But as I looked over at a teen-
age boy in diapers, his face deformed by a scarlet birth-
mark, a monstrous jaw, I understood this abandonment
more than I understood families who kept a child like this
at home.

All the children at Hills and Dales go to school. Some,
too sick or too damaged to respond at all, are kept within
the building. Sometimes "school" means being talked to
and held, or having their bodies positioned and exercised
so muscles don't atrophy.

We suggested at the original staff meeting that Zachy go
"out" to school ("He likes car trips," we explained) to a
class for the nonambulatory profoundly retarded in the
city. Now we were told that this was working out well,
although Zach usually fell asleep in the van coming back to
Hills and Dales and was zonked for the rest of the afternoon.

The staff said that Zach was making a good adjustment,
that he continued to cry to be picked up a lot, but that he
was eating and sleeping well and was generally alert.

"He's discriminating," said Sandy, a young nurse who
has come to be our friend. "He doesn't smile for everyone."

"Does he smile for you?" we asked.

"You bet. He's my boy," Sandy replied, unabashed at her
favoritism.

Later that day the workers set up elaborate relay games:
two long lines of wheelchairs, and each staff member had
to thread a long rope through the spokes of the wheels to
connect them. The kids hardly knew what was going on but
the adults jumped up and down, cheering on their team like
color war at summer camp.

I held Zach in a rocking chair, feeding him some blended
peaches. Then Joe, Gabi, and I took him out for a walk—
there was a cemetery right nearby, and Gabi, walking along

the paths, looked with great interest at the headstones of children.

Back at Hills and Dales we changed Zach's diaper, powdered him up, and put him in yellow pajamas.

Out in the dayroom someone had brought in a rather complicated sound system. Wheelchairs made a circle around two of the workers who were dancing as disco blared from three different speakers.

I bounced Zach around till he smiled and passed him on to Joe for some serious boogying. We left Zach, all grins and giggles, in Sandy's arms with a set of instructions: "Just make sure he gets asked to dance."

2

I was two when my brother Ricky was born, twenty-seven years ago. He, too, was inward and could not hold up his head. He cried all the time and slept very little—no more than two or three hours a night. But he was gorgeous, like Zach—blond, beautiful (to this day he has the longest, curliest eyelashes I've ever seen).

My parents put Ricky in the New Hampshire State School for the Retarded—for life. I don't know—to be honest—whether they would have done so quite so early (before he was three) without the firm prodding of our family physician. He knew what it would be like to care for a three-month-old baby who got larger physically but not much older mentally.

I think Ricky is content; my folks visit him one or two Sundays a month and take him out for rides. The concepts of "mother" and "father" are too abstract for him, but he recognizes them—knows Dad is good at games of turning the car radio on and off—and his relationship with my mother can only be termed mother-infant bonding: his feeling for her is special, he holds her hand, touches her cheek. A sister is even more removed and he no longer even recognizes me now that I have moved away and my visits are on an infrequent basis.

At any rate my point in writing to you is to tell you that from Gabi's viewpoint (mine) this decision is the only one that can be fairly made.

I had a wonderful time growing up—help when I needed it, attention, love, peace, lack of tension—all of which would have been impossible if Ricky had been home.

Although Ricky's condition touched me (when I was little, I used to punch anyone who told "retard" jokes) and has strongly in- fluenced my career choice (biochemistry—studying the basis of cellu- lar errors causing retardation), I don't think I was damaged in any way—as I might have been had my life been redefined to provide care for Ricky's enormous needs. And I love him—in a complicated blood- tie way, which I don't think could have been possible.

But I grew up as an only child with Ricky always in the back- ground. I caution you to watch Gabi for symptoms of the trap I fell into without my parents being aware—well, not a "trap" really, just a misconception of the world. When I was young, and did so well in school, I figured God had goofed and given me a portion of Ricky's brains as well as my own—which made me responsible for his achievements or lack of them. I always felt I had to be the best, the top, number one—not because my parents pressured me in any way, but because I felt I couldn't dare let them down because everything I did, I did for both Ricky and me. Even when I got old enough to know that wasn't logical, I still did everything I could to make my parents proud.

Actually I'm glad in some ways—I have a very rewarding career —but I was well into my twenties before I realized they would have been just as proud and pleased with me if Ricky were normal and could make them proud on his own.

It has always been a part of my life to have a retarded brother— a fact, not a tragedy. And that it was not a tragedy for my family was due to my folks' courage in choosing to not have Ricky live with us.

I have a son of my own now, Eric (we call him Ricky sometimes), and this miracle of health, this normal happy little boy who runs and

talks and laughs and understands has brought my parents so much
happiness. For all of us, each step is like a double miracle as we've
seen it fail to occur in Ricky. . . .

—Marilyn

One night Gabi and I were chatting as she readied herself
for bed; Gabi told me that she felt very sad at school that
day. It was fire prevention week, and a young fireman had
come to talk with the class about safe exits during an emergency. "How many of you have a younger brother or sister
at home?" he asked.

Gabi did not raise her hand.

Her friend Teri said, "Gabi, put your hand up." But she
didn't.

"Well, you were right," I offered, "because your little
brother is not at home."

Gabi said, "Yes, but I felt awful, just sitting there with my
hands in my lap."

It is a disloyalty of sorts, a denial, even though it is absolutely true; she does not have a little brother at home whom
she has to save from fires.

The question everyone kept asking us was "How is Gabi
taking it?" I thought she was really okay. She was concerned with the affairs of her own life: learning how to add,
opening junk mail addressed to "occupant," waiting for
Teri's birthday party. That was how it should be.

Last year when we were having one of our talks, I asked
her how she felt about having a brother like Zach. She
said that it sometimes made her sad, "but really he is *your*
baby."

Even so, on a Christmas wish list she brought home from
school, she forsook three-speed bikes and Barbie con-
dominiums on the last line of the sheet, which read that "If
you had only *one* wish, what would it be?" and penciled in
her neat print: "That my brother would be normal."

It's hard to know what goes on in children's minds. For a while during the first year with Zach, the big going-to-Iowa-City-seeing-doctors year, Gabi was so excluded. We weren't getting our questions answered, and we really didn't know what questions *she* needed answered. One time, two weeks into kindergarten, she came to me in tears: Many of the children in her class knew how to tie their own shoes, and she didn't. I explained that this was her first pair of tie shoes, she had always wanted buckle shoes, tending to favor anything that looked "partyish." We sat and practiced tying for a while, and when she failed to catch on right away, she turned to me, clutching her chest in horror, "Oh, Mommy, do you think *I* am developmentally delayed?"

So that was part of her suspicion all along, that as she sometimes got Ann's cold, as Teri had given her brother chickenpox last winter, so whatever it was that Zach had that made him "developmentally delayed," a phrase she had heard us use—whatever it was that prevented him from sitting and crawling about like normal babies—was catching.

So while I usually think Joe and I are too verbal and tend to tell Gabi too much, here I had overlooked the obvious —I had failed to tell her that she would never get whatever it was that Zach had.

It upset Gabi the most seeing Joe and me upset. To be a little person, not quite sure of the world, and see your parents, those rocks, shaky and scared themselves, must be hard. And having seen us upset so many times for so long, she does not want our lives to be upset anymore.

Solicitous, she watches my face if we see a curly-headed blond little boy in front of us on line in the supermarket. ("Do you think he looks like Zachy, Mom?" she'll ask, patting my arm.)

We talk about Zach, and Gabi looks forward to bringing him home for visits. But now, not living home, Zach simply does not dominate our lives anymore.

I think that Gabi is really okay. She is compassionate, and

that's good. She is sometimes too good, and that's bad. But she has lots of friends, and she does well in school, and she never has bad dreams. So I'm just *not* going to worry about her now. In twenty years she'll probably have a lot to tell her analyst.

Gabi called from school one morning and said in a small voice that she had a stomachache and could she please come home? I, at the time, had been reading Jane Howard's book *Families* (I should have been correcting student themes), and felt a rush of warmth and maternal concern as I ran right over to school and got her. I'm so grateful that she is part of my "family" that I feel a greedy desire to hold her and kiss her, glad to be so needed by her that it interrupts the normal course of the day's events. I anticipated us spending the day together in bed drinking herb tea and reading *Little House on the Prairie.* She was waiting, her red jacket already zipped, outside the classroom door, accompanied by her friend Teri. Before I was at her side, Gabi reached her hand out for me. It felt warm and very little. We turned to go, and Teri told me that *she* thought "it's only heartburn." Gabi nodded in serious affirmation, never having before been a victim of such a malady. Before Teri returned to the classroom, she touched Gabi's shoulder. "I hope you feel better very soon," she said solemnly.

Gabi and I walked the two blocks home from school together in respectful silence of her heartburn. At home, after a peanut butter sandwich and a glass of milk, a story (each of us taking turns reading a page), and two trips to the bathroom, Gabi told me she really felt fine and wanted to go back to school, kissing and patting my arm, leaving *me* in bed with books piled high on the night table as if *I* were the one who was sick. "Bye," I yelled downstairs as she was out the front door. "Have a good day."

"I will," she promised, just as she had only three hours ago that morning.

Normal kids, I thought. So undependable. Here I

planned to give up my day (even relishing the sacrifice), and she went back to school.

Often lately I feel how much Joe and I depend on Gabi, how much more precious she is to us. It's not as if we *did* choose to have an only child, but that's the way we are living. We're somehow maimed by Zach's loss (actually his presence and his loss); the unit is missing a part. It's not as if we are a three-person family: we're a four-person family —the one idealized in tea for two with a boy for you, a girl for me—only broken.

To have one such damaged child makes the other appear so much more vulnerable. I just finished reading *The World According to Garp* and one element of its appeal to me was Garp's obsessive "awareness of the mortality" of his children.

Last year, when Gabi and her friends started to walk by themselves to the stores two blocks away, I started cautioning her about strangers. Growing up in New York, I heard these warnings always, about "sick men" (my mother, who accepted humanist-liberal-psychological interpretations for human behavior, said no one was "bad"; he was "sick") who could "do things" to little girls that would hurt them. I tried delicately explaining these unsavory facts of life.

"Are they kidnappers?" Gabi asked, wide-eyed after my description of those who would offer candy to little girls and invite them inside their cars.

"They may be," I said, acknowledging a label that she at least felt familiar with, "although, of course, *most* people are not," I concluded optimistically. "Especially in Ames, Iowa."

Gabi added, remindful of how enthusiastic I was to New York friends about the joys of small-town living. "Yes, especially in Ames, Iowa."

Later that week Gabi and Ann, delicious as candy in their pastel summer dresses, tanned little legs sticking down into white sandals, walked by a fraternity house on the way home from Dairy Queen. Four boys who were playing Frisbee on the lawn acknowledged their presence. One turned to the other with joyful scorn, and said "and here's a couple of girls for *you*, Doug." "Doug" turned to Gabi and Ann and said in a mock leer, "Want a piece of candy, little girls?"

"So what did *you* do?" I said to Gabi after she reported the entire scenario.

"Well," she said, "I just put my hands on my hips and said, 'I'm sorry, but my mother does not allow me to take candy from strangers.' " Then, seeing me smile, she said, "You know, Mom, I *knew* they were just kidding around with each other. They weren't really, you know, 'like that.' " I don't know how well I explained what "like that" meant. But I knew she understood.

So that's a relief. I don't have to worry about strange men molesting my daughter—or at least not with her acquiescence. But as John Irving wrote about Garp, "There was so much to worry about, when worrying about children."

One day as I was doing dishes, I heard a car meanly screech outside. I ran, soapy-handed, to the front window, almost colliding with Joe, who, hearing the same sound, had jumped up from his typing at the dining-room table. We saw Gabi happily playing hopscotch on the sidewalk. Probably, at the corner stop sign, was a teen-ager in a jacked-up car who liked to make obvious his comings and goings.

Before he went back to his typing, Joe said, "If anything ever happened to her, I think I would kill myself."

Joe would rather bring Zach back to Ames than stay and visit in Dubuque. I can't say that I blame him. A few times we all went up together, got a motel room, and tried to pretend we were on vacation. But we were all depressed. Also eating out in restaurants is hard. If Zach gets all chokey, then I have to start moving him around a lot.

In the winter, when Zach was home for a visit, we'd sit by the fireplace and watch the snow. Sometimes we had friends over for bridge. I would be nervous about the roads going to Dubuque when it was time to take Zach back. Often Joe would make the trip alone with Zachy and I'd stay home with Gabi.

One time Joe called from Dubuque, very blue, planning to go to the bar, drink, and watch a fight on TV. Maybe do some dancing—there was a live band in the lounge; country and western, but he was desperate.

A careworker at Hills and Dales had innocently asked Joe if we were going to pick Zach up again next week to take him home for Christmas.

"I told her we were going to Florida to see your folks, Fern," Joe said, "and I felt so guilty saying that—that we were going away for a vacation; that we weren't taking our son home for Christmas."

I tried to console Joe: We had seen Zach all this week. What difference if we had seen him on December 12 or December 25? *Zach* didn't know what day it was. *He* didn't know it was Christmas.

But even as I said it, I was feeling a little guilty myself. Our son . . . Christmas Eve . . . So far from home.

Not until I hung up the phone did it hit me. I got the number of the Holiday Inn and called Joe right back: "Hey, we're Jewish. We don't even celebrate Christmas!"

Even so, that first holiday was hard. It was a family vacation—lots of beach and bridge-playing till the wee hours and everyone feeling good in each other's company, but relaxed enough to read or take naps or just be. I love my family. My brother's little boy is exactly Zach's age, and it did take me a while to see him without thinking about Zach and what could be. When they were born and we all spent part of that first summer with my folks in New York, Lynn and I called them "the boys" and compared Zach's dimply thighs with Abram's skinny, kicky legs. Abram was a fierce, scowly, extra-alert baby (or so I thought then—compared to Zach; the babies were just a few months old and so it was

Before We Knew). But I did get over thinking about "What could be." Well, that is, I didn't exactly "get over it," but I just didn't dwell upon it. I talked a lot with my brother, who told me that not a day goes by that he does not think of Zach, and that has made Abram infinitely more precious to him.

My parents kept on saying how good I was, how good I looked, how all okay things seemed between Joe and me. This was all true. We were all "doing well." But the feeling of incompleteness was always with us, sometimes only as a blurry dullness. Other times, like when we met my brother's friend at the beach, he with his little boy, my brother with Abram, and Joe out in the waves alone, the pain pierced so intensely that I could not speak. I was so sad. My sister-in-law and my brother's friend's wife were both pregnant. They sat in beach chairs at the water's edge talking distractedly as they watched the boys. I felt as if I were from another planet.

Sometimes when I see an older couple with a retarded child/adult, I am amazed at how they endured so many years of tension and pain and still somehow look normal themselves. Sometimes I think that they don't—maybe that is just my perception of them (or how I think *I'd* be after living so many years with that burden). At a restaurant in Florida there was an older couple with their Down's syndrome adult daughter. There was a pallor, a certain grayness about both the parents. Did I imagine the tightness in their throats, their labored breathing?

In the airport, waiting for our plane back to Iowa, we saw a woman checking in—with her a boy about eleven, leaning heavily on the counter, making gurgling noises and waving his hands. Joe and I looked at each other like silent conspirators with our painful secret. A half hour later we were sitting across the aisle from them—seats 10A, B, C, they in D and E. (Who planned that?) The boy was drumming on the seat in front of him and rocking in his own, straining against the seat belt his mother had clasped across his lap.

She took out a bag of Kraft Miniature Marshmallows, opened a small hole in the top, and offered it to him. He spent the next ten minutes or so fisting three or four marshmallows into his mouth. The woman took out a book *(Far From the Madding Crowd)* and began reading. Out of the corner of my eye I was transfixed by this scene. No, lady, I thought, you are not fooling me, there is no way you can be coolly reading a Hardy novel, pretending this is just an ordinary plane trip with your child. Soon the boy was finished with the marshmallows and started his thumping. The man in the seat in front of him moved to the seat next to the aisle (the plane was rather empty). The boy was making noises that sounded like *"maaaa-ah-ah,"* and the woman took out a toy for him, a Fisher-Price music box with nursery-school pictures on it (Zach has one—will it continue, too, to amuse him for ten more years?).

The stewardesses were serving lunch. They didn't know what to make of this scene, so they just plopped the trays down and hurried along. The mother was cutting the boy's meat into tiny pieces. I saw that she helped him hold his glass when he drank. She was absorbed by every messy spoonful, balancing the tray, guiding his flailing hands. She managed to eat a few bits herself, in between spills. The boy was very much like an eighteen-month-old—curious, noisy, wanting to do things on his own. But, of course, he was not cute. By the end of the meal his face was covered with drool and bits of food, even with all his mother's wiping.

Later Joe moved to the back, so he could put the armrests up and sleep across three seats (the plane was *very* empty), and I moved closer toward the aisle, across from this woman, so Gabi could put her head in my lap and stretch across the seats to sleep. I turned to the woman before I could think and said, "I have a retarded child, too. I just want to tell you that I think you are really brave to make this trip by yourself." So then, in between more miniature marshmallows, her holding and hushing and moving his

hands (he pinches), we talked a little. Mike was her only
child . . . Her husband died two years ago; she was visiting
her parents for a "vacation." She was a university mathe-
matics teacher. She talked about "looking for a place" for
Mike. She talked as if she still has time, as if this is something she will "have to face sooner or later," as if this is
something she *wanted* to put off. I didn't understand her,
and the plane trip was too short for me to try. It was as if
we'd been through the same war together but had come
away with different visions of the experience. At the end of
the flight he was trying to sit on her lap and she was uncurl-
ing sticky fingers from her hair.

I read someplace that the divorce rate for parents of
handicapped children was over 70 percent, double the national average—and this for a study done in the *Midwest!*
(In California there are probably only two couples still
together in the entire state.)
    For a while after Zach left, Joe and I went separate ways.
It was as if someone had unhooked the chains; we did not
have to begrudge time, we were not so dependent upon
one another to survive the day.
    Gabi was usually with one of us, but she flowed with her
friends easily in and out of weekends. There were moments
of cherished spontaneity: I'd take Gabi to a matinee and
after the show go out and pick up Chinese food for supper
—surprise Joe with pea pods and black mushrooms.
    We look at each other's changing faces: Now we have the
time to ask, "How are you?"
    I can tell when Joe is thinking of Zach, even if I do not
see his eyes. I look at his back, and sometimes there is a sad
slump to his broad shoulders, deflated, like a kicked tent.
    Silently I walk up behind him, my arms locked in love
across his chest; we stand like this a minute and
sway. . . .
    I still (always) feel sad. We talk about Zach almost every
day—if not talk, pictures flash—we share these with each
other. Joe gets a certain look of warmth and sorrow. We

romanticize Zach, recalling to each other only his physical beauty, his sweet, slow smile, the smell of his hair. We live every day with these strange feelings, like fond memories of someone who died, only there he is again: a call from Hills and Dales to say that Zach is sick (we can't go up this weekend), a bill from Social Services for seventy-five dollars for the monthly foster-care service. So Zach, who is not with us, is very much always with us. Joe went shopping one day in Des Moines to buy some clothes. Coming back, he thought of Zach turning three and had to pull off the road because he was crying so hard.

But now Joe and I have the energy to support each other. That's what you need for caring for someone else's pain—energy. When Zach was home, we were both all used up from him; we coveted our own alone-time, we couldn't handle the burden of someone else's needs.

Joe and I are together and strong; there is a softness in him now. Having a child like Zach is humbling, and I know that there is a part of Joe that hurts more than I, maybe that part where baseballs are tossed around in his head, that part that longs to see a son whose body is in his own image.

And if Joe is softer, then I am stronger, if only a little worse for wear.

So I would say that having Zach did bring us closer together in the final analysis, though I don't think we could have *stayed* together had we kept Zach at home. There is, in marriage, that tenuous balance, and ultimately, I think, the care of such a needy child would have so destroyed the balance—I know the damage would be irreparable.

Maybe short-term crises, the car-accident-I-almost-lost-you-in kind, pump up the marriage adrenaline and inspire new commitments. But a long-term crisis, the care of a child like Zach, is erosive to a relationship; too much energy is drained, resentments wash away the care.

I think Zach left before that happened. I share something with Joe that no man could ever understand. Matching wounds—like the blue V-neck sweaters we both had in high school. I also have more fun with Joe than with anyone else even still. As far as marriages go, I would say that ours is on solid ground. But having looked over the edge of that ground, I know to what depths we can plummet. I make no promises.

The article "A Place for Zachariah" came out in *Redbook*'s "Young Mother" series, the cover boasting "7 Beautiful Body Exercises," "Price Tag Recipes," "A Marriage Checkup." I wrote the article because I simply could not stand one more pap narrative about the "special" member of our family, one more inspirational piece in the Sunday family section showing a handicapped child as a gift of love.

I wanted people to understand that institutionalization (read: "appropriate residential placement") is a positive alternative and *not* a giving-up, not a failure. It can certainly be understood that way if there *were* appropriate placements in good facilities and we really did have choices and alternatives. I shouldn't have to feel "lucky" that we "got Zach in" through pressure and articulate maneuvering. These placements should be offered as alternatives to all parents who have severely handicapped children.

When I think of the priorities in this country, when I think of something like that billion-dollar missile, the millions of dollars spent for car-crash scenes in trashy movies —my God, how can the *National Lampoon* caricature anything when real life is so perverse?

I was grateful that *Redbook* was publishing my story; it took a lot of courage for a magazine that espouses traditional family values, because the article is about placing Zach, about choosing not to have him live home with us. Over many long-distance phone calls, Andrea, the editor of the "Young Mother" series (who is herself young, but not a mother), and I have become friends. She always asks "How is Zach doing?" Andrea thinks placement is a controversial topic, like abortion: people will feel strongly on both sides.

My friend Barbara called from New York, worried about

me. "I'm afraid people won't like you for doing this. They won't understand."

The first day the magazine was out on the stands in the supermarkets, I got a call. It was a woman named Rita who was calling me from New Jersey. Next week, she was moving her severely retarded daughter, age two, into a children's home. She was plagued by this decision . . . "Oh, but what you wrote helped me so much. I know I'm not alone."

Fifteen minutes later the phone rang again. It was a woman from a small town in Georgia who has a severely brain-damaged six-year-old, still at home. "Oh, I've been trying to get up the nerve to do what you have done. It's so hard because the places around here are all so depressing . . . I have been so afraid of what people would say. . . ."

Those next few weeks were crazy. Hundreds of letters, calls. Only a dozen or so were negative. One was an obscene letter that began, "You Bitch, You Slut, I Hope You Rot In Hell" . . . the writer taking out her anger in a frenzy of capitalization.

Some of the supporting calls and letters were from social workers and teachers of special education. (". . . Five days a week I spend teaching retarded children—I truly love my job; but every day I thank God that my own children are normal—that I do not have these kids to come home to.")

But most of the letters and calls were from mothers who had damaged children. They ranged in age from a young mother, nineteen, in Mississippi ("How far away is Iowa? Do you think I could come and talk to you sometime?"), to a woman whose retarded "child" was fifty-two years old ("He's living in a group home now, a real good one, and he's happy. But you know, it still pains me some to see a man my son's age in church, with his own family.").

I cried with one woman who told me that she took her son out of a state institution in the South, "because he had sores on his hips and back from rubbing against the wheelchair. No one ever moved him around. I couldn't leave him there—I couldn't care for him at home. What choice is that? I took him home, I think, to kill him. I planned it all out. Just a pillow over his face as I held him. A social worker called last week about an opening in a private home. We qualify 'cause we don't make but eight thousand dollars a year and my husband pays child support to his two other kids. So I didn't kill T.J. God, I can't believe I am telling you, a stranger, all this. What you must think of me. Could anyone else understand this?''

One night the phone rang during dinner. It was a woman from Illinois. She was thirty-four, had an eight-year-old daughter and a three-year-old little boy who was severely brain-damaged at birth following a complicated delivery. Now he lived in an ''infants' home'' some fifty miles away, and she saw him only on monthly visits. We talked for almost half an hour, and when I went back to my spaghetti, the sauce now cold and runny on the plate, Gabi asked, ''Did you know that woman, Mommy? You talked as if you knew her.''

I said I guessed that I really did.

Jan called to say that she sent copies of the article to all her friends, all the teachers in Eddie's old school, all the doctors who ever examined him. She said she's still learning how to fill the time since Eddie left. Both she and Roger were in therapy. ''We kid around that we're supporting psychiatric America . . . but I think it's working!''

At the end of the first year that Zach was placed at Hills and Dales, we noticed a change. He was not using his hands at all, not even to clumsily bat a balloon the way he used to. We knew he was being worked with every day, more so than he had been by therapists when he was home with us. And yet the changes were unmistakably there: his weakened head control, an increased spasticity in the legs.

Joe blamed the lack of control on the new adaptive wheelchair that Hills and Dales had built—it was a very supportive chair, with Velcro straps to go over Zach's chest, shoulders, waist, with stirrups and straps for his feet. Our first look at Zach in his chair made us both swallow hard.

"Boy," Joe said to him when we picked him up one week-end, "do you look handicapped." Zach smiled, leaning against the back of the chair, blond curls in a fluffy halo over the headrest.

When we got home, Joe decided to cut Zach's hair. It was warm enough that Saturday afternoon, so that Zach was wheeled in his new chair out to the backyard. Joe clipped away. It made me sad to see Zach's long curls blow away in the wind. Joe was pleased with his barbering job. "There," he said proudly as he maneuvered the wheelchair past the back porch and into the kitchen. "Now he doesn't look like a baby anymore. Now he looks like a real little boy."

Jan called me the next week. She had just come from seeing Eddie. She said, "The only change in Eddie during the past year is that his hair is slightly darker. I want it the way it was. I want his hair white blond still."

A few months after Zach's third birthday, Hills and Dales called and told us that they wanted to schedule an appointment to have another brain scan for Zach. They measure his head every month as part of a routine exam, and it seemed that his was growing disproportionately—though not alarmingly so. Also, they agreed with us about the loss of head control: Zach seemed less able to hold his head while sitting in the chair and "rested" it a lot against the adaptive headrest. Joe insisted that the new chair was giving Zach too much support—that's why he was regressing.

I didn't know what I thought.

Hills and Dales Resident Evaluation:

Zachariah Kupfer

NURSING SERVICES
Zach's general health this past quarter has been fairly good. He is eating and sleeping well and his bowel function is good with the use of Senokot. Zach has no known allergies.

Due to an increase in Zach's head size along with notable head lag and a decrease in energy level, nursing consulted with Dr. M. A CAT scan was scheduled. Following this, Zach received a physical checkup by Dr. M. The results of the CAT scan were then reviewed.

It was Dr. M.'s decision to make an appointment with University Hospitals in Iowa City, Iowa, in the Pediatric Neurological Department, to review the CAT scan and evaluate Zach. Zach tires very easily. Because of this, he is attending school on a half-day basis in the morning and returning to the center at noon. Zach appears to be more cheerful and responsive in the morning.

RECREATION THERAPY SERVICES

Zach's recreation program consisted of such in-center activities as music, stories, and sensory stimulation. His response to the various activities depended on his mood. Zach was often fussy during recreation sessions, which warranted his being placed in bed for a nap. At times Zach did respond positively to music, i.e., he smiled and vocalized.

Zach's fussiness and poor head control has made fine-motor programming difficult. It has been noted that he does not play with toys as frequently as he used to. He also does not seem to enjoy looking at books or catalogues anymore.

Zach participated in a number of community activities, i.e., a picnic at Eagle Point Park and a trip to the Kennedy Mall. He seemed to enjoy all of these activities; however, at times, he appeared to be very sleepy.

Zach has two Big Sisters and a Foster Grandparent.

POSITIONING

The positioning program recommended by Habilitative Services has been changed since last quarter. The floor positions include prone on a floor mat, flexed sidelying on either side in a beanbag or on a floor mat, and supine in a beanbag or on a wedge. Zach may also be placed on an air mattress in a prone or sidelying position. Zach has not been tolerating floor positions very well, crying soon after he is placed on the floor. We have tried rolling him on the cage ball before placing him on the floor. He will tolerate the floor longer when we do this, but his favorite position is being held by grandparent or staff. When placed in a prone position and toys are provided, he will lift his head; however, he is unable to keep it up for more than ten seconds.

FAMILY INTERACTION
The parents, Joseph and Fern Kupfer, retain custody and guardianship of Zach. These parents have continued their involvement with Zach since his placement. Over the past quarter, the Kupfers have accompanied Zach to Iowa City for a medical evaluation, have taken him for two home visits, and called Hills and Dales frequently to check on his condition. The Kupfers are to be considered an important resource in all program planning for Zach.

But it wasn't the wheelchair. It was Zach. A CAT scan showed that the ventricles in his head were enlarged. He moved even less than ever, and except for a few cerebral palsy thrusts, while on his back, reached out not at all.

The pediatric neurologist suspected hydrocephalus. That was unusual since this fluid on the brain usually occurs at birth (unless it is "invasive"—from a growing tumor or something). Hydrocephalus was what the doctors thought when Zach was six months old, but none of the tests supported this diagnosis. The neurologist said that sometimes (rarely) hydrocephalus could develop as it seemed to be doing in this case. I questioned whether there was an original misdiagnosis, but the doctor (of course) rejected that idea, saying that the fluid would build up and Zach's head would grow more than it has in the past three years.

If hydrocephalus was absolutely indicated, they would put a shunt in Zach's head to drain off the fluid and relieve the pressure.

As usual Joe and I responded to this trauma with our

totally different visions of the world. I saw this as the beginning of a series of tests, of operations (once a child is
"shunted," as they say, he needs to be checked, regulated,
sometimes "reshunted"). One thing about Zach that I was
always thankful for was that, although Zach was severely
damaged, his problems were not medical. Unlike a lot of
other kids at Hills and Dales, he didn't need special medica-
tions, operations, etc. Now I saw all this changing. It just
didn't seem quite fair that with so little going for him, he
now had to have operations, too.

Joe, on the other hand, saw the operation as a chance to
finally "do something." That is, for the first time since
recognizing Zach's disability, there was something to do.
Joe liked this aspect of control. And Joe, still the optimist,
thought that these operations could somehow "fix" Zach a
little. (Just a little. Joe's just an optimist, not a fool.)

I was looking toward the operation with dread, already
picturing Zachy in pain, confused, more helpless than ever.
And probably bald. They would have to shave his head. Joe
was almost rubbing his hands in anticipation—as if this
operation would be a birth of some sort. So, of course, Joe
and I were not feeling close.

Gabi, who listened to my conversation with the social
worker and heard the word *hydrocephalus,* recalled with horror the grotesque hydrocephalic child we had seen in one
of the institutions, and who had never been shunted. "Zach
won't look like that, will he?"

The staff at Hills and Dales was reassuring, compassionate, interested. They stayed with Zach and us in the hospital
and met with all the doctors.

It was very difficult to feed Zach because he rested his
head, and it was impossible for him to swallow. So we held
him, draped across our laps, to get some food in. Oh, to see
him lose ground when he had so little to begin with. . . .

The next week Sandy called us from Hills and Dales. The
doctors she spoke to concluded that Zach was not hydroce-

phalic; there would be no operation; they could give no reason for his regression except to say that sometimes "that's the way it is with these children." Maybe in six more months they would do another brain scan. I didn't know what that would show, except perhaps further abnormalities, and those we could see by looking at Zach.

Sandy said that his condition appeared "stable" and that he was eating all right. They were concerned that he was not getting enough liquids, but he seemed to be taking them now with a little spoon attached to the top of a baby bottle. "And last night," Sandy said, "he and some of the kids went out with us for pizza." She brought a food grinder and Zach's special bottle.

Sandy told me about this scene: At another table a family was eating pizza, trying not to stare at the Hills and Dales kids being spoon-fed their pureed pizzas, but the little girl of the family slipped out of her seat, came over to Zach, and demanded, "What's the matter with that boy?" While her mother frantically beckoned her back to her own table, Sandy told her that his name was Zach and his brain was damaged so that he couldn't walk or talk like she could. The little girl added optimistically, "But he sure does like pizza!"

Dear Fern:

I don't know how to begin this. I'm still in shock. Only I'm angry and still in shock. Roger left. Roger left me, the house, Amanda—mostly me. He said he "doesn't want to be married" to me anymore. The next day he packed up and moved in with a friend (male) until his apartment downtown is "ready." I can't believe this is happening. And I feel so dumb because I truly don't understand any of it, didn't see it coming.

We had gone out last week to dinner and a show. I have been feeling really together lately, about Eddie, about my painting. I had two new shows to prepare for and in the past few months have even been making some money. Anyway, as we were driving home, I'm babbling on about how good

I feel, how well I think Roger and I have been doing. Then he lays it on me. He wants out. He's going through "changes," he needs "space." God, every cliché in the book. Why doesn't he just reread *Passages*? I don't understand how he can actually *leave* just following a period of dissatisfaction.

He says he's been "working on the relationship" for almost a year. (Ergo the reason he went back into therapy.) That drove me crazy. How can one work on a relationship alone? Why didn't he tell me? I'd have worked with him. It seems so unfair to me. I feel so deceived, betrayed. I am so angry that for the past few days I don't even know if I *want* him back if he decides on a reconciliation. And how could my own feelings change so, in just a few days, following thirteen years of what was, I thought, a loving marriage?

The night he left, I stayed in the bathroom for two hours with diarrhea. I lost five pounds. I'm scared about money. I can't make a living with my painting, so I'll have to start thinking about getting a job. If I go into the city, that will mean commuting and leaving Amanda alone a lot after school. I don't think she's ready for that. Amanda is very angry, too. It's like Roger left these *two* women who are just not going to make things easy for him. I try and explain to Amanda that Daddy left *me*, not her, but somehow it doesn't ring true. I am trying very hard not to use her to sort out my feelings and not to bad-mouth Roger to her. ("He's still your daddy, he really loves you," etc.) Still, I feel I'm not really being honest with her. I feel like shrieking "He's your daddy, and he's a selfish asshole; he's ruining our family, and he's ruining my life."

We've already divided some things up. (And, God, the body isn't even cold yet.) Roger took the big color TV. Amanda was upset at that one. But really he's in front of it most weekends, watching any ball game. I wanted his mother's antique wardrobe that we have in the bedroom. Roger was upset about that. ("It's *my* mother's.") I told him no one was asking him to leave. If he wanted it, he could stay and use it.

I feel as if I'm getting everything and nothing. I have this enormous house and all the trappings, every piece of furniture we ever bought together (some we even had made); I have the new car (if Roger was thinking of leaving, why would he buy a new car?), and I have Amanda. Roger has a studio apartment downtown, a color TV, and expense-account lunches. Apart from my rage (*the* main emotion right now), I am also jealous. Roger is free. He has an exciting job, which he loves. I get to call the plumber when the garbage disposal breaks down and to drive Amanda to birthday parties. (But no, no way I would want Roger to have her, if that's what you're thinking.)

Strange, this is the first time in years that Eddie is peripheral to our troubles; he is not the trouble. (Roger was so taciturn. He was always helpful to me, but I was never really sure just how he felt about Eddie.) I wonder how Eddie figures in all this. Were we just "hanging on" for all this time with Eddie, then when things calmed down, Roger felt he could split? Why didn't I know any of this? Did having a child like Eddie drain us of all the lightness, the joy?

I have a lot of support here. My friends have been wonderful. Even Roger's mom called, sympathetic and warm.

Please call. I'll really try not to be too hysterical.

Love always,

Jan

I asked Joe if he thought it frivolous if I flew to Chicago for the weekend just to see Jan. He thought it was, but if I really wanted to go, it would be okay with him. "Can we count it as your next birthday present?" he asked. I agreed, thinking what a great deal as I called the travel agent. Usually, Joe buys me a robe.

The next Saturday morning, Jan met me at O'Hare. I saw her red hair, now long and wild, popping up over the crowd. She was wearing a black cape and high-heeled black boots. We hugged warmly, telling each other how good we looked.

"This is my mourning outfit," she told me.

Amanda was at a friend's all-day, all-night birthday party. We spent the day in the city, easily, like old friends, touring the galleries, stopping to eat a spinach salad, have a beer. And talking, talking about our lives, the children, choices, our men, the pain. We walked through a current exhibit, the Luminists, large incandescent canvases of lights across the water, fields of glowing wheat.

"Do you think Roger has another woman?" I asked.

Jan shook her head. "I thought of that. He says no. I don't know if that would make me feel better or worse. He said he doesn't love me anymore. Maybe I wouldn't be so hurt if he loved someone else—that's why he was leaving. To go to someone else, not just to get away from me."

Later we bought French pastries and wine, some fruit and cheese for dinner.

It was about an hour's drive to Jan's, and in the car we polished off a Linzer torte and a chocolate eclair. Jan said, "I'm okay when I'm outside and busy, but I dread going home."

Jan's house was terrific. A lot of levels and light, wood and fabric. Jan's paintings were everywhere, hanging down stairwells, across a big wall in her dining room; vibrant abstracts, complicated spirals.

In the hall was a photograph in a silver frame: Jan and Amanda, in a park, looking outdoorsy and happy, a smiling Roger behind them, one hand protectively on each female shoulder. Jan took me to her studio on the top floor of the house, a big room filled with half-squeezed tubes and buckets of brushes and canvases already with splats of purple and orange.

"I love working here. All by myself. I don't know how much I'll love it without knowing that Roger will be coming home for dinner. Is that what I hate giving up more than Roger himself? The traditional arrangement of family life?"

We went down to the kitchen to start cutting up sour

apples, slicing cheese. Jan opened the refrigerator and pulled a piece of wilted red cabbage from the crisper.

"Oh, shit. There's still food in here from before he left."

We sat at a table set with candles, cloth napkins, and woven placemats, the wine sparkling in crystal. Jan said, "I like to do this. Maybe I just have to get used to doing it for Amanda and myself. Maybe just for myself. Amanda is happy enough to eat Spaghettios off paper plates."

After dinner Jan and I took the rest of the wine down to the den and arranged ourselves face-to-face on the ends of the couch, covered by the same afghan.

Jan talked about a job she was offered in a new, rather avant-garde gallery, arranging exhibits and doing public-relations work.

"The pay is not terrific, but with child support, and if I sell a few of my own paintings, I can manage okay. I have to get over this anger, though. Anger is very unproductive."

I made a toast, "to a new life," as we gave our wineglasses a gentle clink. Jan shrugged.

On the side table was a photograph album, and I started leafing through: Jan and Roger as young marrieds, he with black-framed glasses on a boyish face; Jan with light lipstick, a tight scarf pulling back straightened hair. Later, lots and lots of Amanda as a baby: naked in the tub, bonneted in the carriage, smiling from a backpack. Then the foursome: proud Roger, holding his new son, Eddie, Jan and Amanda smiling beside him (Before They Knew).

I saw the later pictures of Eddie at a year, after he was diagnosed ("something is wrong"), but he looked very happy and normal, sitting sweetly under a Christmas tree. (Unlike Zach, Eddie could sit and hold his head.)

We finished off the wine, laughing and crying over the album. Jan said, "I remember that picture. We were at Roger's brother's for Christmas. The doctors had just told us of the possibility that Eddie was severely brain-damaged.

I was heartbroken the whole time, but we went through the motions of a joyful holiday, eating turkey, opening the gifts. I remember one remark Roger's sister-in-law made to me. We were sitting by the tree while her older daughter, Tina, was opening a gift, a blazer with the Girl Scout insignia. Tina was babbling on enthusiastically about how many boxes of Girl Scout cookies she was going to sell that year, and then she started talking about camp. My sister-in-law turned to me; there I was sitting with this baby on my lap whom the doctors thought was probably retarded, and she said, 'You just don't know how tough life can be until you have a daughter in Scouts.' "

Eddie was missing from the later pictures. Now I think Roger will be—like those insurance commercials on TV where an invisible force zaps out the husband as the family walks together through the park. (A voice-over booms, "Who will take care of *them,* if you're gone!")

I remembered that after the article in *Redbook* came out, I got one letter from a woman whose husband said "Goodbye, toots" the *day* her boy was positively diagnosed as mentally retarded. She realized, of course, that she was well rid of him. Maybe having these "special" children forces out certain life decisions that are necessary. We can no longer dawdle along our merry (or not-so-merry) blind ways. But there is not a control group for handicapped families. I wondered if Jan and Roger would have stayed together had they not had a child like Eddie. How could we ever look at this objectively?

Before we went to bed, Jan asked, "Do you think this will make a good ending for your book? With Roger and me getting divorced, I mean."

I told her it wasn't a novel. I was not searching for an ending that "worked." I was just trying to describe what happens in the lives of some who have retarded children. Besides, I said, I had no control over this.

"I know," Jan sighed wistfully, "I wish you did."

The University of Iowa: Genetics Clinic Evaluation:

Zachariah Kupfer

REASON FOR COUNSELING: Questions about Zachariah's mental retardation.

HISTORY: Zach has been seen several times at the University of Iowa. He is now a resident of the Hills and Dales Child Development Center in Dubuque. A summary of his history is that during gestation, his fetal activity was less than that of his sister. At about three months gestation Mrs. Kupfer had some vaginal bleeding. She says she has always felt that this may have been contributory to Zach's problem. Zach weighed eight pounds, twelve ounces at birth. His sister, Gabi, weighed nine and a half pounds. He was seen first at five and a half months at the University of Iowa because of developmental delay. At that time several examiners found that he had hyperreflexia with 3+ DTRs at the knee. His skull X ray at that time was normal. Serum amino acids were normal and urine metabolic screen was also normal. PKU was done which was normal. An EEG was done which was described as being within normal limits. His head circumference was 46.5 cm which was less than the 97th percentile at that time. He was seen a few weeks later, at six months of age. He had an EMG that was normal. He had a CAT scan of the brain which was normal. At that time he was also described as having thumb and palm positioning of his hands.

At fourteen months of age, a slit lamp examination was normal. The examination of the fundus was described as being normal and the only abnormality described was a mild strabismus and possibly more fixation with the right eye than with the left.

Zach was next seen at eighteen months at the U. of I. in both Hospital School and Pediatric Neurology. At that time, his head circumference was 51.3 cm, which was greater

than the 97th percentile. His DTRs were decreased throughout; they were described as being 1+. There was also some
scissoring and spasticity of the lower extremities.

At three years of age there was a question of a rapid increase in head circumference over a short period of time. At
that time, his head circumference was 54 cm which was at
the 30th percentile. There was increased tone of his lower
extremities. He was admitted for evaluation for possible hydrocephalus. CAT scan of the brain at that time showed enlarged ventricles with cortical atrophy which raised the
possibility of a degenerative white-matter disease.

He was evaluated by the neurosurgeons at that time and
they felt that there was no indication for placing a ventricular
peritoneal shunt.

Zach did develop a few skills which he has lost. These
included holding objects and attempting to feed himself.

FAMILY HISTORY: A review of the family history revealed
that both parents are Jewish. Both families came from Eastern Europe . . .

SUMMARY: The parents think they will probably have no
more children but are not completely certain at this time. I
discussed my inability to prognosticate about Zach's future.
This inability stems from the lack of having a specific diagnosis. I feel that Zach's history of loss of developmental mile-
stones coupled with his changing head circumference and
CAT scans suggest that he has a degenerative brain disorder. Which of the several degenerative brain disorders he
has is difficult to determine by clinical evaluation. The lack
of seizures, the report that an eye exam at fourteen months
of age was normal plus the CAT scan suggests that perhaps
Zach has entity called spongy degeneration of the brain
(Canavan's disease). Homocystinuria and hyperglycemia can
cause the same morphological appearance of the brain but
these two entities have been ruled out by amino acid analysis of his serum.

At this point in time I feel that, regardless of the specific diagnosis Zach has, it is very likely an autosomal recessive disorder. This means that both parents are carriers and

each subsequent child is at a 25 percent risk for having the same entity.

Dear Jan:

How life changes around. In the past week we have been hit with news that stuns us to our core.

1. That Zach's damage was possibly due to genetic causes, both of us carrying a recessive gene hidden through generations and possibly linked to our being Jewish. (It is not Tay-Sachs—it's something even more exotic, but something that cannot be diagnosed "for sure.")

2. That Zach's slight regression in the past year has taken a dramatic turn. He was home this weekend and was a total blob. Doctors in Dubuque do not expect him to live "a normal life span." (Months? Years?)

The past few times Zach has been home have been so hard. He has been sick—earaches, respiratory infections, so much that he has been on antibiotics for most of the winter. He's been so weak that he could barely manage to smile. Even when Joe asked him if he wanted to play "Captain Cuddley."

Also, Zach is losing weight—almost seven pounds since last year. First we just thought he was growing "normally," losing his baby fat at four, but just recently his body has begun to have that wasted look that some of the other children have.

Anyway, though this is apart from Zach's condition, for some time now I have been planning for us to see a genetics counselor. Since the diagnosis of Zach's brain damage remains "etiology unknown," we still have so many questions.

I suppose the thought of having another baby has been with me all these years. Why at thirty-four would I romanticize it so? In my head I know that I do not want to start over, that our lives have settled into a pattern of care and tranquility. We—Joe, Gabi and I—have time to squander on each other, on ourselves. But there is that yearning, that body call. Do all women feel that?

I don't know if our questions about why Zach is the way he is will ever be answered.

Iowa has a traveling genetics-counseling service (I suppose that makes it sound as if they operate from a tent—really the doctors and nurses are part of a group based at the Iowa City University Hospitals), which was going to be in Ames at the Student Health Service, right on campus. So I set up an appointment, had all Zach's medical records sent to the genetics department, and last week we met with Dr. Bartley—young, nice, very undoctorish, who spent most of the afternoon asking questions, offering possible hypotheses.

I suppose I wasn't prepared for any "news," so it took a few days for us to really absorb what we talked about. The gist is this: because of the difference in Zach's brain scans (the infant ones are normal; the recent ones are abnormal, showing atrophy of the brain itself) and Zach's general deteriorating condition, these doctors feel that the problem *is* genetic, probably the result of a recessive gene that Joe and I both carry. They wanted to see Zach in Iowa City and continue with a further series of tests to see if they could come up with a diagnosis.

So I went back with him to Iowa City Hospitals where they ran through a series of esoteric genetic tests. It was like experimenting on a corpse, for Zach cried only when he was truly in pain—otherwise he just lay there. It was such a painful day. We also saw an eye specialist who ascertained that along with atrophy of Zach's brain cells, the tissue behind the retina had worn away. Zach no longer sees.

I cannot put into words how devastating it is to watch the deterioration. It seems so damned unfair.

It's very confusing. Dr. Bartley kept talking about Zach having a brain "disease." The idea that Zach could actually have a disease, a syndrome, something we could label and research and read about, is strange after all this time. When I think of his first two years, all the questions that I had that couldn't be answered ("What is the matter with him . . . What will he become?"), the horror of it was the unknown. . . . I think if you find out that your child has a fatal illness, you are devastated, but the sick feeling that I had with Zach for so long, and the nauseating terror that crept in in the early-morning hours before he awoke, was because of *not* knowing.

I looked up the description of the disease, No. 27,190 in a book called *Mendelian Inheritance in Man.* Zach has all the clinical features—hypotonia, retardation, the slightly larger (but not hydrocephalic) head, and now the "eventual blindness." The text said that these children die "at eighteen months on the average"; although in one of the later journal articles I read, there was one child who lived to be nine years old. In this country the degenerative disorder has been seen in "infants of Jewish extraction whose ancestors lived in Vilna." We looked up Vilna. It was somewhere in Lithuania, although history has not been kind to stable Eastern European borders (nor Eastern European Jewry for that matter). Anyway, it is our ancestral turf.

A friend who's a biochemist explained about genes. Seems everyone has a lethal half-dozen or so genetic rotten eggs. But it is only when the specific gene matches someone else's lethal gene that an abnormality is produced. The odds against this, for Joe and me to have this specific gene for a disease that has only been recorded in a handful of families, are indeed very great, a drop in the ocean of calamity. Yet, here we are, generations away, blond and blue-eyed in Iowa, betrayed by some tribal memory: the final pogrom.

It is very different to see Zach as a dying child rather than a severely handicapped child or a retarded child. Joe and I were talking after a retarded citizens meeting. Joe said, "You know, I don't feel like them anymore" (the parents of retarded children). Another change. He dissipates so much of the anger.

We explained what we understood to Gabi . . . of course, she's listened to us talk about Zach getting worse for a while now, so she knows that now he is "sick" as well as handicapped.

Sometimes Gabi is so grown-up and sensitive that I forget she's really a kid, asking a kid's questions.

The other day we came in from grocery shopping, and as we were lugging in the sacks, she asked, apropos of nothing, "Hey listen, if Zach dies, can we get another baby?"

Intellectually I know it will be better for Zach's life to end; it's too cruel for him to grow physically only to become a giant infant who can do nothing at all. Emotionally, however, I feel a real sense of loss, so sorry about the whole travesty that was his life, apologetic to him for having to put him through it.

I spoke to the nursing staff at Hills and Dales and requested that no extraordinary measures be taken to prolong Zach's life—no CPR, no respirators. Joe typed out a formal statement last night and we both signed it. Then we walked to the mailbox together.

There is an image I have from Zach's last time in the hospital. We were in the ophthalmology department. Zach was lying still on a table, feverish, whimpering. We were in a cubicle with black walls and the technician, a young girl with a ponytail, was going to put an instrument like an eye cup over each of Zach's eyes, to hold them open as an electronic machine flashed eerie bleeps of light in the darkness. I held Zach's hand. Even laid out, wired up, he looked beautiful, other-worldly. Would that I could believe in angels, then in another time and place he could be whole and at peace.

My parents called last week after they had visited my brother and Lynn in Tulsa. My parents were careful not to talk at all about my brother's little boy—as if he weren't there. They thought it would hurt me. It would. Joe will always ask my brother "What is Abram doing?" and he gets angry at me because I don't. "For God sakes, Fern. Do you wish your brother had a brain-damaged kid, too?" Of course I don't. But I also don't think I care to hear about the cute ways of a normal four-year-old little boy as I picture blobby old Zach deteriorating into vegetabledom.

We still want to bring him home for visits, as long as he is able to make the trip. When Joe went to pick up Zach, Hills and Dales was having a "talent show" for a parents' night. Joe described it—sad and laughing. The children, all in wheelchairs, were arranged in a circle and "decorated" with various signs depicting their characters (Zach was Woodstock in a Charlie Brown skit) and moved appropriately by staff personnel to a record playing in the background. The children, oblivious to choreographic demands and dramatic intent, continued to whine, howl, seizure, and thrust. Joe said, "Oh, Fernie, they weren't even very good props."

I think I've mellowed. It doesn't drive me nuts anymore. I still won't go to birthday parties the center plans for Zach —that's too personal, individual, and wounding. But I think a certain attempt at celebration, a community planning, is good for staff morale. It is really normalization for the staff —to make them feel like regular teachers! And anyway, who really knows what goes on in the kids' heads? Damaged as they are, who knows? Doesn't everyone like applause?

Zach is "home" now, asleep for the night. He is so thin, so fragile looking. We just hold him and rock him all day long. The social worker was here. (This counts as a visit, so she won't have to drive all the way to Dubuque.) This was a different social worker, one who hadn't seen Zach in a while. She said, "He looks so sad." That made Joe cry.

Zach still loves to be walked. We took home a red wagon from Hills and Dales and propped it with pillows for a trip around the block. He lay, legs and arms draped regally over the fluffy cushions; Joe calls him "The Prince of Vilna."

You sounded so good when we last spoke. The job at the gallery sounds exciting. You *can* get lonely sometimes.

You're entitled. But this job will open up all sorts of possibilities. Shades of *An Unmarried Woman.* (Listen, honey, if Alan Bates ever comes along, you better take him!)

Cheers to you, Jan. To *your* new life! (I finished off your glass of wine along with my own.)

Love, Fern

Hills and Dales Resident Evaluation:

Zachariah Kupfer

NURSING SERVICES
Zach's general health continues to be stabilized at the present time. Periodic fussiness continues to be noted at mealtime and throughout the day. Zach's eating patterns are fair. Sleeping pattern is good.

Zach's weight continues to fluctuate. A slight decrease has been noted over the last quarter. Zach continues on six small feedings daily. Some changes to his diet have been made to include three ounces 2 percent milk at 3:00 P.M. and three ounces Sustacal pudding at 9:00 A.M. His total diet is included in his Individual Program Plan and the Medical section of this report.

Zach's head circumference increased .7 centimeter/¼ inch over the last quarter. The increase is not considered significant. Monitoring will continue.

Zach continues to receive postural drainage four times daily. One episode of possible dyspnea, lasting two to three minutes, was noted. Emergency procedures did not have to be initiated.

No dental examination was scheduled for this quarter. Zach continues to receive daily brushing and flossing.

FEEDING
Zach remains dependent in the feeding program. He has continued to receive six small feedings daily. Zach tires quickly during feeding and is somewhat reluctant at the be-

ginning of each feeding due to occasional choking. When this happens, the feeding is stopped until Zach can be relaxed enough to continue with the feeding.

Zach is fed on the trainer's lap. His feeding equipment includes a regular dish, a Plexiglas youth spoon, and a small, cutout plastic glass. Zach receives postural drainage before the first, third, fifth, and sixth feedings.

REHABILITATIVE SERVICES

Zach's abnormal muscle tone continues to cause significant problems. Generalized hypotonia has resulted in a complete lack of head control and proximal joint instability. Spasticity is present in the extremities with a pattern of strong shoulder retraction present in the upper extremities and a dominant extensor pattern present in the lower extremities.

Zach was seen by Dr. R. at the Hills and Dales orthopedic clinic for a recheck of his hips because of the significant adductor spasticity. Hip X rays were taken. The results were discussed with the physical therapist. Hip X rays revealed bilateral hip dislocations. Various alternatives were discussed, including possible bracing and surgery. Bracing was ruled out because of the tremendous amount of spasticity, which would resist against the brace, and Dr. R. did not feel that surgery was indicated because of Zach's medical status.

Zach's therapy sessions have emphasized relaxation and maintenance of range of motion. Direct care staff have been instructed in relaxation techniques and are encouraged to use them periodically throughout the day.

Zach continues to be positioned on a pillow bed in a reclining wheelchair (reclined to approximately 50 degrees) for transportation. A specially constructed foam abduction wedge is used between his knees and small bolsters are placed lengthwise on either side in the seat to provide optimum hip positioning.

RECREATION THERAPY SERVICES

Zach was involved in a number of in-center activities, i.e., arts and crafts, vestibular, auditory, and tactile stimulation.

Zach did not tolerate a handprint painting activity. He was

resistive to hand-over-hand assistance and he cried; therefore the activity was discontinued.

Zach received vestibular stimulation through use of the cage ball and tilt board. He seemed to enjoy this and seemed to be very relaxed. Zach responded positively to soft tactile stimulation to his arms and face. He also responded positively to soft music. Zach received assistance in shaking bells that were attached to his wrist.

Zach participated in a Team I picnic at the park. He seemed to tolerate it well.

Zach has two Big Sisters. He went out with his Big Sisters on four occasions this quarter. Zach has two Foster Grandparents who spend a great deal of time holding and rocking him.

FAMILY INTERACTION: The parents, Joseph and Fern Kupfer, retain both custody and guardianship of Zach. These parents have continued their involvement with Zach since his placement. Over the past quarter the parents have visited Zach at Hills and Dales and have taken him for a home visit. The Kupfers are considered to be an important resource in all program planning for Zach.

Zachariah at five. He has become a mythology. The essence of who he is ripples profoundly, forever, through our lives, so much stronger than the reality of who he is. Five years old, five years high, but an infant still. A child who did not grow.

I had a dream the other night that hung sweetly about through the day, making me feel so vulnerable and soft, like the memory of old good-night kisses, filling me with longing. It was Zach sitting in his blue recliner chair, a molded plastic "feeder" seat which I ordered three years ago, $49.95, out of a handicapped products catalogue when I admitted that the sturdy infant seat could no longer hold two-year-old Zach and that Zach could not hold himself. In the dream Zach sat, blue-eyed against blue plastic, thin and lovely, his legs scissored and spastic as they have been these many months, his hands crossed peacefully across his chest. I came in from the outside.

"Hi," he said gently, seeing me framed in the doorway. It was Zach's voice, and though he has said not a word in his life, I know it was the voice he would have if he could talk.

"Can you say, 'Hi, Mommy?' " I asked, surprised and tentative.

Zach smiled proudly, a smug look he has sometimes when he lies comfortable in my arms after crying to be picked up.

"Hi, Mommy," he said. And then raised an eyebrow as if to add, "How's *that?*"

The daytime fantasies wash over me quick and fast even still. I suppose they always will. Now Gabi runs in the door, breathless from some third-grade news: she is learning cursive, and they have just done the letter Z. I have a flash of turning to a normal little boy, her brother. "Oh, now she can write your name." Brother and sister, my two kids playing.

This fall my neighbor's little girl will be starting kindergarten. We make backyard talk about whether or not little Claire is ready; would another year at nursery be better? She is such a tiny girl. It is not until I come in my own back door and see Zach's picture on the refrigerator that I realize that he, too, would be starting kindergarten this fall and before I can blot the image, it's there—of a normal Zach, walking down the block through autumn leaves going to school, knapsack and all. In my fantasies I put him in overalls, navy blue crewneck sweaters, and never cut his blond hair. Hey, it's my fantasy, and I like visuals. For although I can never remember a phone number of a single friend, though I can never remember at the store what it was we needed—peanut butter or mayonnaise—I can remember, I can *picture* in my mind's eye, the most mundane scenes from ordinary life of even years and years ago: being lifted by my father from a bath and wrapped in orange towels trimmed with black and gold; of seeing my new brother in his crib for the first time, his face lined and segmented, "like a grapefruit," I told my parents. Similes at four. I remember walking to school myself in the fall—the first day of sixth grade with a new pink looseleaf notebook and my first "straight" skirt, a brown and beige plaid with an inadequate kick pleat, which forced me to assume little mincing steps that at the time I fancied as exotically Oriental. And yes, feeling at the top of the world.

There were no days when Zach lived with us for those two years and four months that I felt on top of the world. And I must say, quite without melodrama or hyperbole, that I think that if he had lived with us for the next two years, the world would have crushed me.

Zach and the fact of who Zach is will always make me unutterably sad, and it is something that I have come to live with, those fantasy flashes of who he could have been. But these are brief; they rest now in a smaller space of who I am.

We got a phone call a few days ago. It was Hills and Dales. Zach had a fever of 105 degrees and was taken to the hospital, where he received a massive dose of penicillin. The nurse, Sandy, is on the phone, and she sounds upset. She dearly loves Zach. She tells us to wait and to call the next day. In the morning Joe and I are on the phone, and Sandy tells us that Zach has "pulled through," his fever is down, he ate a good breakfast. She and Joe talk, relieved. Afterward Joe asks me why I was so quiet on the phone. I say that I am not sure how I feel about Zach "pulling through." Pulling through toward what? My heart burns from his fever. I want this to be over for him. Honestly, not for me now, but for him. Joe says he is not ready to say good-bye, to let him go. Joe is a very tenacious person.

Being with Zach on his visits home is bittersweet. I cry when Joe pulls up in the driveway, and I see Zach stretched out in the backseat, smiling and staring. I cry when we all drive to Dubuque to bring Zach back to Hills and Dales, driving up that hill past a hospital, then a church, then a cemetery—a telling landscape.

In between, when Zach is "home" in our house, the work is grueling. We give him six small, blended meals a day— he is fretful and scared when the swallowing doesn't come easy. We try to loosen his body tone in the bath, gentle against the strength of his rigid limbs. As an infant he was always hypotonic, "floppy," we said. Now he is stiff as an ironing board.

When Zach is home, my teeth ache. I don't eat well when he's here; energy seeps from me like slow-drip coffee.

When I move him in the night, so he won't sleep through locked in only one position, I wake him with kisses until he smiles, half-foggy with brain-damaged dreams, opening big eyes to me that no longer see. And, oh, I do still love him so. When Zach is home, the clocks stop ticking; everything is put on hold, as we join him in his world. Joe holds him and chats with me in the kitchen while I stir the chocolate pudding. The day is defined by the most ordinary events: giving Zach food and drink, the bath, his bowel movement, putting him down for naps. Millie still comes and helps us. Joe and I still divide the days—time for me to correct some papers, time for Joe to go to the gym.

When Zach is home, he fills up the house and makes us feel like a whole family again.

When Zach is home, I think about when he's going back.

I remember, sometime in that first year after he left, when we decided to take down the crib in his room. A student at school, a woman without much money, was having a baby, and I asked her if she'd like a crib. She was very grateful and offered a number of times to pay.

"No," I said, "I don't want any money. It would please me that a healthy new life would be in it." She didn't know about Zach.

I washed and folded all the crib sheets and set them on

the mattress along with the rubber pads, the bumper with the frolicking lambs, a musical mobile. Joe stayed home the afternoon her husband came with the pickup truck and I left to go shopping.

Slowly, we added bookshelves to the room, bought a portable open-up loveseat for guests. (Zach was our first guest and we surrounded him with pillows in case he rolled off; but it was an unnecessary precaution, for he didn't roll anywhere.) I did one wall with a bamboo textured wallpaper and bought matching shades. I took down the old rocking chair, recovered it, and put it on the front porch. I took up an old desk from the basement, painted it with white enamel, and set out sharpened pencils in a ceramic jar.

But still, years later, painted and spackled and recarpeted and built-upon, we call that small space in our house, a space that shows no sign of boy, no rubber balls, Legos, marbles, or string, we call that space "Zach's room."

Zach has not lived with us for more than three years, but Gabi remains loyal. In New York this summer, Joe was talking on the phone to an old college friend. "Did you all come in?" Charlie wanted to know, thinking that maybe Joe had made the trip alone to see his family.

When Joe said, "Yes, we're all here," Gabi was furious.

"We are *not* all here," she said pointedly. "Zachy is not here."

It was in New York this summer that I found out that this book would be published, the half-finished manuscript was sold. I go to meet the editor and as we talk about the book, we both begin to cry. "What kind of hard-nosed, New York City, big-time editor are you anyway?" I say, looking around for tissues on her desk. We stay in her office for two hours, and we talk with the door closed, an intimate sharing. When we walk out together past the receptionist, toward the elevator, I feel like when the lights go on after a sad movie.

Joe and I celebrate by taking the family out for dinner at Tavern on the Green in Central Park, a tourist treat for native New Yorkers.

Waiters, lean in black tuxedos, hurry by as we sit on a loveseat before entering the outdoor restaurant, and Gabi looks at me long and hard. She knows what "being published" means, growing up in an academic community where "perishing" was the unenviable alternative. And we are celebrating not just "an article" that got published, a cause for Joe's coming in with a better-than-cheap wine for dinner. This is a *book*.

Gabi turns to me, her green eyes narrowing. "So *now* are you glad that you had Zach?"

The truth catches in my throat like stale popcorn hulls.

"No, I could never be glad to have a child like Zachy. But I can still love him in a special way. And I can still be happy about getting the book published. Can you understand that, Gabs?"

She nods, shrugging a bit in resignation—as if she knew I would say that.

Do I have to explain to anyone why I would write a book like this? Is it a rationalization, a public anguish—to lay the blame, heal the hurt, share the pain?

This is the *tsuris* genre—the popular books about other people's problems, those cancer-operation–dying-spouses–crippled-athlete stories. Oh, I love them myself. I, too, can still be awed by the indomitable human spirit of those survival sagas and sway under sentimentality. I, too, can feel as I watch a made-for-TV, "true" drama about a young mother's fight with leukemia. "Whew, I'm glad that is not me." Now another voice answers: "So? You have it so good yourself?"

There are such ironies in writing about one's life when the distinguishable "marketable" feature of that life is a welldeep pain. No, I could never be glad to have a child like Zachariah.

A lesson: What happened to me could have happened to anyone. To prove a point—it does, to different anyones, every single day.

Those of you who are reading this and have normal children, those whiney miracles, fall to your knees by their bedsides; let gratitude burn forever in your breast, an eternal pilot light.

Driving back from New York this summer, we stopped at Jan's in Chicago. She and Amanda have moved into a loft downtown in a cooperative shared by four other artists and their families. Jan has a small, private "sitting room," and sit we do, cross-legged on pillows around a low wooden table while Jan serves "nori," some mysterious brown grain tightly bound by a fishy-smelling seaweed.

"A Japanese delicacy," Jan proclaims as she bites into the viney skin.

"Interesting," I say, doing the same. Gabi smirks across the table. *Interesting* is a code word for us. When she first started dressing herself for school, choosing her own clothes, she would come into our bedroom, wearing stripes and plaids, a plastic pin of a bunny rabbit on her chest. "Interesting," I would say, determined to let her set her own standards.

"That means you think it's awful," Gabi would say, getting to the core of the matter.

"These are pretty awful," Jan says, looking down at all the oily little rolls arranged neatly on an earth-toned platter. "But look how pretty they look. Aren't they aesthetically pleasing?"

"They look like dog turds," Amanda observes, not unkindly.

This sends Gabi, released from the burden of trying a nori of her own, into gales of laughter.

Jan brings out a green salad, some sourdough bread, a tray of cheeses, and cold meats.

Joe and I are a little stiff with each other in front of Jan, awkward about showing any affection across the table. We look in each other's eyes.

Joe's eyes are gray-green flecked with yellow, although sometimes they look blue. When Joe fills out the form to renew his driver's license, he puts "steel gray." They are not a color easily recalled to the mind's eye. Gabi has these selfsame changeable eyes. Like Joe's, they also turn down at the corners.

"Droopy eyes," I once said to him years and years ago.

"Jack Kennedy has droopy eyes," Joe once said when we were all still in Camelot's golden glow.

Joe looks lovingly at me now, and when Jan gets up to answer the phone in the next room, we meet together across the table for a kiss, gentle but promising.

Later Joe plays Uno with the girls while Jan and I bring dishes to the sink.

"We have to organize our time a lot. Roger to see Amanda twice a week—it's easier now that I'm downtown —me, to go see Eddie. I've weaned myself. I only see him every few weeks. And I don't make Amanda go if she doesn't want to. I'm okay. My work is fun, though I'm still always worried about money. I don't have anyone to depend on about that and it's something I'm still not used to. I don't miss Roger. I miss being *a family,* but I don't miss him as a person. So maybe he was right . . . and we didn't have a good marriage after all."

I hear Joe laughing with the girls in the next room. "Oh no, you didn't say 'UNO.' You can't go out now. Those are the rules."

He yields to Gabi's request for a second chance only with the promise that he, too, be allowed such a slipup in future games.

Early the next morning we leave Chicago to get a good jump on the day, only to find ourselves exiting wrong and reentrancing on the Dan Ryan Expressway, off and on again; and I am laughing, I can't help it, as Joe pounds the dashboard with his fist. Crazy drivers . . . rush hour. No one's letting us off. Joe cuts off a carful of angry-looking Latinos in a rusted out Ford. I'm waiting for one of them to reach into the glove compartment for the gun.

We're part of the traffic now, the molecular chain.

"Just go with the flow," I say. "We'll get off eventually."

Joe is hunched over the wheel, ferocious. "That's a really stupid thing to say. We could be here for goddamn forever!"

From the back Gabi says, "Really *forever,* Daddy?"

And I picture us, a Didion No Exit, growing old on the Dan Ryan Expressway.

But soon we're off, only a half hour wasted at the most; the tension lifts from our shoulders as we edge the city, moving on toward the bland country of the Midwest: big sky and endless plain.

We both sigh; aren't we glad we don't live in a big city now? We make a northern detour to go and see Zach.

Around Dubuque the countryside changes; real cliffs and valleys, and as we come up over a hill on a county road, we find we are immersed in cows. Two red-faced farmers are running frantically up the road from behind, shooing the Bessies toward the barn on the other side of the road.

We can't figure it out—did the cows get loose, a hole in the fence?

"Maybe the farmers just cross them here every day," Joe says. City-boy hypothesis.

We are creeping along with them, ten miles an hour. Bovine bodies as big as Toyotas push up against the car.

Gabi is nervous. "Don't hit them, Daddy."

Soon there are more cows behind than ahead, and after another half mile we're alone again on the road; looking back, we see the herd cutting off toward the barn.

Joe is thrilled. "Wasn't that fantastic?"

We approach the familiar driveway to Hills and Dales; young careworkers on their breaks are sitting along a brick wall, drinking Pepsi and smoking cigarettes; a little boy, propped with pillows, is being pushed in a swing, thin legs hanging: no pumping.

Inside, someone directs us to Zach, lying on a wedged cushion on the dayroom floor, quiet, not crying. This is one of the first times we have come in and not seen him being held. Everyone tells us, shamelessly, proud even, how spoiled he is—they hold him all the time.

Joe kneels down wordlessly in front of Zach. No response. It's true, he doesn't see.

"Hi, Zachy, your daddy's here," Joe says, a smile in the words.

Zach lights up—a big, spastic, shit-eating grin; his arms tighten in anticipation. *Ahhhh,* unvoiced from his open throat, soft Zachy noises.

Joe picks him up, and I say, "Hi ya, sweetie. Hi ya, babe," as I kiss his cheek; Gabi holds on to one of his dangling legs.

Outside we go for a walk, pushing him in his reclining wheelchair, awkward, like moving a hospital bed.

We walk past neat brick houses, fire hydrants painted like little soldiers or cartoon figures: it must have been some civic pride project; the whole crazy city has these painted fire hydrants, little gnomes at attention, policing each block.

Zach smiles over the bumps in the sidewalk, turns to the sun, warm on his face, ashy lashes; stretched out in the sick chair, supported by bolsters and Velcro straps: the original Heartbreak Kid.

What can I say to you, Zach? That I'm sorry I gave you this life, this lousy long haul?

In a park we walk, Joe and Gabi racing up ahead toward a swing. Under a clump of trees a shirtless teenager lovingly rubs wax onto the hood of his car. Rock music blares from his radio: oldies but goodies, a blast from the past. Do you hear the music, too, Zachy? Do you wanna dance?

"Oh, baby, oh, baby," I say. "Come be my dancing boy." Ripping back the Velcro, I bend to lift Zach from the chair. I hold him in my arms, twirling him under that big August sky.